War and the Illiberal Conscience

War and the Illiberal Conscience

Christopher Coker

WestviewPress

A Division of HarperCollins*Publishers*

Copyright © 1998 by Westview Press, A Division of HarperCollins Publishers, Inc.

Published in 1998 in the United States of America by Westview Press, 5500 Central Avenue, Boulder, Colorado 80301-2877, and in the United Kingdom by Westview Press, 12 Hid's Copse Road, Cumnor Hill, Oxford OX2 9JJ

A CIP catalog record for this book is available from the Library of Congress.
ISBN 0-8133-3369-5 (hc)

The paper used in this publication meets the requirements of the American National Standard for Permanence of Paper for Printed Library Materials Z39.48-1984.

10   9   8   7   6   5   4   3   2   1

Cocteau had been showing a journalist his apartment, filled with various mementos and awards and afterwards the visitor asked the usual question: "If the house burned down and you could choose only one thing to take with you, what would you choose?" To which Cocteau replied, "The fire!"

—Michel Tournier, *The Wind Spirit* (1989)

It happened that a fire broke out backstage in a theatre. The clown came out to inform the public. They thought it was just a jest and applauded. He repeated his warning. They shouted even louder. So I think the world will come to an end amid general applause from all the wits who believe that it is a joke.

—Søren Kierkegaard, *Either/Or* (1843)

It may be that when we look back on this time [the twentieth century] we will suddenly see that the very great artists . . . were surrealist jokers [like] the artist Jean Tinguely who built immense structures which he then set on fire, saying "I want this to be ephemeral. I want it to have happened only once".

—George Steiner, 'Talent and Technology', *Prospect* (May 1996)

Contents

Preface

Carlyle: a man of strong words and attitudes, a rhetor from need, constantly lured by the craving for a strong faith. . . . The craving for a strong faith is no proof of a strong faith, but quite the contrary. If one has such a faith, then one can afford the beautiful luxury of scepticism.
—Nietzsche, *The Twilight of the Idols* (1889)

In June 1917 the perceptive, left-wing social critic Randolph Bourne wrote an article for the *Seven Arts* magazine entitled 'The War and the Intellectuals'. In it he criticised the American intellectual community for its uncritical support of Woodrow Wilson's decision to take the United States into the First World War against Germany.

For a man who still retained an implacable animus against war, it was a bitter experience to see the unanimity with which most American writers had rushed to support the war effort. Indeed, not content with merely supporting the war, they also claimed to have effectively willed it in the face of a national indifference as to which of the belligerent powers would prevail. Bourne objected to an intellectual class "guiding a nation through sheer force of ideas into what other nations entered only through . . . popular hysteria or militarist madness"—helped, to be sure, by "an indubitably intellectualised president", Woodrow Wilson.

Bourne was scathing of an intellectual class who "might have turned their intellectual energy not to the problem of jockeying the nation into war but to the problem of using our vast neutral power to attain democratic ends for the rest of the world and ourselves without the use of the malevolent technique of war". Instead, the era had been wasted.[1]

Bourne was not alone in that criticism. Wyndham Lewis, writing from the perspective of the right and as a member of the English intellectual elite, also berated his colleagues for supporting a society of millionaires and war profiteers who had been interested only in making profits as quickly as possible. He condemned them, in particular, for what he called their "barbarous optimism" in the future.[2]

The idea that intellectuals were modern barbarians, however, was voiced more often about the writers who were prepared to lend their support for war to illiberal regimes rather than democratic governments. Julien Benda called them *"barbares, honteux de leur barbarie"*—barbarians unashamed of their barbarism.[3] These were the men who supported regimes that were willing to plunge the world into war not to make it safe for democracy (Woodrow Wilson's declared objective when he took the United States into the First World War) but to remake mankind, or to forge a new order, or to appropriate history in the name of a nation or a race.

"I am an intellectual, not a politician," wrote the most famous French philosopher of his generation, Jean-Paul Sartre, in 1967. "My duty as an intellectual is to think without restriction".[4] But this is precisely what Sartre did not do. As Alfred Fabre-Luce wrote in an article entitled 'A Barbarian Amongst Us', Sartre persistently betrayed those who had the right to expect the writers of the age to support truth against oppression:

> Sartre, 1950, justifying the North Korean aggression, refusing to take a position on the Russian labour camps, assimilating in the proletarian countries opposition to rebellion. Sartre, 1952, leaning more and more towards Stalin. Sartre, 1954, observing in a journey to the USSR, "a complete freedom of criticism". Sartre, 1956, suddenly awakened by the Hungarian revolution.[5]

This was a factual but partial summary, of course, by a man who had himself betrayed his compatriots by his collaboration with the Germans in 1940 (when Sartre had found himself a prisoner of war). The problem was that Sartre was not alone in this "treason of the intellectuals", as Benda called it, this barbarism of modern life. He had followed another major philosopher of the hour, Maurice Merleau-Ponty, in excusing the trials of the Stalin years in terms of the "dialectic of History" in his claim that the trials were fair and the verdicts pronounced in good faith.[6]

Before the Second World War Benda had lambasted the intellectuals of his own day for the support they gave to political creeds and secular religions that threatened the lives of those who embraced them. He called them barbarians for sanctioning the language of political extremism on both the left and the right, for sanctioning rather than challenging the prejudices and ideas in which the great dictators of the age increasingly traded. They were even prepared to applaud the organised hatred of the intellect that was such a prominent feature of political life in the 1930s.

Benda was particularly scathing of the intellectual class for its

> wish to confuse intelligence with reasoning of a dry and uninventive sort, in order to thoroughly misrepresent it; to believe that the great discoveries are due to a function (the 'intuition') which 'transcends intelligence' . . . its delight at witnessing what it believes to be the setbacks, the 'failures' of science (instead of regarding them as a misfortune). . . . This violent dislike, conscious and orga-

nised, of the intelligence—'intellectual' has become almost a term of contempt in our salons—constitutes something entirely new in French society. . . . This dislike will be the mark of our time in the history of French civilisation.[7]

Not even Benda could have foreseen that in the Nazi period the word 'intellectual' would become the code word for 'Jews' (as it had, of course, in Dreyfus's France).

Benda's criticism was well taken on one count. Those who should have known better were prepared to be associated with acts that should have been unacceptable in an intelligent age. But his critique ignored three important elements of the age in which he wrote, which form the backdrop to the arguments of this book.

1. In involving themselves in political life the intellectuals were responding to a new need of philosophy. As George Lichtheim wrote in his history of French Marxism, philosophy was required to become real. Its principles were no longer to figure as ideals unrelated to human practice. They were to descend from the sphere of speculation and assert themselves as the actual practise of a society. The twentieth century demanded that a society could no longer be suspended between blind empiricism and the passive contemplation of transcendental aims not realised in actuality.[8]

Intellectuals such as Malaparte, Spengler, Jünger and Weber (all of whom appear in this book) were setting a precedent in reworking philosophical ideas into their own work—the ideas of Hegel and Schopenhauer, and of course of Nietzsche, who was appropriated by more writers than anyone else. In Shaw's concept of the Superman or Wedekind's attempt to produce a new sexual morality, Nietzsche's ideas found a voice.

What made their role unique was their engagement in political life, their commitment to a cause or a political leader. In other eras, of course, there had been thinkers who had identified with causes as well, particularly the *philosophes* with their devotion to the Enlightenment and its ideas. But for the most part, they had promoted liberal ideas or a liberal programme that put an emphasis on religious tolerance, reason and civil liberty. Those of an illiberal temperament reacted a hundred years later to what they considered to be a dangerous programme that had gone too far and undermined social life. In their estimation faith in reason was inadequate to sustain men and women in the face of the challenges of modern life.

This led to a degree of didacticism in their work that was particularly strong in twentieth-century thought. Even liberal writers responded to the demands of the hour. The theories of psychoanalysis, for example, may have been at times tentative, incoherent and often contradictory, but they were expressed with a self-confidence that was almost authoritarian in nature. Indeed, there is much truth in the accusation that psychoanalysis not only claimed to offer a new science for a new era, but that it also saw itself as a new faith with its own doctrines and dogmas, its own sacred texts, its priesthood and its line of apostolic successors—not to mention its different sects, each fighting over the truth, and their dissent from Freud, the founding father.

Like the psychologists, liberal and illiberal thinkers alike formulated programmes, agendas and initiatives to save Europe from nihilism, barbarism or both. This was an intensely intellectual age. That is why what happened on the Alexanderplatz in Berlin on 4 November 1989 was so important. The fall of the Berlin Wall marked more than just the end of communism. It also marked the end of the tyranny of nineteenth-century ideas, that rusting infrastructure of concepts that formed the decaying legacy of post-Enlightenment thought. What the people of Central Europe wanted, declared a German historian, was "to be spared the political systems of redemption produced by the nineteenth century".[9] What happened in Berlin was not the end of history but the end of the nineteenth-century world of opposing ideals and visions. In November 1989 the people of East Germany were impatient for the twentieth century to begin.

2. We must always remember that ideas cannot be divorced from the social and economic context in which they are formulated. Ralf Dahrendorf, for example, was quite right to criticise "the German propensity for synthesis, the attempt to evade conflict or abolish it in superior authorities and institutions." He was right to regret the influence of Hegelian thinking on German political life.[10] But we must appreciate why modernity was more alienating in imperial Germany than it was elsewhere, especially in Britain.

One explanation is that Germany saw the most rapid industrialisation in history, coupled with the fastest process of urbanisation. By 1907 only half of the 60 million Germans lived at their place of birth. For industrial workers who were crowded into cities unprepared for their arrival, living conditions were appalling. Alienated from their previous social relationships, many workers became attracted to socialism. By contrast, many middle- and lower-middle-class Germans, fearing that the socialist movements would bring anarchism, became increasingly attracted to authoritarian movements. Many of the illiberal theories and creeds of the modern age were addressed to a reality that we associate with modernity: the conflict at the centre of social life.

The liberal democracies paid insufficient attention to the concerns and anxieties that were at the heart of the modern condition. The modern era was one in which people felt that they were losing control of the forces that governed their lives. They believed that the moral fabric of the world was unravelling around them. These concerns were not addressed by a political philosophy that presumed that individuals had sovereign choice, that they were free agents in their own future. Frequently, liberal writers were far too dismissive of the desire of many of their own citizens to retain those communal and religious traditions, those "habits of the heart" that Tocqueville saw as a corrective to the debilitating individualism of the modern age.

3. We must also see Benda's age as a moment in European intellectual life. The substitution of an emotionally charged ideological structure for the world of reality was in fact a desperate challenge to reality, and it was symbolic of the need of the moment. It could not be sustained, as Jacques Ellul so clearly pointed out, beyond that moment.[11] It was self-destructive.

Even so, at this century's end the liberal world confronts a paradox of its own victory. It is a paradox that Sartre had read into the development of the life of one of his antiliberal heroes, Jean Genet. "The secret failure of every triumph is that the winner is changed by his victory and the loser by his defeat".[12] In triumphing over its enemies in 1989, the liberal world, although still convinced of the truth of its own first principles, is no longer enthusiastic about acting on them. The liberal conscience no longer spurs it to action. In our postmodern world it seems to make cowards of us all.

There are many explanations for that outcome, which I will discuss in the last chapter. But one of the principal ones is that the West has begun to recognise, belatedly to be sure, that liberal values cannot be transformed into an ideology without grave cost to the world. It has begun to recognise that it has a greater responsibility still: not only to make the world safe for democracy but also to ensure that democracy can be made safe for the world.[13]

Origins of This Book

In writing about what Benda called the *"méfaits des intellectuels"*, the misdemeanours of the intellectuals, I have drawn inspiration from three principal works. The first is Michael Howard's *War and the Liberal Conscience*. Howard's book is based on a series of lectures he delivered at Cambridge in the mid-1970s when the Cold War was still at its height. In the preface he tells us that he chose the term 'liberal conscience' because the word 'conscience' implies not simply a belief or attitude but also an inner compulsion to act upon it. And by liberal he meant in general all those writers who believed that the world should be profoundly different from what it was and had faith in the power of human reason and history to attempt to change it for the better.[14]

Howard details the long debate about the value and importance of liberalism in a two-hundred-year cycle of history. At times in the twentieth century that faith was tested to the utmost. "We all lost the war", wrote D. H. Lawrence in his First World War novel, *Kangaroo*, "perhaps Germany least".[15] What the English lost was an unqualified faith in the future as they lamented the passing of a golden Edwardian age that was more imagined, of course, than real. If after the First World War they were not reconciled to becoming a cold and unimportant little island, they became increasingly unwilling to fight their way back into history as they were drawn into even closer contact with some of its more abrasive realities.

The English may not have lost their faith in their own liberal values, but they were no longer able to take them on trust. In the darkest days of the Second World War an American writer noted the dual character of the liberal age. As a student he had viewed the last decades of the previous century as a glorious stage in the progress of the West towards liberty, social betterment and the scientific control of nature. Some thirty years later, however, these decades appeared to him quite differently. In retrospect they appeared to have been a "fertile seed time" for "a quite different harvest of personal dictatorship, social degradation and mechanised destruction," the nineteenth century's legacy to the twentieth. It was, he felt, the dual character of that age that had invested it with "its particular interest and significance".[16]

In short, liberalism had to be fought for and defended, often at great cost. "The parapet, the wire and the mud" had now become "permanent features of human existence," complained one British soldier as early as 1915.[17] War, alas, soon became the central theme of twentieth-century life (not peace, as the English had fondly assumed when they were at their most self-confident, in the middle years of the Victorian era). In paying tribute to the intellectual power and persuasiveness of the illiberal imagination (in a way that few liberal writers did at the time), my aim is to show how remarkable it was that the liberal world never lost faith in its own first principles.

The second work that I have found particularly inspiring is Fritz Stern's *The Failure of Illiberalism,* a collection of essays on the political culture of modern Germany. By 'illiberalism' Stern meant not only the structure of a political regime, such as the restrictions it might choose to impose on electoral suffrage, but also its state of mind. Illiberalism in German life meant more than a failure to engender tolerance or dissent in political life. In Bagehot's celebrated phrase, Germany lacked "the nerve for open discussion". It was overwhelmed by challenges ranging from the threat of class war at home to attack from outside. It tended to mask its fear with the rhetoric of strength and heroism. Because its margin of confidence was slim, there was always a latent readiness to rely on force. Because its fear of the future was so profound, it tended to take refuge in the state and in state repression.[18]

Afraid of change and conflict in political life, Germany's intellectuals denied the need for either. Unreflectively, they came to think in terms of an endless struggle against enemies more imagined than real. It was an escape from reality. That is what Nietzsche meant when he wrote "apparent heroism—to throw oneself into the thick of the battle can be a sign of cowardice".[19]

In an essay on Thomas Mann's last great novel, *Doctor Faustus,* his critical enquiry into what had gone wrong with Germany in the course of the twentieth century, the critic Georg Lukács identified some of the principal themes of the illiberal imagination:

an arrogant rejection of economic solutions to social problems as "shallow", touching only the surface of human existence; the equally arrogant repudiation of all questions and answers based on reason and understanding; the *a priori* acceptance of the "irrational" as something higher, more fundamental, beyond reason and understanding; above all, the fetish of the *Volk*—which still took the "purely intellectual" form of the natural superiority of the Germanic to both East and West.[20]

In the course of this study I shall look in detail at four of these themes: the belief that war and peace could no longer be distinguished, that struggle was the essence of life; the belief in the sentence of History; the obsession with nationalism; and finally, the belief in the power of the human will, all material obstacles notwithstanding, for obstacles there must be if life is to be seen as a perpetual struggle.

Lukács, of course, was a Marxist with an implicit belief in positivism, a philosophical view that claimed that all true knowledge is scientific, that it is in accordance with demonstrable laws of science established by experiment and verifiable by the evidence of the senses. In later life he wrote a polemical tract entitled *The Destruction of Reason*. It was not aimed at the antirational spirit of fascism but at the lack of faith in the Marxist critique. By the 1970s the world seemed to have lost faith in positivism's as well as Marxism's ability to state anything that was universally true. Lukács particularly deplored the postmodern contempt for a perfect, rational, compassionate world, postmodernism's challenge to the modern world's faith in technology and planning, its detached, self-mocking attitude towards culture and progress. He despaired at the irony and self-reference that had become the hallmarks of the late twentieth century, an age that mocked linearity and rationality and the idea that both were necessarily progressive. As August del Nove remarked, Lukács's last book was pervaded with the secret fear that Nietzsche might triumph over Marx.[21]

The third book whose insights I have found invaluable is Peter Gay's *The Cultivation of Hatred,* the penultimate volume in his study of the Victorian mind. Illiberalism was not only to be found in illiberal societies. It was to be found even in the heartland of liberal England. What distinguished most English intellectuals from the Germans was what Gay calls their "liberal temperament". Liberal and illiberal views alike drew their inspiration from the same roots. What distinguished the former was not the certainty of its beliefs but its willingness to tolerate uncertainty, to accept the need for a large element of ambiguity in life.[22]

At the heart of the modern consciousness we find an acceptance of ambiguity: the right to learn from our mistakes, rather than act on blind faith; to reinterpret the world in accordance with our own experiences, and not have our actions dictated by an ideology that brooks no self-questioning.

In the end the liberal conscience prevailed in the Western world because it rang true. It verified a world that was experienced at many levels, sometimes intellectually, often not. At the end of the twentieth century, however, liberalism cannot (as it once sought to do) stand by some of its more all-embracing claims. That is why its victory has been conditional. We live in a world that has to accept the absurdities, the inescapable dangers and inherent contradictions of existence. We now recognise the elements of defeat in victory and victory in defeat. We acknowledge the loss of opportunities inherent in every choice. Those of a liberal disposition recognise the disorder that often follows upon the attempt to achieve order. The liberal conscience does not disparage the inevitability of loss, but it does allow the process of grieving to go on so that we may celebrate life despite all its miseries and afflictions, and thus have a reason to live on.[23]

It was not on such limited ground, of course, that the liberal world originally engaged the illiberal imagination. But it was the ground on which it eventually prevailed in the long struggle against its critics.

Chapter One

War and the Liberal Conscience

What a pity to see a mind as great as Napoleon's devoted to trivial things such as empires, historic events, the thundering of cannon and men. He believed in glory, in posterity, in Caesar; nations in turmoil and other trifles absorbed all his attention. . . . How could he fail to see that what really mattered was something else entirely.
—Paul Valéry, *Wicked Thoughts and Others*

G. K. Chesterton and the English Tradition

As a child I was beguiled by stories of Napoleon. Since his death at St. Helena the English have conducted a strange affair with him. Without him there would have been no legend of Nelson at Trafalgar, no stirring stories of the Duke of Wellington's victories in the Peninsula. The long Napoleonic Wars form the backdrop to Britain's emergence in the early nineteenth century as the greatest power in the world. In a sense the Emperor was the *metteur en scène* of the British moment in history.

The interest in the Napoleonic myth, however, runs much deeper than this. The wars with Napoleon marked a hitherto irreversible break with the continent. From 1789 the English and the continental Europeans went their separate ways.

Influenced by the great Whig (turned Tory) Edmund Burke, the English (re)discovered the importance of tradition, as well as the virtues of pragmatic, utilitarian thinking. The need to avoid excess and certainly enthusiasm were qualities that seemed to be borne out by the rise of Britain itself to preeminence as an industrial power. And although that preeminence did not last, although doubts about the supposed British virtues began to set in long before the end of the nineteenth century, their success in two world wars confirmed the British in their respect not only for the moral virtues of liberalism but also for its practical application. In a recent book challenging the 'myth' of British decline, its author quite rightly points to the political success of the United Kingdom in the past hundred and fifty years. Indeed, it is quite unparalleled—with one exception, that of the United States, another liberal society that wisely chose the path of peace rather than war when the latter could be avoided. That Britain has been on the winning side in all the wars it fought in the twentieth century is a remarkable testament indeed to the good sense of its rulers.[1]

Not that the English did not occasionally turn their eye to the more romantic and heroic options across the Channel. Even during the Napoleonic Wars the Holland House set enthused about Napoleon's "grandiose" conceptions, which contrasted so markedly in their scope with the "reactionary", unexciting patriotism of Lord Liverpool's administration. "A streak of divine folly runs through all his work", one of the Romantic poets wrote of him. Sir Walter Scott, who thought of himself as "the grand Napoleon of the realm of print", later wrote a biography of the Emperor which Goethe claimed had confirmed him in his admiration for Napoleon as a man. "What could be more delightful to me than leisurely and calmly to sit down and listen to the discourse of such a man?"[2] The historian Thomas Carlyle went one stage further, arguing that, with Goethe, Napoleon was one of the few really great men that the nineteenth century had produced.[3]

In the main, however, as much as the Emperor had and still has his English admirers, they were happy to be spared the misfortune of experiencing him at first hand. Enthusiasts are dangerous; secular redeemers even more so. Sometimes it is more comforting to adopt other people's heroes rather than to produce one's own.

No one sneered more at continental enthusiasm than G. K. Chesterton, that quintessential English author, who these days is mostly remembered for his series of detective stories featuring a uniquely English hero, Father Brown. Inevitably, the good father's eternal foil is a Frenchman, Flambeau, the Napoleon of crime. Unlike most writers of detective fiction, Chesterton undertook to explain the inexplicable rather than the obscure, and what the detective had difficulty interpreting were crimes based on metaphysical ideas, the bizarre rather than the pragmatic. As the genial priest remarks of the murderer who appears in "The Actor and the Alibi": "You talk about these highbrows having a higher art and a more philosophical drama. But remember what a lot of the philosophy is. Remember what sort of conduct those high brows often present. . . . All about 'the will to power' and 'the right to live' and 'the right to experience' . . . damned nonsense and more than damned nonsense—nonsense that can damn".[4]

Chesterton was never more in his element in challenging the nonsense of metaphysical thinking than in his novel *The Napoleon of Notting Hill*

(1908). In the first chapter he set out the plain Englishman's creed, the distrust of high ideas and secular prophecies, of overly intellectual thinking. Not for the English the prophecies of the hour—and there were many as the country transited the nineteenth century into the twentieth. As a people, Chesterton wrote, the English were prepared to listen politely to great minds and even greater egos, but only in the spirit of a wilful child who awaited the death of a prophet so that he could do something else entirely, without being impolite.

The way the prophets went to work in the early twentieth century, Chesterton noted, was that they took something that was going on in their time and extrapolated from it something extraordinary, some time in the future. There were those who, like Edward Carpenter, thought that in a short time man would revert to nature and live like the animals. There was Tolstoy and the humanitarians, who forecast that the world was growing more merciful and that in future no one would wish to kill anyone else. There was Cecil Rhodes, who thought the greatest institution of the future would be the British Empire and that there would be an unbridgeable gulf between those who were members of it and those who were not. (To be born British, Rhodes once wrote, was "to win first prize in the lottery of life".)

The problem with the twentieth century, Chesterton concluded, was that there were so many prophecies that it was difficult to elude all their ingenuities. Whenever a man did anything free and frantic and entirely his own, the horrible thought struck him that it might have been predicted by someone in the past. "Whenever a duke climbed a lamppost, when a dean got drunk, he could not really be happy, he could not be certain that he was not fulfilling some prophecy". He could never be sure that he was an agent with free will rather than a man whose actions were determined by history.

What Chesterton had grasped was the dilemma of life in the twentieth century, the pain of being 'modern'. In the Western world consciousness of history had transformed itself from an opening of doors at the time of the Enlightenment into the most insupportable burden of self-consciousness at the end of the nineteenth century. It had become impossible to express individuality through action that did not remind the actor of something that had been already achieved or predicted by someone else. Men were no longer free agents but 'functionaries of the Absolute' (as de Maistre once called them), the agents of higher historical, social or cultural forces or a mixture of all three.

In short, Chesterton grasped the deep sense of alienation produced by history. Modern man was constantly thinking backwards to what his predecessors had predicted. As a result he was frequently devalued. He was denied the self-respect that comes from the exercise of free will. Chesterton's own response was a liberal one, to do exactly the opposite of what the prophets expected, to act in defiance of History's laws.

In his own day the English clung ever more tenaciously to the principle of free will, unacquainted as most were with the deterministic systematising of history by the great German philosophers, particularly Hegel. In the eyes of the common people, Chesterton added, of the sailor at sea, or the peasant in the field, one could see a look of mirth. These were the men who enjoyed playing the game of 'Cheat the Prophet'. They had no intention of fulfilling other people's prophesies, not even their own.[5] Unlike the nations across the Channel, which, even as Chesterton wrote, were beginning their slow descent into the First World War, the English were far too intelligent, too sensible, perhaps too obtuse or dull, to follow even their own prophets to perdition.

Chesterton saw himself as the spokesman for the ordinary man who accepted the terms on which life had to be lived. In that sense he was the voice of liberal England. Possibly, Ezra Pound was once heard to complain, Chesterton *was* the mob. In his *Short History of England,* which was published during the Great War, in its penultimate year, 1917, he spoke of how the English people had entered history "with the noise of trumpets" and turned themselves in only two years into one of the iron armies of the world. They had done more. Not for them the 'heroic' struggle to pursue a well-defined destiny at the behest of those who had defined it, the intellectuals and the philosophers. Instead, in rejecting the metaphysical *idées reçues* that are the subject of this study, they had become for the first time the hero in their own story.

Such, at least, was the mood and sensibility that I was told, as a child, was the essence of English history that distinguished it from that of its great continental adversaries—France and later Germany. Only in later life did I learn to recognise that the English view was only a point of view that it was much easier for the English to adopt, safe as they were behind the Channel.

Indeed, Chesterton extolled liberal individuality without especially appreciating how fortunate his own countrymen were to enjoy it. Looking back on the twentieth century, I am struck by a passage in *The Napoleon of Notting Hill* that is often overlooked: "They stone the false prophets", Chesterton wrote, ". . . but they could have stoned true prophets with a greater and juster enjoyment. Individually, men may present a more or less rational appearance, eating, sleeping and scheming. But humanity as a whole is changeful, mystical, fickle, delightful. Men are men, but Man is a woman".

So runs the second paragraph of the book, one that bears an uncommon resemblance to a passage in Nietzsche's *On the Genealogy of Morals.* "Unconcerned, mocking, violent—thus wisdom wants *us:* She is a woman and always loves only a warrior".

What sort of warrior is unconcerned, asks one of Nietzsche's more perceptive critics? One for whom the means is an end, for whom war making is not so much what you do but what you are. There is, he tells us in the first essay, "no being behind doing . . . the 'doer' is merely a fiction added to the deed".[6]

If this is the understanding of the warrior's morality, what does the warrior mock? Clearly, those who are locked in a world of goals and purposes, and subscribe to hypothetical imperatives, who fight for causes rather than for themselves, who go to war for its own sake. The true warrior, of course, is one whose campaigns happen to be philosophical, who not so much loves wisdom as he is, like a warrior, loved by wisdom.

Up to this point there was nothing in Nietzsche's case with which Chesterton would have found fault or to which he would have taken exception. But Nietzsche went much further than Chesterton in arguing that you can only challenge or mock the prophets of war if you have an argument, if you are prepared to philosophise. As he adds elsewhere, the warrior mocks, for mockery is the violence of the metaphysician, and if one's writings are to be mocking and violent, they must *hurt* if they are to penetrate at all. As a philosopher he called himself "an artillery man"—he wanted his barbs to hurt so that they would hit home.

As we shall see later, one of Nietzsche's main criticisms of English pragmatism was that the liberals did not think profoundly enough about war and its consequences, they did not philosophise "with a hammer", they were ignorant of the forces working towards conflict in early twentieth-century Europe. In short, their thinking was too shallow.

Chesterton himself had little time for Nietzsche. He dismissed him as an incorrigible romantic, "a useless anarchist" whose works, when translated, had ushered in an "epoch of real pessimism".[7] He saw him as a fanatic, a wild dreamer, a man out of touch with the humanity he wished to save. In the end, however, the prophet who was vindicated was the visionary, Nietzsche, the philosopher who first foretold the coming of an age in which liberalism would be hard pressed to survive. In the course of the twentieth century over 70 million people lost their lives in wars, the majority for the pursuit of ideas that most liberal writers were too quick to dismiss as immature, irrational or simply childish.

Chesterton and his fellow liberals must be judged harshly on two counts. The first is their not taking war seriously enough, treating it as a social aberration. One of the reasons why *The Napoleon of Notting Hill* is a flawed work is that the novel ends with a battle with real swords in which nobody gets killed. It is a silly ending because real swords kill. It is an account that could only have been written by an Englishman, and then only before the First World War.

In a curious tribute Albert Speer once claimed that in the portrayal of one of its characters, Adam Wayne, Chesterton's novel had forecast "the frightening consequences of mass psychosis" played upon by a Caesarian demagogue who in his powers to move a crowd was not unlike Hitler. But Chesterton, we should remember, was on Wayne's side. He approved of his violence. Only the honesty with which he recognised other people's faults in himself predisposed him against embracing some of the illiberal ideas of his age. If he was one of the first writers to condemn Hitler it was because he recognised in himself the seed of anti-Semitism.

Secondly, with a few exceptions, most English intellectuals were insufficiently responsive to the fears and anxieties that predisposed people to embrace illiberal ideas, the fear of losing control over the forces governing their lives. It was a concern that was not addressed by the prevailing liberal belief that individuals were 'unencumbered selves', sovereign in their choice of values. Nor was it helped by the hasty dismissal of those religious and other 'irrational' observances that Tocqueville, in calling them "habits of the heart", had seen as a corrective to total reliance on the market. As Wyndham Lewis recognised, the apparent 'soullessness' of liberal society was itself responsible, in part at least, for driving men to more radical visions of life, and more radical solutions. If the Anglo-Saxon "commercial idea", he warned, ever gained the day in the world as well as in England, even "the British Chestertonian small-holders of the future [might] curse their rich neighbours across the Channel for their soulless individualism".[8]

Many of those illiberal forces, alas, seem to be dominant today in much of the outside world. Some of them are even reappearing in the heartland of Europe itself. All of us who are fortunate enough to live in a 'postmodern' world may be required to take illiberal ideas a little more seriously than did Chesterton and his contemporaries in 1908.

Who's Afraid of Leonard Woolf?
The English and Philosophical Quackery

"Let's be superficial and pity the poor philosophers."
—Elyot, in Noel Coward's *Private Lives* (1937)

I am glad about the military development of Europe . . . the time of rapture and Chinese ossification is over . . . the barbarian in each of us is affirmed. . . . Precisely for that reason philosophers have a future.
—Nietzsche, *The Will to Power* (1884)

In the late 1920s the young Indian novelist and art critic Mulk Raj Anand came to Britain. He chose voluntary exile rather than be committed to gaol as his friends in the noncooperation movement back at home had been, that long, protracted, but largely peaceful revolt that marked the closing years of British rule in India. He soon found work as a part-time proof-reader for the Hogarth Press, through which he met and befriended two of its principal authors, E. M. Forster and Leonard Woolf. Forster was about to publish *A Passage to India,* the last and perhaps most important of his novels. Woolf had served as a district officer in Ceylon and was interested in the colonial question.

In an essay recounting his meetings with most of the members of the Bloomsbury set, Anand described an episode at Woolf's home, where he first met the novelist Virginia Woolf.

> "Of course, you Hindus have the advantage of always looking inwards. You people lifted veil after veil—and some of you have *seen.*"
>
> "I think they overdo it", Leonard commented. "Of course, they may be right about that 'far off divine event to which the whole creation moves' which Tennyson talks about."
>
> "Our roots have always been in Heaven," I said. "The *Gita* says the branches of the sacred tree spread downwards." I paused, smiled sheepishly, but then continued with a strain of mockery about the Hindu boasting. "The downward branches stretch towards"—I made a gesture towards the earth. "Actually the ancients returned with a negative answer. It is neither this—nor that."
>
> "And so the earth is hell", murmured Leonard Woolf. "That is why some people here say you Indians should go on your upward path and leave the earth to us practical people".[9]

Throughout his life Leonard congratulated himself on his 'practical' view of life. He had no time for the metaphysical speculations of other people, either Indian gurus or German philosophers. He gloried in the pragmatic nature of the English mind. Virginia, Anand tells us, had criticised her husband for thinking that all men were "Bertie Russell mathematicians", a reference to the greatest of the English empiricists who with A. J. Ayer developed a version of logical positivism that tried to produce a logical reconstruction of everyday reality. In his most famous book, *Principia Mathematica,* Russell attempted to account for the complexity of experience in a system based on mathematical reasoning.

Leonard was distinctly unimpressed with his Indian friend's metaphysical musings. He reminded his young guest that "there was much hocus pocus"—or what he would later call "quackery"—"about the yogis", particularly those of the European variety such as Spengler and Nietzsche.

In an earlier encounter with Woolf and E. M. Forster, this time under a chestnut tree in Tavistock Square while drinking sherry in the sun, Anand had been ticked off for bringing Nietzsche into the conversation. "Nietzsche has said it well. . . . Christianity gave the European poison to drink. He did not die but degenerated into vice". At the mention of the German philosopher's name Forster had raised his eyebrows in disapproval; Woolf had rapidly passed on to another subject.[10]

Leonard Woolf is little remembered these days except for his autobiography and what it, in turn, had to say about the world of the Bloomsbury set and Fabian socialism. If he is remembered at all it is as the long-suffering husband of Virginia Woolf, who is still the towering figure among twentieth-century women novelists. But he was an influential writer of his day, a man distinguished by the company he kept. When he was at Cambridge he was invited to join the Apostles, the secret society that numbered among its members one of the most famous British traitors of the century, Kim Philby. It was as a member of this exclusive Cambridge intellectual and aesthetic circle that Woolf first met John Maynard Keynes, E. M. Forster, Lytton Strachey and above all, his tutor, the philosopher G. E. Moore.

Keynes in particular was profoundly influenced by Moore's philosophy of common sense. What Moore gave his students, he recalled in later life, was a view of the world that amounted almost to a 'religion'. Like many other members of his generation, he confessed, he had been "permanently inoculated with Moore and Moorism".[11] It was a philosophy, Woolf later wrote in his autobiography, that constituted an intense love for "the pure light of plain common sense".[12] His own preference for plain speaking stemmed from one of Moore's principal teachings—that all essential truths are simple truths that can and must be expressed in simple language. Common sense, Moore once wrote, was "that degree of judgement which is common to men with whom we can converse and transact business" (a telling phrase that recalls the belief of the American philosopher William James in "the cash value of ideas"). A man of common sense was a sensible man, not to be identified as one who holds an arcane view of the world and everything in it. If a man holds ideas he should hold those intelligible to everyone, and not merely to members of the philosophical school to which he belongs.[13]

Woolf was merely expressing the views common to many Englishmen of his generation who shared his innate scepticism of all things metaphysical. Perhaps one of the best examples of the English response to the illiberal challenge is his book *Quack, Quack,* which he published in 1934. It was rightly seen at the time as a clarion call for liberalism. In it he defended the ideals in which he passionately believed, particularly the League of Nations. He was a great exponent of international government, a development whose origins he traced to the nineteenth century:

> A profound change in international relations has taken place since the beginning of the nineteenth century, and . . . the people who repeat and repeat again that international government is utopian, and international agreement must betray national interests, simply shut their eyes to the fact that in every department of life the beginnings and more than the beginnings of international government already exist.

Indeed, he claimed, the recognition that national interests were international interests and vice versa was "the great social discovery of the last hundred years".[14] It is not surprising, therefore, that halfway through his life he was appalled at the rise of totalitarianism in Italy and Germany. In fascism, more than in communism, he saw the potential undoing of all that had been achieved so far in terms of agreement between states.

In *Quack, Quack,* which was perhaps the most wide-ranging and stimulating of his political tracts, Woolf set out to analyse the deep roots of European authoritarianism with reference to the findings of anthropology and even psychoanalysis, which had been made fashionable by Freud and Ferenzi. Never a man to engage in a bland critique, Woolf laboured hard in the 1930s to expose what he considered to be the philosophical and metaphysical foundations of the illiberal conscience. The rise of the dictators, he believed, owed much to the pernicious influence of intellectuals, especially German philosophers (and their English admirers, notably the historian Thomas Carlyle).

> Long before the Duce or fascism had been born, German philosophers and historians were quacking with the greatest brilliancy and subtlety in order to give a new philosophical foundation to the most ancient of political barbarisms and to console the victims of that old Moloch "the absolute state" with the knowledge that they were at any rate being sacrificed in accordance with the doctrines of the Hegelian dialectic.[15]

Woolf complained that the rejection of standards of intellectual integrity by intellectuals themselves had manifested itself in a number of ways. He singled out two in particular. The first was a pseudohistorical attempt to provide arguments in favour of imaginary social superiorities or class inferiorities, or proofs that unreason, intolerance and violence were both desirable and historically inevitable. The second did for religion and philosophy what the first did for politics and history. It discredited science, reason and common sense and paved the way for the rejection of all unpalatable facts that conflicted with superstitions about the universe. It provided arguments for retaining a religious and metaphysical belief in magic and myth.

Woolf, of course, was not the first in the field in his criticism of illiberal thinking. His misgivings were shared by a number of other writers, the most important of whom was Julien Benda, whose book *La trahison des clercs* (The Treason of the Intellectuals) had an enormous impact when it first appeared in the bookshops in 1927. Woolf may also have been influenced by the writing of the American philosopher George Santayana, although he does not refer to him by name. It was Santayana who had written the most popular critique of German metaphysical thinking, *Egoism and German Philosophy,* a work that had appeared almost twenty years earlier than Woolf's, at the height of the First World War.

Traditionally, all three writers argued, intellectuals had been indifferent to, or opposed to, popular passions. Formerly detached from political life, they had dedicated themselves, like Goethe, to intellectual pursuits, or been persuaded, like Kant, that good conduct should be guided by abstract principles. In the late nineteenth century, however, they had betrayed their own kind by descending into the political arena. The modern *clercs* had enthusiastically adopted the political passions of ordinary men, and in so doing had placed their art and thought at the service of the worst demagogues and politicians.

Before the nineteenth century, political passions had also been considered to be natural or instinctive. In the course of the twentieth century they were rationalised or philosophised into a system, translated into scientific or historic laws, and transformed into ethical principles. In this respect the betrayal of the *clercs* was only a particular instance of a widespread movement towards illiberalism in European intellectual life.

These charges, it should be added, appealed particularly to the English because of their opposition to men of ideas. When the English spoke of an educated person or scholar they generally meant someone who stood above the mêlée of political life. When the continental Europeans spoke of an intellectual (a word not much used in the English-speaking world) they meant someone who was prepared to fight in the midst of life with words rather than deeds.

Woolf's own contribution to the debate was to take it much further by attacking the metaphysical presuppositions that he found embedded in German philosophy. He concluded his book with a particularly savage attack on such thinkers as Oswald Spengler and Henri Bergson for their great faith in intuitive rather than rational thinking. Both men, he insisted, had dealt a fatal blow to the structure of reason that had been the chief feature of the European Enlightenment: "Civilisations are not destroyed by the Herr Kubes or even by the Herr Hitlers, they are destroyed when the M. Bergsons have to be numbered among the intellectual quacks".[16]

Kube was a Reichstag deputy and Nazi propagandist, and Bergson a philosopher who believed in intuitive understanding as the best way of appreciating the truth. Woolf insisted that the intuitive could not be proved or demonstrated to be untrue until societies had been committed to political ventures well beyond their strength, when it was far too late, of course, to change tack.

Unfortunately, he concluded, modern society appeared to be suitable material for quacks. By metaphysical quackery, he wrote, "I mean the abandonment and contempt for reason as a means to truth in nonpolitical speculations and the substitution for it of so-called intuition, magic and mysticism".[17] He was particularly dismissive of the beguiling and bewitching language in which writers like Nietzsche and Spengler engaged—the 'quackery' of the quack doctor's aura of magic and mystery, "the destiny of culture, fate, the predetermination of history, the Man of Destiny, the Elixir of Life, the Philosopher's Stone, Doctor Ben Ezra's Magic Panacea for the Cure of Rheumatism and Cancer".[18]

It was necessary to point out, he conceded, that not all the assertions of quacks were necessarily untrue, just as not all the medicines of the quack doctor were necessarily valueless. A true statement that could be stated in ordinary, plain language and for which ordinary proof could be given only became quackery if it was wrapped up in a high-flown, metaphysical, obscure language and then announced as a mysterious discovery of direct intuition. In Spengler's best-selling book *The Decline of the West*, he found a particularly vivid example of methods that had been characteristic of quacks and magicians since time began:

> Herr Spengler's assertions about "cosmic beats" and "destiny" and "the logic of time" and the "morphology of history" may or may not be true. There is no reason for believing that they are true and there is every reason for believing them to be quackery, because (a) they are stated in words and language the meaning of which is never clear, so that neither Herr Spengler nor his readers can ever be certain of the exact meaning of the truth which he claims to be asserting; (b) the proof that the statement is true is said to be the fact that they are direct intuitions . . . but there is no more reason to believe that Herr Spengler's or my metaphysical direct intuitions about the course of history are true than for believing that those of an African witch doctor are true; (c) Herr Spengler is perpetually telling us that he is discovering something which no one has ever discovered before and at the same time is appealing to those emotions in us which are roused by mysteries and magic.[19]

Such criticisms had been raised much earlier by Santayana, who had alleged that metaphysical language was a reflection of a third characteristic of German philosophy: a romantic egoism that counted subjectivity as its most conspicuous feature.

Santayana condemned a wide range of views that he found in German philosophy, including wilfulness in morals, subjectivity in thought, uncompromising self-assertion, the notion that truth and fact were a mere "fiction of the will", a contempt for happiness, their own as well as other people's, and above all, as the title of his book suggests, a pronounced egoism. It was an egoism that "assumes if it does not assert that the source of one's being and power lies in oneself, that will and logic are by rights omnipotent and that nothing should control the mind or the conscience except the mind or the conscience itself".[20]

What Santayana sketched so vividly was a portrait of an entire national *mentality,* an inner worldview that in 1914 had been translated outwardly into a monstrous assertion of will. "Not that the German philosophers are responsible for the war, or that recrudescence of corporate fanaticism which prepared it from afar. They merely shared and justified prophetically that spirit of uncompromising self-assertion and metaphysical conceit which the German nation is now reducing to *action.*"

The Germans had put together a secular religion that had "its prophets in the great philosophers and historians of the last century, its high priests and pharisees in the government and the professors, its faithful flock in the disciplined mass of the nation". It even had its heretics in the socialists and now "its martyrs by the million". Here, indeed, was one of the first and most violent attacks on the illiberal imagination, one that predated Benda's by several years.

What all three lines of attack had in common—the criticism of intuitive thinking, the metaphysical language of German thought, and the subjectivity inherent in the German tradition—was the belief that they were all associated with the most important development of the first half of the twentieth century—the revolt against positivism. It was to colour the period from 1890 to 1945, and can be said to have ended only with Germany's partition by the two superpowers eleven years after the publication of Woolf's book.

The origins of positivism lie in the empiricist school of philosophy of the seventeenth and eighteenth centuries. The positivists were opposed to any attempt, in particular by metaphysics, to go beyond the world or what was scientifically demonstrable. They were given to an observation of the real world from which they derived their first principles and ultimate ends. For positivists the key word was 'analyse'. It was the role of philosophy, they believed, to explain the scope and methods of science and its implications for life. They did not believe it could be used to obtain knowledge that could not be verified or tested by the scientific method. Indeed, they went much further, insisting that philosophy could only investigate methods of representing reality; it could offer no independent guide to reality—independent, that is, of experimental science.

The great nineteenth-century positivists held strongly to the belief that every brand of knowledge would be found eventually to conform to scientific rules. Most British philosophers such as Bentham and the two Mills, considered themselves to be positivists, as did evolutionists such as Herbert Spencer. Theirs was the vastly influential project of knowledge that for many years came to be identified with the English-speaking world.

It was this feature that distinguished them most from philosophers such as Kant and Fichte, who instead of attempting to describe the world in order to understand it, had criticised the world in order to reconstruct it. It was this phenomenon that made the alliance of philosophy and politics so disturbing in an age in which war could be used to restructure reality, with its promise to make man for the first time autonomous of history.

Positivism may have failed in the course of the twentieth century, but it was held to tenaciously by the English. England became the home of a number of exiles from the Vienna Circle whose members tried to develop the discipline of logic into a mathematical theory of logical systems. Between the two world wars Ayer and Russell tried to save positivism by creating a mathematical language for philosophy.

The positivist programme undoubtedly had an appeal to the English as something hard-headed and commonsensical. Russell was widely applauded at the time for trying to systematise empiricism. Wittgenstein was popular with his English readers for his attack on metaphysics as essentially unverifiable and, being unverifiable, neither true nor false but simply meaningless. The task of philosophers, he insisted, was not one of establishing philosophical doctrines but of elucidating meanings or calling attention to the lack of them.

Woolf's own critique would be of little interest if it did not reflect so faithfully the attempt to engage in logical thinking. This was the basis of the liberal conscience for much of the century. Liberal writers took great pride in the claim to engage only in straight talking and pragmatic thinking. They boasted of their clearheadedness and respect for language. They were also deeply suspicious of metaphysical ideas, which they regarded not only as profoundly illiberal but, worse, profoundly un-English.

Philosophical ideas, of course, reflect the reality of the age in which they are formulated or held. In the case of Britain, the most powerful and most industrialised state of the nineteenth century, positivism accorded with a business ethic that was scornful of intellectual life, especially the speculative. "It is the extremely *practical* character of the English people that distinguishes them from the French", wrote John Stuart Mill: "In intellect they are distinguished only for a kind of sober good sense . . . and for doing all these things which are best done where man most resembles a machine, with the precision of a machine."[21]

The English public, wrote Mill in 1833, thought nobody worth listening to except when they were being told of something to be done, and only that when the something to be done required immediate action. What they wanted was specific proposals that could be acted upon at once. As a result, philosophical thinking had declined quite dramatically, not only in the universities but also in public life. The mid-Victorians seemed to have a profound distrust of "speculation of any comprehensive kind upon deep or extensive subjects". Britain, he added, a country that in the eighteenth century had produced some of the greatest abstract philosophers in history, such as Berkeley and Hume, had lost interest in "the investigation of truth *as* truth".

It was the French historian Hippolyte-Adolphe Taine who compared an Englishman's mind to a *Murray's Guide,* a great many facts but few ideas. After visiting England he reported that he had found only half a dozen men who were given to philosophical speculation, and even then they "paused . . . half way, arriving at no definite conclusion". Another mid-nineteenth-century visitor, the American writer Ralph Waldo Emerson, found many intelligent men who could talk with force and knowledge on subjects such as free trade, but who were quite at a loss to discuss philosophy, especially metaphysics.[22]

Mill had no hesitation in tracing the origin of such anti-intellectualism to the industrial revolution and the business ethic to which it had given rise. There was little recognition, he regretted, that from philosophical enquiry into the nature of man and society "a single important *practical* consequence could follow". Even an aesthete like Ruskin complained that "busy metaphysicians are always entangling good and active people and weaving cobwebs among the finest wheels of the world's business". Even in Ruskin's writings the business ethic was pronounced.[23]

It was this approach to which Nietzsche (Woolf's principal candidate for quackery) was so opposed. I will discuss his work at much greater length in the pages that follow, but for the moment I want to discuss his own critique of the liberal conscience, for it encapsulates the main themes of the present study.

In the foreword to *Twilight of the Idols* Nietzsche tells us that his book should be seen as a "grand declaration of war" against the facile nature of English liberal thinking.[24] Woolf may have made great play of the 'quackery' of illiberal thought, its tendentious statements about the future, its metaphysical language, which often obscured more than it revealed, its tendency to treat its own ideas as revealed wisdom. But Nietzsche, for one, had no doubt that a counterclaim could be made about liberal thinking, about its complacency or self-satisfaction (especially when the writers were English); its preoccupation with plain speaking, which often disguised an absence of sustained thought; its denial of what people wanted most—a reason for living. What he set out to do as a philosopher was to challenge "the quack doctoring" with which liberal writers had hitherto "been accustomed to treat the illness of the soul".[25]

Although Nietzsche never wrote a work on political philosophy as such, his writings are replete with political observations, some of which even struck a chord among many of his English readers—or at least those who were honest enough to recognise that in the troubled twentieth century liberalism could no longer be taken on trust.

Let me identify five central propositions of his critique, beginning with his criticism of English thinking for its lack of imagination. "They are no philosophical race, these Englishmen", he wrote in *Beyond Good and Evil*. He accused Locke and Hume of debasing the value of philosophy. Mill and his school had done even more damage, for they had positioned themselves "in the middle regions of European taste" where their "narrowness, aridity and industrious diligence" appealed to mediocre minds. Perhaps this would not have mattered much but for the age in which Nietzsche lived. It was an age in which men had to live with the terrible knowledge of "the death of God", a discovery Nietzsche was the first to make public.

The English themselves, of course, had played a part in the secularisation of the late Christian mind. They too had challenged the metaphysical foundations of belief in God. Their own scientists, such as Darwin and Huxley, had played a leading role in undermining many of Christianity's most deeply held beliefs. The English more than any other people had been in at the "death of God", but they had survived it better than his own countrymen. They had not found it necessary to create a metaphysical system to take God's place. They claimed that they did not require one, that they knew of their own accord, "ironically, intuitively", what was good and bad. Indeed, was that not the basis of Moorism?

"For the Englishman", Nietzsche complained, "morality is not yet a problem". His objection to English philosophy was that its avatars always claimed to know the truth from their own experience. The United States comprised another society that had experienced so much success in its comparatively short history that it never saw the need to enquire too deeply into the human condition. None of its great liberal philosophers of the twentieth century, neither Dewey, Peirce nor William James, sought to fill the gap bequeathed by the Enlightenment—the gap between knowledge and truth, power and authority, existence and purpose, history and meaning. One of the reasons, Nietzsche suspected, was that they were even unconscious of the fact that such a gap existed. Their own material success discouraged speculative thinking.

Unfortunately, the pragmatism that became America's chief contribution to Western philosophy could not help its own disenchanted citizens, those struggling at the margins of the American Dream. In the first chapter of *Walden* Thoreau complained that America could boast no "philosophers, only professors of philosophy", men who were unable to deal with "the lives of quiet desperation" led by the majority of his countrymen, whether they were immigrants trapped in the tenements of New York or settlers eking out a subsistence living on the western frontier.

America's preoccupation with happiness even puzzled the English on occasion. Commenting on Dickens's first trip to the United States in the 1840s, Chesterton noted that "he was quite prepared to be pleased with America. He would have been better pleased with it had it not been so much pleased with itself". Later he added that Dickens "was annoyed more with its contentment than its discontents", in particular its exaggerated sense of its own good fortune.[26]

Whatever the misgivings of the English might have been, they were muted in comparison with the criticism of continental philosophers. Like Nietzsche many of them complained that liberals had started out with the intention of making the good of society the good of the individual. They had ended up in making the individual good fortune of one country into a doctrine that supposedly applied to the rest of the world. Utilitarianism, Nietzsche wrote, had slipped from an interest in the general welfare into the "happiness of England".[27]

Nietzsche of course can be faulted for failing to grasp the fact that democratic life involved far more than the pursuit of happiness. It frequently forced citizens to address issues that made them very unhappy indeed. It often required them to take a stand on a particular collective good. If not always tragic, more often than not the choice entailed an arduous or painful sacrifice. It often required the citizen to make a choice between family and friends and between class and church. It often detached people from their communities, or estranged them from the groups into which they were born. Or, if they chose to put community first, it often forced them to support causes to which they were in principle opposed.

In the course of the twentieth century the democratic world frequently asked its citizens to put principles before people, or ideas before interests. In taking the democratic citizen as quite literally "an unencumbered self" without any obligations to others apart from the duty not to commit unjust acts, Nietzsche ignored an important element of democratic life that was particularly intense in a century in which the democracies had both at home and abroad to battle for their existence.

Where Nietzsche was on stronger ground was in his suspicion that one day democratic governments would be more interested in advancing procedural rights than in pursuing the good of society. He praised the Greeks for not taking themselves too seriously, for "not reflecting on their rights. . . . They commanded: that sufficed". They had a purpose, the good of all.[28] He was disturbed that one day democracies, rather then ensuring that they discharged their responsibilities to society, might conclude that the only legitimate role of the state would be to adjudicate citizens' rights against each other. Such a minimalist view of citizenship is of course one with which we are more familiar today. We have still to discover whether it can possibly provide the will to fight for the common good, especially when that good is challenged by market forces that threaten to isolate people in individual struggles for survival.

Secondly, if liberals attacked German philosophers for their objection to happiness, their own as well as everyone else's, Nietzsche had an acute insight into the material soullessness of the utilitarian ethic. What he took exception to most was one of the most influential contributions the British had made to European thought—mid-nineteenth-century utilitarianism, with its principle of "the happiness of the greatest number".

"Man does not strive after happiness, only the Englishman does that", he once complained.[29] He was particularly scornful of the liberal tendency to "regard states of distress in general as an objection, as something to be *abolished.*" Such a philosophy could be disastrous in its consequences. It would be "almost as stupid as would be the will to abolish bad weather—perhaps, from pity for the poor". The abolition of unhappiness would deprive existence of "its great character" and devalue man's perpetual striving after truth. Unfortunately, he added, the English preferred to preserve their existence "as much at the expense of *the truth* as at the expense of *the future*".[30]

Like most German philosophers of his time he found himself engaged in a fight against the English "mechanistic doltification of the world," in criticism of which Hegel and Schopenhauer for once had been of one mind.[31] Stated so bluntly Nietzsche's objections may sound harsh, but they explain why some people were drawn to illiberal philosophies by the failure of liberalism to offer them any idea to which they could commit themselves, or any set of values they found worth defending.

There were a few liberal writers who were aware that in denying man transcendence to a higher state of being, liberal societies ran the risk of alienating men from modern life. John Stuart Mill, for one, was critical of the secular nature of the moral regime proposed by Bentham, and called for an explicit reintroduction of belief in heaven and hell and for making that affirmation an obligatory ground of liberal thinking.[32]

As Nietzsche acutely perceived, the nihilism that lurked at the heart of late-nineteenth-century Europe could be traced not only from the death of God in the theological sense but also from the failure of other metaphysical faiths to fill the void left by his absence. None of the God surrogates that had served humanity since antiquity, including the positivist faith in science, could take his place.

Science in particular could not redeem humanity. It might have undermined religious values, but it could not create them. It could not tell man how to live or how to behave. In that sense, it was nihilistic because it had destroyed belief in God for no reason. It had challenged man's faith in such absolutes as truth, including the very belief that truth existed. What, asked Nietzsche with concern, "if nothing turns out to be divine any longer unless it is error, blindness, lies—if God himself turns out to be our largest lie?"[33]

He accepted that the scientific ethic was in many respects the highest expression of endeavour in the modern era. But some of its implications were deeply despairing. With the acceptance of Darwin's hypothesis on human evolution, the West had crossed the last great epistemological frontier. It had entered the intimate realm of the self. It appeared to offer a chance to restructure human nature.

It was not enough to claim, as most positivists did, that because science was value free it could not be put in the service of political movements or parties. The twentieth century exposed that illusion early on, when the chemists became a party to the invention of poison gas, to that unique marriage of technology and bureaucracy. Freed from any moral constraints or religious scruples, modern scientists were quite prepared, in Nietzsche's vivid phrase, "to vivisect the human soul".

Thirdly, Nietzsche was not blind to the other danger, the overly metaphysical nature of German philosophy. He regretted that Germany had produced most of the great ideas of the nineteenth century. As he remarked in an entry in his *Notebooks* of 1880, the most original thoughts were often foolish. Unfortunately, the Germans suffered from a "rage for originality".[34]

In the unoriginality of English thinking, however, he saw no consolation. To him it seemed to provide few reasons that made life worth living. It seemed to offer only an escape from the dilemmas that made life challenging and worthwhile—for it is metaphysics and the debate about values that have been at the heart of Western philosophy from the time of the pre-Socratics. It is the continual questioning—what is man, what is the meaning of history, and what is man's relationship to it—that has distinguished the Western consciousness from every other.

The Anglo-American school of philosophy has paid a high price for the attempt to purge philosophy itself of its metaphysical dimensions in order to produce clarity of expression. It is a characteristic, of course, of all speculative enquiries that its most influential thinkers are those who find the most compelling vocabulary in which to express their own ideas. Writers like Freud had a genius for metaphor and a marvellous power of imagination that contrasted notably with the austere language of the empirical tradition. That is why liberal writers have so admired them. Auden called Freud "not a person but a whole climate of opinion", and Harold Bloom more recently, "the central imagination of our age". By contrast, the language of empiricism was singularly uninspiring.

The empirical school has also degenerated into word games and an interest in semantics, which has made it largely inaccessible in the popular imagination. In continually reflecting upon itself, philosophy looks like the embodied doubt of its own possibility.

It is a predicament that Nietzsche himself anticipated. Once the philosopher lost faith in his ability to communicate any metaphysical truths, he would become imprisoned in his own subconsciousness. Nothing would speak to him anymore, he wrote, "except his own speech; and deprived of any authority from a divinely ordered universe, it is only about his speech that his speech can speak with a measure of philosophical assurance".[35]

Fourthly, Nietzsche also took exception to what he considered to be the excessive importance that the English attached to political thought. For their own part, of course, the English frequently criticised the disengagement of German writers from the political realm that was such a marked feature of German culture for much of the twentieth century. But as Michael Hamburger reminds us, although German thinking before 1945 was indeed bedevilled at times by a scepticism towards politics, the English have been in danger of the opposite fault, of giving politics too large a role in life. Their imagination has been cramped by a literalness, a notion of realism, that is so intellectually limiting that it has invested life with a drab efficiency, without enriching or refining our experience.[36] Even today English writers, in their obsession with common sense, have been largely hostile to any attempt to question the importance of the *political* in human life. It is a fault, claims Milan Kundera, that can be found even in the work of George Orwell, one of the few liberal writers with an insight into the nature of the totalitarian experience. It was, however, a one-dimensional insight, which ensured that even his novel *1984*, despite the high opinion in which it is still held, was a flawed work. It is not a novel at all, but propaganda.

It was not even useful propaganda, Kundera claims, because of its unremitting bleakness. Its power resides in its implacable reduction of reality to the political dimension alone, as well as its reduction of that dimension to what was exemplarily negative about it.

In his obsession with the 'political', Orwell excluded everything else that made it possible in real life for people to survive the totalitarian experience. In Kafka's totalitarian vision, by contrast, there is always hope, there are always moments that are life enhancing. His characters retain to the end a freedom of decision that makes them human. In Orwell's depiction there is nothing but a war on life, there is nothing that is uplifting. His depiction of a totalitarian society is reduced to "a simple listing of its crimes".[37]

One explanation is that very little importance is attached to aesthetics in the empirical mind. In his later years Thomas Mann drew an important distinction between the two totalitarian faiths of the age. Communism, he claimed, wanted to politicise art; fascism wanted to "aestheticise" politics. One reason why communism wanted to politicise art lay in the knowledge that art affords a retreat, that its rationale and justification are to enhance the private rather than the collective life, and in the process increase our enthusiasm for it. One of the reasons why national socialism tried to aestheticise politics lay in its recognition that art was, in Nietzsche's words, "essentially affirmation, blessing, the deification of existence".

Art can transform the way we look at the world. It can help us transcend our political condition and enrich our life in a way that politics, on its own, rarely can. As Nietzsche once wrote, "one possesses art lest we perish of the truth".[38] Art engages the heart as well as the intellect. Political truth, by comparison, often tends to be one-dimensional. The Nazis wanted to enhance the political; the communists wanted to politicise the senses. Both failed. Their failure was a significant factor in the collapse of both the Third Reich and the Soviet Union. It is one, nonetheless, that has been almost totally neglected by liberal writers.

Ultimately, however, what Nietzsche found most objectionable in English thinking was its refusal to acknowledge the historical contingency of its own beliefs. The fact that England's philosophers identified so closely with their own experience is what he found particularly meretricious. Their thinking, he wrote in *Genealogy of Morals,* was "by nature unhistorical". The utilitarians, for example, had mistakenly taken the contingent traits exhibited by nineteenth-century Englishmen as universal features of human nature. The English, he wrote, had unwittingly gazed across time and beyond their frontiers through the distorting lens of their own moral convictions.

In their intense positivism most liberal writers had transformed a set of propositions about life in the West into a universal ideology—at which point, added Santayana, writing after the Second World War, it ceased to be "empirical and British" and became "German and transcendental". At that point moral life was reduced to the development of a single spirit that was obtainable "through a series of necessary phases, each higher than the preceding one".[39]

Santayana was not the only liberal thinker to express his misgivings about the conviction that the United States offered the rest of the world a glimpse of its own future. Another critical voice was that of the English philosopher Michael Oakeshott. In an essay that was never published in his lifetime, he drew an important distinction between "the politics of faith" and "the politics of scepticism", making explicit, as nowhere else in his published work, the historically grounded nature of thought.

It had been the work of the seventeenth-century sceptics such as John Locke, Oakeshott argued, to remove religious 'enthusiasm' from the discourse and practise of politics. Locke had argued that it was inappropriate, for example, to ask any government to define an eternal religious 'truth'. If government were to enforce any form of belief it must be on account not of the 'truth' but of the disorder and insecurity that often springs from the absence of established religion.

In this regard Oakeshott took particular issue with the American model of liberalism, which had allowed the sceptical faith in universal suffrage and popular government that appeared in the writing of Bentham and James Mill to become the idea that there was only one form of government appropriate to man. It was, he wrote, an 'illusion' that was more appropriate to the politics of faith.

Liberal societies were always loud in their defence of preserving links with the past, or building upon them. Yet in the course of the nineteenth century liberal regimes had often trampled upon the traditions and conventions of every society except their own. What was scepticism, asked Oakeshott, but an understanding of politics as "a conversation in which past, present and future each had a voice"?[40] Yet it was that voice that the liberal powers had tried to stifle in their conviction that what was true for them had to be true for everyone else. It was on that principle that the Americans had gone to war: to make the world safe for their own understanding of democracy.

It was a quintessential liberal response to history. If the Americans rejected the idea that there was a plan to history that could be decoded

(Hegel's thought of God that can be detected through reason), they themselves were quick to draw an invisible line of rectitude through history and in that way take power over it. Against the awesome "thus it was" of history they set the overawing majesty of "it might have been". Even if liberal societies had to live with the fear that their values might not win out, that would still not have challenged the validity of their beliefs. "The line of rectitude would still traverse history".[41]

Looking back at Nietzsche's critique of liberalism we can see why a society like his own found itself in an irreconcilable dispute with the West. There was never really a dialogue between them. Given the circumstances of twentieth-century Europe, the only dialectic possible was war.

At best, they found themselves engaged in a dialogue of the deaf. If a country like the United States (like Britain before it) rarely subjected its convictions to close scrutiny, its self-confidence enabled it to win all but one of its wars. Liberal societies were all the stronger because of the strength of their convictions. But the liberal conscience was often powerless to prevent wars from breaking out. It did not address the deep anxieties that often made the illiberal response to history so compelling. Perhaps it could never have succeeded. Perhaps the issue had to be resolved on the battlefield. Nevertheless, the greatest indictment of the liberal creed was that it showed little understanding of other people's fears and anxieties. Like all the important ideologies of the twentieth century it took few ideas seriously except its own. It was intensely self-regarding.

The Problem of Not Reading Nietzsche Correctly

The liberal world paid a heavy price for not taking Nietzsche seriously enough. There was in the brightly lit optimistic world that it painted a parallel, dark, silent world in the unconscious mind of Europe, a world in which doubts and resentments hovered and grew, waiting to be clothed with the name of thought and action. The predisposition of Woolf's generation to dismiss illiberal writers as obscure, obscurantist or even silly proved almost fatal in 1940 when Britain came within a narrow margin of defeat.

The danger was made clear to the philosopher L. T. Hobhouse during the Second World War. In a preface to his book *The Metaphysical Theory of the State,* he tells us that he had been annotating Hegel's *Philosophy of Right* when he heard German planes bombing London. His first impulse had been to throw down his book with a sense of the uselessness of philosophical speculation. His second was the kind of recognition that also inspired Karl Popper during the war: to recognise that without Hegel the Second World War might never have occurred.[42]

At least Hobhouse had checked himself in time. Others did not. Take the case of Arthur Koestler, a political refugee whom André Malraux met in

1936 just after his release from a Francoist prison cell where he had spent months under sentence of death.[43] One night during the Blitz he recalled listening to a discussion on the radio comparing the relative merits of American and English novels. The first speaker had just finished his presentation when an air raid warning sounded. After a brief interval the discussion continued. The third speaker was a crumpled, tweedy, loveable little man who attacked the American writers Hemingway, Faulkner and Dos Passos for their morbid preoccupation with violence. "When you read their books", he complained, "you would think that the ordinary man spends his life punching people's noses or being hit on the head". In fact ordinary people rarely met with violence in their lives.

At that point another bomb whistled and crashed some blocks away and the antiaircraft guns started firing. Waiting patiently for a lull, the professor calmly continued: "What I mean to say is, violence rarely plays a part in ordinary people's lives, and it is positively indecent for an artist to devote so much time and space to that kind of thing".[44]

Here was an implacable belief in liberal internationalism. Unfortunately, the real world in which British intellectuals lived in 1940 was not a Bloomsbury salon any more than it was Hobbes's state of nature in its most brutal and unqualified form. It was a world in which nations, like their citizens, paid dearly for their dreams and illusions.

Leonard Woolf's autobiography bears testament to the contrast. It reveals an imperfect understanding of the terms on which life in the twentieth century had to be lived. As a Jew he had all the more reason to try to understand them, to grasp the deeper realities behind history. "As a woman", complained his wife, Virginia, "I have no country"—"as a woman my country is the whole world".[45] As an internationalist, Leonard might well have said the same about himself, but the times were not propitious for internationalist thinking. Whether or not he chose to claim citizenship of a country, membership of a community in Nazi-occupied Europe was determined by others.

In any event, neither Leonard nor his wife had any intention of waiting to find out their fate. An entry in Virginia's diary, dated 13 May 1940, records her entering into a suicide pact with her husband. If the Germans had reached London it would have had to be honoured if Leonard was to avoid deportation or worse. On 9 June she wrote: "As a sample of my present mood: capitulation will mean all Jews to be given up. Concentration camps. Go to our garage", which had been turned by her husband into a "suicide shed". If the worst happened they intended to douse it with petrol and set it alight with themselves inside.[46]

After Virginia's death Leonard became more realistic. The title of the last volume of his autobiography, *The Journey Not the Arrival Matters,* suggests as much. In his long journey through life, he confessed, he had arrived at no goal and achieved little of what he had hoped to accomplish:

Looking back at the age of 88 over the 57 years of my political work in England, knowing what I aimed at and the results, meditating on the history of Britain and the world since 1914, I see clearly that I achieved practically nothing. The world today and the history of the human anthill during the past 57 years would be exactly the same as if I had played ping pong instead of sitting on committees and writing books.[47]

Woolf's autobiography was, in a very English sense, an existential enquiry into who he was, who he might have been and what he had become. The future tense is crucial in the making of any autobiography. By turning back we seek to move forwards so that life can begin again. For Woolf this was too late. Instead, looking back at fifty-seven years of endless discussions on how to prevent war and promote universal government, he reckoned he had sat through "between 150,000 and 200,000 hours of perfectly useless work". He and his generation certainly worked hard to achieve a better world. They were sustained by a rare enthusiasm and emotion. Unfortunately, the earnestness with which they talked into the night to avert another war was underpinned by a peculiar deficiency of imagination.

In his defence he claimed that this was due not so much to personal failure on his part as to the general human condition. But that is precisely the point. He misread human nature. He failed to grasp its frailty as well as its aggressiveness, its fears as much as its hopes, the anxieties that drove ordinary men living in quite extraordinary times to find some security in the illiberal agenda.

Woolf's influence could have been considerable. His ideas were influential in creating the League of Nations. He was a coarchitect with Philip Noel-Baker of the first Labour Government's foreign policy. But he expected too much of human nature as well as of the times in which he lived. If for much of his life Woolf was out of sympathy with the times, the times were also out of sympathy with him. Sadly, he ended his life out of sympathy with himself. When reading his autobiography it is hard not to be reminded of Samuel Beckett's *How It Is,* which, its title notwithstanding, tells us only how it *wasn't.*

The Liberal Temper

Goethe has an excellent aphorism defining the state of mind which he calls thatige skepsis—*active doubt. It is doubt which so loves truth that it neither dares rest in doubting nor extinguish itself by unjustified belief.*
—Thomas Huxley, 'The Darwinian hypothesis',
The Times (26 December 1859)

One of the books whose insights I have found invaluable is *The Cultivation of Hatred,* the penultimate volume of Peter Gay's monumental study of the Victorian mind. Illiberalism, as he writes, was not only to be found on the continent. It was to be found also in the heartland of liberal England. Both the English and the Germans developed alibis for aggression and justifications for war.

The nineteenth-century bourgeoisie engaged in continuous debates about the moral nature of aggression. These were particularly intense when nation clashed with nation or class with class. Sometimes they were conscious of the aggression in themselves; sometimes they were unaware of it. In the 1930s the black poet Aimé Césaire claimed that he could hear "the white world stumbling in great alibis" of aggression.[48] Gay uses the same term to describe the beliefs and principles that inspired Western man to attempt to master nature, geography and the 'other', and ultimately, of course, 'self'.

I shall look at three "alibis of aggression" in the liberal imagination to illustrate the fact that the key difference between the liberal and the illiberal consciences was as much a factor of attitude, or belief, if the two can be distinguished. All three alibis provided a collective identification that was both inclusive and exclusive at the same time. All three helped to identify the "outsider" who was to be bullied, ridiculed or exterminated at will. All three cultivated hatred in both senses of the term—they at once fostered and restrained it while providing excuses for natural aggression.

The difference was that however angry they might be at the world, the most intelligent Western writers were prepared in the end to live with ambiguity. Gay finds most of his examples of his "alibis of aggression" in nineteenth-century Europe. But they were even more evident in the twentieth-century imagination. They figure prominently in the work of three authors who are frequently identified with the liberal cause.

Conan Doyle and the Lost World

> There was the grizzly thing again. It was coming across an open space, running almost on all fours in joltering leaps. It was hunchback and very big and low, a grey hairy wolf-like monster. At times its long arms nearly touched the ground.

This is how H. G. Wells described Neanderthal man in his short story 'The Grizzly Folk', seen through the eyes of the first 'true man' drifting north into the lands of the primordial world. Here we have all the themes of fear of the 'other'—a perception (based on both fear and disgust) of a different stage in human evolution—a fear that has survived in the Western imagination; in time the Neanderthals, who had been displaced by Cro-Magnon man, were gradually displaced in the psychic imagination into the ogres and giants of nursery folklore.[49]

In fact, modern science has largely challenged the nineteenth-century version of events. The Neanderthals were probably not killed off. They gradually yielded to a race that had a competitive advantage in its genetic inheritance, particularly in the invention of a spoken language. The 'new men' left the Neanderthals alone. Unlike the Europeans themselves as they fanned out and occupied the world in the nineteenth century, the new men apparently lived side by side with the Neanderthals, probably happily enough. Rather than killing them, they ignored them.

Of course this was not the early-twentieth-century understanding of primitive man. Take the work of Arthur Conan Doyle, a man who spent a considerable amount of his time and personal fortune in a variety of liberal causes from penal reform to the abolition of capital punishment. In *The Lost World* (1912), however, there is little liberalism. In the words of Lord John Roxton: if he had fifteen men with rifles, "I'd clear out the whole infernal gang of them and leave this country a bit cleaner than we found it". The 'them' in question are ape-men living on a plateau the size of Sussex, which they share with various Jurassic life forms, including dinosaurs, who have been cut off from time, exempt from Darwinian selection.

With the help of Professors Challenger and Summerlee and the amiable reporter Malone, Roxton goes on to exterminate the savage ape-men, in part to advance the evolution of the Indians who also live on the plateau, trapped by an accident of time; the Indians, although savage, are distinctively closer ancestors to the Europeans. Indeed, at the end of the novel the leaders of the expedition congratulate themselves on ensuring the survival of one race over another. As Challenger declares, the conquest of one nation by another nation is a trivial matter in comparison.

The modern age spent much of its time constructing the 'other' inside or outside society—whether in the form of the bourgeois enemy, the malign revolutionary, or the irredeemable native. All three were themes of pseudo-scientific discourse. Politicians contrived to discover great historical engagements in which they were involved in a life-and-death struggle, between Anglo-Saxons and Celts, Aryans and Semites, whites and blacks. "Indian hating", Herman Melville puts in the mouth of one of his main characters in *The Confidence Man* (1837), "still exists and no doubt will continue to exist as long as Indians do".[50]

Liberal England had its own Indians—the Irish. Carlyle had a radical answer to the Irish Question: "black-lead them and put them over with the niggers". The Webbs thought them worse than Hottentots. The eminent historian James Froude described the people of Catholic Ireland as "more like tribes of squalid apes than human beings". On a visit to Ireland in 1860 the novelist Charles Kingsley complained of finding thousands of "white chimpanzees . . . along that hundred miles of horrible country: "To see white chimpanzees is dreadful; if they were black, one would not feel it so much, but their skins, except where tanned by exposure, are as white as ours."[51] As James Joyce has Madden point out in *Stephen Hero,* the Irish Celt is libelled as "a baboon faced Irishman that we see in *Punch*".[52] It was precisely to offset such race libels that he set himself the task of redeeming the Irish nation.

In Conan Doyle's account the ape-men have to be exterminated because they have crossed the racial divide. Ultimately, however, they have to be destroyed because they are a mirror image of the white man—in this case of a race not that removed from ape-men: the Irish.

"Ever since I ran wild in Ireland I have been a bold and skilled tree climber", remarks Malone. His genealogy already has been observed by Challenger:

> "Roundheaded", he muttered. "Brachycephalic, grey eyed, black haired with suggestions of the negroid. Celtic, I presume?"
> "I am an Irishman, sir."
> "Irish, Irish?"
> "Yes".[53]

As an Irishman, Malone feels particularly threatened by the inferior species, which reminds him all too acutely of his own distant cultural affiliation. Towards the end of the novel, with the uncanny insight that Conan Doyle often displayed throughout his life, he makes Malone return to the plateau later in life. Killing has aroused in him a blood lust, first for sport, then for hunting other species. Later still be becomes a war correspondent, awaiting that European war two years later that would also transform pre-1914 Europe into "a lost world" for so many of the soldiers who returned from the front.

George Bernard Shaw and
The Simpleton of the Unexpected Isles

Another alibi to which Gay refers is the cult of manliness that was to find its apotheosis in the homoerotic literature of the First World War. Manliness was a liberal virtue too. Leslie Stephens, in an essay on Macaulay, the great Whig historian of the early nineteenth century, admitted that he suffered from "a certain brutal insularity" but praised him for being "a thoroughly manly author . . . combative to a fault".

This, writes Victor Houghton, was the criterion of an intellectual—not a modern intellectual, of course, but a Victorian, one whose roots were in the same soil. In the case of Stephens and Macaulay, this was literally true, for both grew up in Clapham, where their fathers were evangelical businessmen. That explains why, despite recognising Macaulay's limitations, Stephens fundamentally identified with him. He too was proud of his manly success, so much so that he attacked John Stuart Mill, the greatest liberal thinker of the age, for lacking virility, for needing "some red blood infused into his veins".[54]

Across the Atlantic an American version of manliness soon grew up. It was expressed most compellingly by the first of the twentieth-century presidents, Theodore Roosevelt, who preached the virtues of courage and patriotism and "aggressiveness in well-doing". He had no doubt of the moral necessity of heroic action: "you can be just as decent as you wish as long as you are prepared to fight. If you fight hard enough you are bound to secure the respect of your peers".[55]

Much of the work of George Bernard Shaw reveals a similar insistence on the need for heroism in life, together with a willingness to write off any group that gets in the way of its own redemption. This is particularly true of his last plays written in the 1930s England. One of the most interesting, *The Simpleton of the Unexpected Isles,* was written in 1933 when Shaw was seventy-seven.

It is a neglected curio. Divided into a prologue and two acts, two-thirds of the play is meant to be an entertaining satire on modern Britain. The prologue opens in the emigration office of the Unexpected Isles, a tropical outpost of the British Empire. Hyerling, a sweaty, alcoholic emigration officer, is startled by the arrival of a young woman who drags him outside for a tour of the island. During the tour they meet Pra, a native priest, who persuades both them and two English tourists to take part in a eugenic experiment. As a breeding ménage à six, they plan to raise children who will embody the best attributes of Eastern and Western cultures.

Twenty years later, four children, two of each sex, have been raised. They are all beautiful and talented to be sure, but they are also preternaturally idle and amoral. "We have no minds", they insist, "we have imagination".[56]

At the end of the play the Angel of Death appears in person. The Last Judgement is at hand. Love, Pride, Heroism and Imperialism promptly snuff it, as do bankers, politicians, doctors and other "useless people, mischievous people, selfish somebodies and noisy nobodies". This is not the end of the world "but the end of its childhood". Some lives, the audience is told, have no use and are better terminated. "We are being valued", says someone, but *who* is doing the valuing and what criteria are being employed in "weeding out the garden"?

When Shaw was writing the play, Stalin's purges were already under way and Hitler was in the second year of his chancellorship. The world was closer than ever to a real last judgement. That is why Shaw's preface to the play is even uglier than the introduction to *On the Rocks* (which was published in the same year), which praised Stalin's secret police, the Cheka, and recommended 'extermination' for those guilty of "incorrigible social incompatibility". Impressed by the pluck of Djerjinsky, the leader of the Cheka, in personally shooting an inept station master, Shaw maintained that if a citizen's life "costs more than it is worth to the community, the community may painlessly extinguish it".

Shaw admired Stalin. He never admired Hitler, but his affinities with fascism were more marked. "The majority of men at present in Europe", he wrote ". . . have no business to be alive".[57] Heroes must be bred and people licked into shape. The only faith he professed towards the end of his life was "life itself as a timeless power which is continually driving onward and upward ... growing from within by its own inexplicable energy, into ever higher and higher forms of organisation". Such sentiments had already been made popular by Mussolini. Well might James Drennan, in his book *Oswald Mosley and British Fascism* (1934), argue that Shaw had "an influence on the development of the fascist conception", and that he had shown in his more recent writings "both sympathy for fascist action and belief in the fascist future".[58] There are few better examples of the treason of the *clercs* than *The Simpleton of the Unexpected Isles*.[59]

H. G. Wells and the Discovery of the Future

When was the future discovered? It is an odd question, perhaps, but it was one that one of the most influential English writers, H. G. Wells, was among the first to ask. It was discovered, he claimed somewhat immodestly, at the turn of the century, in a lecture he himself had delivered in February 1902.[60]

The previous year he had published his first work of nonfiction, *Anticipations,* a 'prospectus' he called it, of his own opinions. The novelty of the book lay in the ambitious attempt to write the history of the future before it happened. The attempt was deliberate as he made clear in his Royal Institution lecture: "It is our ignorance of the future and our persuasion that this ignorance is incurable ... that alone has given the past its enormous predominance in our thoughts".[61]

In the nineteenth century, he wrote, genealogy had given man a clearer vision of the past. In the twentieth century, what he called 'human ecology', a new kind of inductive history—a working out of the biological and intellectual consequences of evolution, would be used to chart the possibilities that the future offered and to provoke men into making sensible use of them.[62]

The future, alas, required Gay's third alibi of aggression, manliness, if it was to be lived on one's own terms. It even required war as a source of manly virtue. Success or survival in the modern world seemed to depend on being more competitive and ultimately more aggressive than one's opponent. Both social Darwinism and Marxism were strategies of survival. Darwinism was widely viewed as one of the most important intellectual forces to have eroded the traditional moral order. By explaining man's animality it is said to have weakened the Christian association of war with sin. It was also suspected of contributing to the cult of violence, one that romanticised force as exciting, instinctive and elemental.

What can be said with greater certainty is that in challenging the permanence of the human condition, Darwin's *Origin of Species* introduced into Western thinking the belief that the logic of knowledge and hence the treatment of morality and religion might be transformed into the logic of struggle instead.

Liberal England worshipped force as much as anyone else. Leonard Woolf's nephew, Clive Bell, records having dined with a British officer soon after the Russo-Japanese War (1904–1905). At one point in the conversation they both discussed what constituted 'civilisation'. The officer told him that he had some difficulty in answering the question but none in answering another: When could a state be said to be civilised? The test in his eyes seemed to be success in war. People assured him that for centuries Japan had a considerable literature and an exquisite art, but the newspapers never referred to it as a 'civilised' country until its war with Russia—until, that is, it had fought and beaten a first-class European power.[63]

Such thinking was not confined to Britain. Many Americans did not take the Japanese seriously until after the attack on Pearl Harbor. In John Hersey's 1947 novel *The Call*, a description of an American missionary in China, the narrator observes that the Japanese seemed to be transported by their attack on the United States. "They had stopped being caricatures of themselves and had turned into real people".[64]

It was, of course, this bellicosity that made its own contribution to the First World War. The volunteers volunteered for many reasons, but one that cut across the grain of everything else was the desire to be 'simple and natural', to revolt against excessive civilisation. This was immediately translated into a medical language in which robust health was seen as preferable to the sickness of a weak and overrefined society.[65]

All these themes can be found in Wells's writing. As early as his novella *The Time Machine* he had painted the sad picture of a humanity grown "indescribably frail" and decadent through many years of peace. The Eloi—like cattle—"knew no enemies and provided no needs". Their end was the same. They became a source of protein for the vicious but aggressive Morlocks, living in their subterranean kingdom, venturing out at night only for food. At the end of the book the time traveller comes to the conclusion that moral strength is the outcome of a need, or a danger, and that security sets a premium on feebleness.

Manliness, Wells wrote, could have no time for the "multitude of contemptible silly creatures, fear driven and helpless and useless . . . feeble, inefficient, born of unrestrained lusts". Contemplating "the spectacle of a mean spirited, under-sized, diseased little man . . . married to some under fed, ignorant, ill shaped, plain and diseased little woman, and guilty of the lives of ten or twelve ugly ailing children", he warned that the leaders of the ideal state would have "little pity and less benevolence" for such inferior types. Precisely what would be done to curtail their "reproductive excesses" was never specified, but there were ominous hints at aversion therapy. For those who fell behind, life would have to be made "unpleasant and difficult"; they "can easily be made to dread it". As he argued elsewhere, the mass of human population was "inferior in their claim upon the future." In that sense, they were historyless.[66]

In the very last years of his life, haunted by the images of Hiroshima and Belsen, Wells found himself looking for a new kind of man, a new species "better adapted to face the fate that closes in more and more swiftly upon mankind". He wanted to be in "at the death of Man—to have a voice in his replacement". As the shadows closed in he painted a revealing mural on the wall behind his house in Hanover Terrace. It was a set of panels depicting the story of evolution, a Darwinian gloss on the Last Judgement. Beneath the figure of man he wrote, "Time to go".[67]

The liberal convictions of the three authors I have cited were in many respects just as prominent as their illiberal opinions. Wells, like Woolf, was a Fabian socialist dedicated to improving the lot of man. Shaw was also a member of the Fabian circle, a man whose plays did much to illuminate the social inequities of middle-class Britain. Conan Doyle was a noted prison reformer. Yet all three advanced ideas that would not have been ill received in Mussolini's Italy.

If their illiberal views have been neglected in the past that is because their readers and devotees have felt uncomfortable about the ambiguity of the modern consciousness: the fact that liberalism and illiberalism can be traced back to the same roots. That is why Peter Gay prefers to talk about the liberal temperament rather than liberal ideology as the sheet anchor of English liberal life.[68]

Gay describes how, in the course of the nineteenth century, even writers who put forward murderous imperialist theories and conflict-centred philosophies had to confront an uncomfortable ethical, religious and political sensibility. Even the most persuasive writers who provided "alibis for aggression" had to contend with the liberal conscience (at least in the liberal world), in large part because their ideas did not "ring true" in the minds of their readers.

It is for that reason that any account of illiberal ideas must begin with a discussion of the liberal consciousness.

War and the Liberal Consciousness

The Zeitgeist of every age is like a sharp east wind which blows through everything. You can find traces of it in all that is done thought and written, in music and painting, in the flourishing of this or that art. It leaves its mark on everything and everyone.
—Arthur Schopenhauer, *Essays and Aphorisms*

If I am right in suggesting that the liberal temperament was no less important than liberal ideas in ultimately determining human behaviour, if people were predisposed to think the way they did, then an understanding of the prevailing consciousness is all-important. The liberal consciousness allowed people to share different perspectives on life. It enabled them to live with self-doubt even at the cost of cynicism. It encouraged, in turn, a tolerance of other opinions. It demanded respect for dissent as a necessary part of self-questioning.[69]

In the twentieth century liberalism demanded a belief in the new scientific and intellectual perspectives on life (with all this meant in terms of accepting ambiguity and scepticism). Inevitably, it also produced a critical response, a rejection of the new scientific principles, an insistence on an unambiguous truth and a collective will.

The basic concept of social and political life, of course, will never be radically transformed by the universal acceptance of a paradigm that can be encapsulated in a neat scientific proposition, such as Einstein's formula $E=mc^2$. But as Schopenhauer asserted, when the Zeitgeist changes, those changes can be found everywhere from literature to politics. As J.G.A. Pocock argued, when a change in a society's self-awareness has occurred, its style of thinking and acting are irreversibly altered: "There may still be much in its traditions of behaviour which has not emerged into consciousness and perhaps never will. What has changed, however, is its mode of being and becoming conscious of itself and its existence in time, and once that has happened a society is no longer what it was".[70]

What is interesting about the early years of the twentieth century is that a number of writers were quite conscious of a profound change in the way people looked at the world. "In or about December 1910", wrote Virginia Woolf, "human character changed". All human relations, she observed, "have shifted—those between masters and servants, husbands and wives, parents and children. And when human relations change there is, at the same time, a change in religion, conduct, politics and literature".[71]

What changed, of course, was not character itself but how it was *viewed*. Literature and art in particular reflected this transformation. Both hold the key to what Woolf grasped without expressing herself particularly clearly, namely, that the world had entered into a new period of subjectivism.

So far, added Giovanni Papini the following year, art had concerned itself only with the external description of ordinary things "on the basis of ordinary consciousness". Now art had "interiorized" itself. The artist was interested in the spiritual more than the material appearance of what he painted.[72]

According to Henri Lefebvre the change came three years earlier than Woolf claimed, in 1907, when Picasso discovered a new way of painting in which the entire surface of the canvas was used but there was no horizon and no background. There was no reference point. In a stroke, Picasso had challenged the Euclidean idea of space that had been dominant for centuries. What he had also done, writes Lefebvre, was to supply a vision that the world had been waiting for; and he had done so just as the general European crisis broke, just as all the reference points in Europe that had once made life seem so fixed were challenged by the Great War.[73]

Two contemporary writers who lived through this change understood its nature quite early in their careers. As the Austrian novelist Robert Musil recognised, the old consciousness had not been swept away by the war. The war was only part of a much wider development. When it came it was something of an anticlimax—even a supernumerary event.[74] José Ortega y Gasset also rejected the idea that what had happened in 1914 was in itself especially important. "An isolated fact, although of the most enormous size, does not explain any historical reality; it must first be fitted into the whole framework of a type of human life".[75]

Whether or not we wish to date what happened to a specific event, or a specific painting, what does seem clear is that the modern world underwent what Lefebvre calls a "change of course", or a change of consciousness. Changes *in* consciousness occur quite frequently in history. Men are made more aware of the external world and respond to it in different ways. They can become, for example, more sensitive to the suffering of others, or more aware of the existence of issues never previously acknowledged. A change *of* consciousness, however, is more profound, for it represents not only a response to the world but a challenge to many old ideas and beliefs, one that is frequently accompanied by a wish to change the world in tune with a reinterpretation of reality.

The change we are looking at was reflected most of all in the scientific imagination. Indeed, arguably this is where it had the greatest impact on politics and political life. Writing in 1923, Ortega y Gasset recounted how, in the introduction of the inaugural issue of *Espectador* in January 1916, some months before Einstein published the first notes on his theory of relativity, Ortega had put forward a brief exposition of the doctrine of perspective, providing references ample enough to transcend physics and include all reality. As he concluded, this correspondence of views was not coincidental, but predetermined. It represented "a similar cast of thought" that had become, in turn, "a sign of the times".[76]

Perspectivism soon went far beyond Einstein. In 1927 the German physicist Werner Heisenberg developed the uncertainty principle, which argued that although there exists a body of exact mathematical laws, they cannot be interpreted as expressing a simple relationship between objects existing in space or time. It is not possible to decide, other than arbitrarily, what objects should be considered part of an observed system and what should be considered part of the observer's conceptual world. No observer can observe a system without obscuring the observed system's truth. An object is distorted and changed in the act of observation.

A year later Kurt Gödel did for mathematics what Heisenberg had done for physics. What came to be known as Gödel's theorem (1931) asserted that there are formally undemonstrable arithmetical truths. It is impossible within the framework of a mathematical system to demonstrate its internal consistency without using principles of inference whose own consistency is open to question. Our powers of empirical perception and our powers of pure logical conception are largely incapable of making total sense of all the facts that make up the truth.

What the new science asserted was that it might not be possible to explain everything or how the world works. This acknowledgement was more than a recognition of the limitation of theory. It was a recognition that knowledge itself was limited, that reason and wisdom are not necessarily the same. More important, it challenged the old scientific proposition that science itself was anchored in an absolute truth. It argued instead that it is impossible for the mind to deal with anything but ideas about reality. Whether something is true is a matter not of how closely its corresponds to absolute truth but whether it is consistent with our own experience. The main thrust of the new thinking was that the proper goal of science was to provide a mathematical framework for organising and explaining our experience of the world rather than providing a picture of some reality or historical dialectic that allegedly lay behind it.

Both the theories of relativity and indeterminacy had a profound impact on mid-twentieth-century Europe. As Einstein always insisted, it is the discovery that discovers the discoverer, not the other way round. What is still puzzling is the way in which ideas in one field such as science find a parallel in others such as literature. We are often moved to interpret the world independently of our conscious observations. Referring to the uncertainty principle, the scientist and poet Miroslav Holub reminds us that poetry and science embarked on the same reinterpretation of reality at the same time.

Heisenberg's famous sentence runs: "Even in science the object of research is no longer nature itself but man's investigation of nature". Holub adds that in the development of modern poetry words themselves turn into objects. To paraphrase Heisenberg, the object of poetic inquiry was no longer nature but our use of words. In the realm of language, poetry moved ahead into the twentieth century in parallel with the new scientific paradigm into areas less comprehensible for a reader accustomed to forming coherent mental pictures from a sequence of phrases, that is to say, one accustomed to the traditional poetic use of words.[77]

Can it also be argued that the artistic imagination anticipates the scientific? Shaw thought so. He once claimed that Einstein was the "invention" of the artists who had preceded him: that it was they who had created a language in common, that there is no discovery without a language of discovery. It is the artist who creates the means of communication, linguistic, musical or pictorial, with which to express changes in the way we perceive or reperceive the world. It is he who creates a unity of feeling.

Let me cite two examples. The general theory of relativity was reflected in the reinterpretation of space and time that was part of that revolution in thinking at the beginning of the century to which Woolf drew attention. In dissecting the objects they painted, artists began to see life *simultaneously* from all sides. To the three dimensions of the Renaissance was added a fourth: time.

Relativism is one of the principal themes of *The Man Without Qualities*, Robert Musil's brave attempt to come to grips with the 'meaning' of the First World War. Seldom has a work of literature had such a long gestation period: nearly forty years in the making. The novel is only half of what was originally projected. At Musil's death it remained incomplete. It was an appropriate outcome because it could never have been completed or rounded off, not least because the author believed that there was no clear direction to history.

Musil paints a picture of an atomised world rushing heedlessly towards war. Why heedlessly? Because there is no common perspective from which to look backwards or forwards. There are only individual perspectives that are more or less true for those who experience them. As Ulrich, the hero of the tale, remarks, the narrative order of the past is gone forever: "lucky the man who can say 'when', 'before' and 'after'". Only the historian can understand the meaning of history, for only he has the correct vantage point from which to look back.

Works such as Proust's *Remembrance of Things Past*, Woolf's *To the Lighthouse*, and Fitzgerald's *Tender Is the Night* all reflect a peculiarly modern preoccupation with the psychological experience of time. In Fitzgerald's novel the Bergsonian notion of personal or subjective time forms the implicit basis of comparison between its two leading protagonists: "For him time stood still and then every few years accelerated in a rush like the quick rewind of a film, but for Nicole the years slipped away by clock and calendar and birthdays". According to one critic, the disintegration of the hero of the book results in part from his "dislocated sense of historical time".[79]

Echoes of Heisenberg's theory can also be found in the artistic imagination. Writing in the 1920s, Walter Benjamin explicitly linked the new physics of indeterminacy to the ghostliness of modern urban existence that Kafka had described so forcefully in his novel *The Trial*.

We can add Arnold Schoenberg's serial compositions to the list. What Sigfried Giedion wrote of some of the architectural designs that appeared for the first time at the Werkbund Exhibition in Stuttgart in 1927 might serve as an accurate description of the serialism of the Second String Quartet: "Here is a continuous energy at work: nothing in our life remains an isolated experience, everything stands in a many-sided inter-relationship: within, without, above, below".[80]

It was this aspect of Schoenberg's method that his pupils and disciples such as Anton Webern seized upon in their own work. As Schoenberg himself wrote, the musical space of twelve-tone compositions functions on different planes at the same time: "A musical idea . . . though consisting of melody, harmony and truth is neither the one nor the other alone but all three together".[81] The challenge to tonality in music, like the abandonment of perspective in art, represented a repudiation of the idea of a single style or timeless standard to which the artist was expected to conform. Instead the artist was challenged to be true to himself, to his own understanding of the external world.

No writer is more interesting in this respect than Nietzsche, the seer who haunts the pages of this study. Although Nietzsche was a nineteenth-century writer, writes Paul Hamburger, "he had a long time fuse and the main explosion occurred after his death,"—in the first years of this century. "Posthumous men like me," Nietzsche wrote of himself, "are not so well understood as *timely* men but *they are listened too much better*". His own conception of himself as "untimely" is to be found early in his life. It dates back in fact to one of his very early works, *Untimely Meditations* (1874).[82]

As Jung added, Nietzsche's ideas meant more to the generation of the 1930s than they could possibly have meant to his own. He anticipated the future. He listened to the collective unconscious "and gathered its meaning long before others noticed it". It had "taken the experience of [the First World] War and the post-war social and political phenomena to get an insight into the meaning of *Zarathustra*", his most poetic work, an insight that was only accessible to the generation that had survived the Great War.[83]

Let me mention a particular example of this phenomenon, a passage in the discarded 1886 introduction to Nietzsche's *Human, All Too Human* that makes one wonder whether Kafka read or remembered it. Nietzsche speaks of one who is in danger of starving because he hardly ever finds *his* table set, or *his* food prepared. He is forced to decline the food others eat and thus may "perish of hunger and thirst—out of nausea if in the end he takes what the cook offers": "From revulsion I pushed away all the tables at which I used to eat and vowed that I would rather live, like cattle on grass, or live not at all, rather than share my meals with 'the gang of actors' or 'higher circus riders of the spirit'".[84]

The passage is a metaphor for the undernourishment of the soul, for the soullessness of modern life. In its reference to the circus it also evokes one of Kafka's most poignant stories, that of a hunger artist, a showman's exhibit, who finding himself out of fashion and deserted by the public is forced to join the circus as a freak. One day the foreman is reminded of his existence, just at the point when he is about to die. In the artist's own eyes his life has been a failure. Worse still, the terms on which he has lived have been fraudulent. His massive fasts have not been the product of will power in the service of art but of biological necessity: "'Forgive me', the fasting artist said. 'Why?' 'Because I have to fast. I can't help it. I have never been able to find the kind of nourishment I like'."[85]

Both passages are metaphors for the undernourishment of the soul in an industrial and alienating age. What is particularly striking about the two passages is that Kafka could not possibly have come across Nietzsche's, for the excerpt I have quoted was never published in his lifetime. It was added much later to the standard text. What Kafka read, rather, was the *spirit of the age,* one that he shared with Nietzsche so closely that not only his ideas but also the language in which they were expressed, were reproduced.

For the most part, of course, the great majority of people did not read the works of Nietzsche or Bergson, or flock to the galleries, or, still less, listen to atonal music. Such arguments, however, miss the point. Many of the twentieth century's most important ideas were communicated to an audience that had been waiting to hear them for some time. They "rang true" for a public that had been "awaiting" them for a long time.

Take, for example, the correspondence in thinking between Bergson and Max Planck—a correspondence that Moritz Moszkowski noted in the 1920s. When Bergson broke the line of continuity by metaphysical means, in ascribing, for example, "a cinematographic character" to human knowledge, he was merely "intuiting" what Planck had already "discovered" in quantum theory. In rather graphic language Moszkowski added: "It was probably not a case of the accidental coincidence of a new philosophical view with the results of reasoning from physical grounds but a demand of time exacting that the claims of a new principle be recognised".[86]

Something of this comes out clearly in the writing of the mid-twentieth-century French philosopher Maurice Merleau-Ponty, whose principal work, *The Phenomenology of Perception* (1945) developed the methods of Husserl and Heidegger in an attempt to describe how we experience the world long before we begin to analyse it in abstract or scientific terms.

"Phenomenology for ourselves", he insisted, had given "a number of his contemporaries the impression, on reading Husserl and Heidegger for the first time, not so much of encountering a new philosophy as of recognising what they had been waiting for". If phenomenology was a movement before it became a doctrine or a philosophical system, this was attributable not to accident but to a "demand for awareness" that can be found in the work of Balzac, Proust, Valéry and Cézanne, by virtue of "the same will to seize the meaning of the world or of history as that meaning comes into being". In this way, he added, it had merged "into the general effort of modern thought".[87]

It is a vivid phrase that finds an echo in the first volume of the autobiography of Elias Canetti, in which the author recounts how as a child he had seen a fire break out in a neighbouring house. What impressed him most, at the time, was not the danger in which he found himself but the image of people milling around the burning building. Only many years later did he learn that those indefatigable tiny black figures whose image remained with him for the rest of his life, had been looters, who had thought nothing of exploiting the misfortune of their neighbours.

Years later in a painting by Breughel he rediscovered the image of these little, obsessed people, busying themselves like ants. The picture was so familiar that he could no longer tell what had entered his mind first: the gallery of his own memories or the series of images by the artist. That part of his life that had commenced with the fire had continued in the paintings as though fifteen years had not elapsed in between. Writing of Breughel, Canetti concluded, "I found him present within me as though he had been awaiting me for a long time".[88] As Nietzsche contended, the great ideas of history are nearly always "inaudible"; they steal upon us unsuspected. They are part of the spirit of the time that only a historian looking back can identify clearly.

There is perhaps no more graphic example of literature anticipating a political phenomenon than the work of Franz Kafka. Why did the future enter the artistic mind before it found expression in political texts of the twentieth century? How was it, asks Milan Kundera, that a man who was so notoriously unpolitical could have had an insight into one of the horrors the twentieth century was about to invent?

The answer is to be found in the question itself, for Kafka's insight stemmed precisely from his nonengagement in politics, from his total indifference to the political clichés of his own age. Kafka had a deep insight into the totalitarian nature not only of early-twentieth-century politics but of twentieth-century life.

The ideal of a totally transparent society in which privacy was not allowed and the guilt of the citizen taken for granted corresponded in his world to that of the exemplary bourgeois family. The abolition of the boundary between the public and private worlds, the denial, for example, of the citizen's right to hide anything at all from the state, was reflected in the increasing submission of children to their families in terms of their thoughts as well as actions.[89]

In the mid–nineteenth century a new vision of childhood became accepted in middle-class life. Among the poor the old attitudes lingered on. Poverty bred proximity and so forced adults and children to share the same world. The private world of middle-class children produced an absence of proximity. In Europe upper-middle-class children were forbidden most of the house and lived in nurseries. They lived in a world dominated by tutors or governesses. They were tolerated on sufferance and monitored closely. They were forced into line by a regime that made children more tractable by denying them self-esteem.

As an artist Kafka was not alone in that vision. Take, for example, August Strindberg's account of his childhood, which, in its own way, anticipated Winston Smith's account of his mature life in Orwell's *1984*:

The certainty that every misdeed will be punished makes every child afraid of being accused of it, and John was in a perpetual state of anxiety lest some such misdeed should be discovered.

One day at dinner his father examined Auntie's flask.

"Who's drunk from this?" he asked, looking round the table. No one answered but John blushed.

"So it's you", said his father.

John, who had not even noticed where the wine-flask was hidden, burst into tears and sobbed, "I didn't drink the wine".

"And now you're lying also!"

Also!

"I'll attend to you after dinner."

The thought of how he would be attended to as well as the continuous remarks about John's "secretiveness" caused his tears to flow without pause.

They rose from the table.

"Come with me", said his father as he went into the bedroom.

His mother followed them in.

"Ask father for forgiveness", she said.

"I didn't do it, I didn't do it." He was screaming now.

"I told you to ask father for forgiveness", said his mother twisting his ear.

His father had brought out the whip from behind the mirror.

"Please, dear Papa, please forgive me", bawled the innocent child.

But now it was too late. Asking forgiveness was tantamount to confession.

His mother assisted at the execution.

The child bawled—in indignation, in rage, in pain, but mostly in shame and humiliation.

"Now ask father for forgiveness", said mother.

The child looked at her and despised her. He felt lonely, deserted by her to whom he had always fled to find comfort and compassion, but so seldom justice.

"Dear Papa, please forgive me", he said, biting his lying lips. And then he stole into the kitchen to Louise, the nursery maid, who used to comb and wash him, and sobbed his grief out in her apron.

"Now what have you done, John?", she asked sympathetically.

"Nothing", he answered. "I didn't do it".

His mother came in.

"What is John saying to you", she asked Louise.

"He said he didn't do it."

"Are you still lying."

And John was hauled in again to be tortured into admitting what he had never done.

And so he finally admitted what he had never done.

Splendid moral institution! Sacred family! Divinely appointed and unassailable establishment where future citizens are to be educated in truth and virtue.

The supposed home of all the virtues, where innocent children are tortured into their first falsehood, where wills are broken by tyranny, and self-respect killed by jostling egos. The family! Home of all social evils, a charitable institution for indolent women, a prison workshop for family breadwinners, a hell for children.[90]

This passage is strikingly evocative for it conjures up the first sentence of *The Trial,* which famously begins: "Someone must have falsely denounced Joseph K. for without having done anything wrong he was arrested one morning." From this opening to the hero's death neither he nor anyone else in the novel ever asks the obvious question—what is he supposed to be guilty of? When he protests his innocence the only response he receives is, "That is right, that is how the guilty are wont to talk".

What the examples I have cited may demonstrate is that artists can intuit *possibilities* that have yet to be realised. As Kundera adds, "History does not *invent,* it *discovers.* Through new situations, History reveals what man is, what has been in him 'for a long time', what his possibilities are." The poem is always there, Kundera notes. It does not require the gift of foresight on the part of the poet. Writers only discover human possibilities that have been latent for a long time that history has yet to discover.

Musil put it with his usual force. Possibility, he wrote, does not destroy reality. It offers merely an alternative to real action. The possibilitarian is a man who lives within a world of imagination. He is an observer, not a man of action. His mood is the subjunctive. Identifying possibilities is a *reflective,* not an active process. It requires a sensibility that extends well beyond political life: "It is *reality* that awakens possibilities. . . . Nevertheless, in the sum total or on the average they will always remain the same possibilities going on, repeating themselves until someone comes along to whom something real means no more than something imagined. It is *he* who first gives the new possibilities their meaning and their destiny—he awakens them".[91]

In that sense too, as I have argued, people were awakened to the possibility of an alternative life at a particular point of history. It was those possibilities that many tried to realise through war. In the course of the twentieth century war became more than just an instrument of policy. It became a medium of progress, social reengineering and political change.

Let me make clear from the outset what I am *not* claiming. I am not arguing that the artist has a privileged access to the truth, still less a unique insight into the true nature of the belief systems of his fellows. That claim, of course, has been made by among others Kafka. "I went with Kafka to an exhibition of French painting in the gallery of the Graben", wrote his friend Gustav Janouch. "There were some pictures of Picasso's. Cubist, still lifes, rose-coloured women with gigantic feet. 'He is a wilful contortionist', I said. 'I don't think so', said Kafka. 'He only registers the deformities which have not yet penetrated our consciousness. Art is a mirror which goes fast like a watch—sometimes'".[92]

At the turn of the century, the art historian Germain Bazin even went so far as to describe the pictorial artist as a "kind of magus gifted with second sight", a prophet whose vision was not so much the product of his own time as the presentiment of a time to come. The work of art, he claimed, at least when produced by genius, was often an anticipation or a correspondence, rather than a consequence of modern life.

Bazin was particularly struck by how the collapse of the old order in 1914 had been anticipated by many of the most challenging artists of the time—in the gesticulation of the Cubists, the turbulent landscapes of Vlaminck, the joyless streets of Utrillo, above all the despairing clowns of Picasso's Blue period. Did not the artists become "torturers of the human body", rendering grotesque what for a thousand years had been worshipped as sacred? Wasn't that anticipation enough of what actually happened?[93]

Gertrude Stein was equally insistent in this claim. When she looked back on the Great War she claimed that the Cubist artists to whom Kafka referred had anticipated it many years earlier: "The composition of this war ... was not one in which one man in the centre is surrounded by a lot of others, but a composition that had neither a beginning nor an end, a composition of which one corner was as important as another corner, in fact the composition of Cubism".[94]

Certainly the new avant-garde writers, including the Cubists before the war, had derived a powerful imaginative stimulus from the energy of the machine age and thus perhaps anticipated the industrialised warfare that marked the First World War. At the same time, their artistic creations seemed to reflect accurately the fragmentation of the cultural order, just as the forces unleashed by the war swept away a political order that had endured for nearly a century. Cubism, in that respect, reflected the incomprehension of the world that was such a marked feature of life at the front.

These claims may sound convincing, but we should treat them with caution. No one in history has a privileged access to its 'meaning,' not even the historian. A less reductive claim that I find more convincing was put forward by Johan Huizinga, the great Dutch historian. He was unusual among his colleagues for looking at the relationship between art and the human imagination in an attempt to gauge the nature of the beliefs and customs of the early modern era. In later life he no longer claimed as he had earlier that it was possible to find in the pictures of, for example, Rembrandt's twilight years, a glimpse of Dutch society in decline. What he now claimed, less reductively, was that the idea of an epoch that works of art often give us is more ambiguous than much of the evidence to be found, for instance, from reading its chronicles or documents.

In that sense art can be said not to anticipate a change in consciousness so much as to cast doubt on the permanence of the existing one.[95] This is what Walter Benjamin concluded when looking at Kafka's work. He too had been inclined to call it 'prophetic' but he resisted doing so. Kafka's experience, he concluded, was "based solely on the tradition" to which he had surrendered. "There was no far-sightedness or prophetic vision". Kafka was a listener, not a visionary, and what he 'heard' was not the onset of national socialism but the failure of the past that had seriously infected the present. The devastation, writes Lawrence Langer, that this disease might wreak as it metastasised in the future into racist ideology and the policy of the Final Solution was not even seen in detail by Benjamin himself, who was one of its early victims.[96]

If this analysis is correct we can appreciate why some of the most intelligent intellectuals of the age were attracted to illiberal ideas and beliefs. Many of them felt estranged from the age. This had dangerous implications, of course, for when one is estranged from oneself one is estranged from others too. Many wanted to impose a meaning on history, or define a national destiny, or were prepared to support a nation or a leader in their will to power, in their determination to impose order on chaos.

Even scientists who should have known better were prepared to revolt against the relativism they themselves had brought to light. In Camus's excellent phrase, scientists like Lysenko in Soviet Russia were ordered to "discipline the chromosomes", a reference to the attack on de Vries's insistence on the role of chance in biological evolution. Just as the intellectuals of the twentieth century espoused nineteenth-century ideas, so scientists in the Marxist world were required to demonstrate the universal applicability of nineteenth-century scientific principles. On more than one occasion Engels compared the findings of Darwin in biology and Morgan in anthropology to those of Marx in political economy and history. Indeed, he could find no higher praise in his eulogy at Marx's funeral than to call him "the Darwin of history". What made Marx the most successful ideologue of the age was his claim to be a "scientific socialist". His science, however, was not that which the next phase of modernity required.

The treason of the intellectuals went beyond the literary world, but it is best illustrated in the literary imagination. In this study I have invoked literature even more than philosophy in an attempt to come to grips with the illiberal conscience and the appeal that it had for so many people who were not malign, stupid or even, by their own lights, particularly irrational.

In the next chapter I shall try to illustrate how three writers both represented and helped to define their generation's emotional response to history. All three took as one of the principal themes of their work the belief that war and peace could no longer be distinguished. All three were convinced that war had become the accredited theme of modern life.

The illiberal world of course understood the importance of the creative arts all too well. Once in power it set out to deny the ambiguity that modern art reflected by silencing its practitioners and censoring its new styles. Both the Soviet and Nazi states tried to emasculate the modern sensibility in art by insisting that it conform to "social reality" or by rooting out its "decadent" elements. The upshot of such attempts was that art and life began to diverge drastically. Both were progressively divorced from experience, which was at the heart of scientific perspectivism.

This is what Benda found most distressing about the treason of the intellectuals: their willingness to declare war on the intellect itself. The result was almost catastrophic for the artistic imagination. After Auschwitz, wrote the art historian Will Grohmann, the human body could no longer be painted; after Auschwitz, insisted Theodor Adorno, lyrical poetry could no longer be written.

Chapter Two

War and Peace

War is Peace: doesn't this typically Orwellian phrase succeed in defining the state of the geostrategic world balance?
—Jean Chesneaux, *Brave Modern World*

In 1926 the economist John Maynard Keynes wrote a review of a book by Leon Trotsky entitled *Where Is Britain Going?* Keynes dismissed the work as a "hectoring gurgle", an example of the temper of "a brigand statesman . . . to whom Action means war".

"They smoke peace where there should be no peace", Keynes caricatured the Bolsheviks' war cry. Trotsky was insistent that peace was a sign of "the canting, imbecile emblems of decay, senility and death", that war alone was "life and the life force which exist only in the spirit of merciless struggle". Trotsky's book, Keynes added, was typical of the times, for the Bolsheviks were not alone in their opinion that political life in the twentieth century had become a war of all against all. So too did the Fascists, who had captured power in Italy a few years earlier. Both believed that "in the revolutionary struggle only the greater determination is of avail". As a man who acknowledged "the uselessness, the empty headedness of force at the present stage of human affairs", Keynes could not but find Trotsky's views intensely depressing.[1]

Unfortunately, war and peace were difficult to distinguish for much of the century. War *was* peace in the eyes of many writers, a fact borne out by the language often used. In the Stalinist era the Soviet press was full of phrases such as "the industrial front", or "the battle for coal", or "the red offensive". Even literature was considered to be "a literary front" where writers were enlisted in the class war against bourgeois influences.[2]

From the beginning, the Third Reich too revealed its military character. The German people were constantly exhorted to fight the subsistence battle or the war against waste, or to surpass themselves on the labour front. Even liberal societies invoked the language of war for their everyday imagery—losing battles but winning the war, mounting attacks or "going over the top". Such language is still used in political discourse. War may no longer be regarded as the most noble activity of all, but liberal politicians have not given up using the metaphor of "fighting" for their principles, or "defeating" their rivals. A new language has yet to be found for "winning" respect.[3]

Three writers illustrate this phenomenon, all of them representing different aspects of illiberal thinking. The first, Isaac Babel, was a Jew, an outsider, a minor writer of distinction, who found in a revolutionary war the chance to become an insider, an opportunity for his own people, the Jews, to transcend the life into which they had been born. Violence and the cruelty of war were, for him, the birth pangs, painful to be sure, of a new world in the making.

In Babel we find an unlikely enthusiast for war as the harbinger of a new era, as a medium of social change, the medium of a transforming fire. He lost his faith in 1940 when he was arrested for no apparent reason and silenced by the Stalinist regime with which he had supped too closely.

Ernst Jünger, writing, by contrast, very much from the point of view of an insider, an *haut bourgeois,* believed in the redemptive power of war; it offered the German people a chance to become an 'authentic' people in tune with their 'inner experience' for the first time. Both writers shared an element peculiar to the illiberal temper: a hatred of the social groups in which they had been born. In Babel's case, it was not so much his Jewishness but the terms on which the Jews had to live in a gentile world. In the case of Jünger, it was a hatred of the supposedly unheroic nature of bourgeois life, with its narrowly defined rules.

Once even he recognised that in the nuclear age war had become a dangerous anachronism, he retreated into scientific research. In later life he even became an enthusiast for hallucinogenic drugs and went on a number of 'trips' with his friend Albert Hofmann, the discoverer of LSD. In the 1960s he even became an unlikely hero of the counterculture. In the end, however, he too fell silent, as he withdrew from the world.

I shall conclude this section with a discussion of Curzio Malaparte. In many ways he is the most interesting, if not the most talented, of the three. His early writings leave very little doubt about his engagement with the century at its most violent and elemental. Towards the end of his life, however, he saw nothing redeeming about war or the great causes or moments of crisis that required men to fight their way into history, frequently at an insupportable cost to everything that made life worth living. In the person of Malaparte we have a revolutionary enthusiast of the 1920s who discovered late in the day that war had become an unacceptably dangerous form of national regeneration. As his fellow countryman, Steffano Jacomuzzi, once noted, after two world wars even literature could no longer love parades.

A Jew on Horseback:
Isaac Babel and the Russian Civil War

I am an outsider. . . . I don't belong. I am all alone.
—Isaac Babel, *Diary 1920*

The revolution does not choose its paths; it made its first steps towards victory under the belly of a Cossack's horse.
—Leon Trotsky, *History of the Russian Revolution* (1931)

During Napoleon's retreat from Moscow Clausewitz was particularly sickened by the behaviour of the Cossack soldiers in the service of the Tsar. He found them to be a cruel people, a reminder of the visitations of the steppes people from the thirteenth century. They were now "pitiless, pony-riding nomads" who harried the stragglers as the French army marched west back to Poland, riding down and wiping out groups that fell behind the main force, selling prisoners to peasants for cash, or stripping the unsaleable ones in arctic temperatures to the bare skin for their clothes.[4] Few Western observers have ever found the Cossacks particularly noble or redeeming. Clausewitz was not alone in feeling that they were undeserving of the title 'soldier'.

Many Russian writers, however, came to a very different conclusion. Tolstoy, in his account of the Napoleonic Wars, thought them magnificent in their primitive energy, passion and vitality. Military experts such as Clausewitz were the men whom he despised and despaired of the most, whom he memorably caricatured in a chapter of his greatest novel, *War and Peace*. On the eve of the Battle of Borodino, Clausewitz and his fellow Prussians who have volunteered to serve the Tsar are criticised for displaying a ruthless professionalism, which contrasts with the more earthy sincerity of the Cossack warriors.[5]

A hundred years later the Cossacks found themselves engaged in another conflict, the last stage of the Russian Civil War. By then the war was in its third year. On one front after another the Red Army had been successful. The capital of the White forces in Siberia had fallen in November 1919. The following month the forces of General Anton Denikin were defeated in the south. Another challenge, however, rose in the west and in late April developed into full-scale war with Poland. In May 1920 the First Cavalry Army was moved to the front, a force of 1,600 men. The Cossack cavalry, in fact, became the main offensive arm of the Red Army. The Russian Civil War, of which from the Soviet point of view the war with Poland was merely a part, marked the last major contribution of cavalry in a European conflict.

One young man who joined the Cossack forces was the writer Isaac Babel, in the role of a war correspondent for the Communist party broadsheet, *Red Truth*. There was from the beginning, of course, an extraordinary anomaly in the decision of a Jew to join a Cossack regiment. Traditionally the Cossacks had been the feared and hated enemies of the Jewish people. They were renowned for being tempestuous and violent in comparison with the Jews, who were traditionally seen as intellectual and humane. They were more than this: they were boorish, brutal and suspicious of ideas of any kind. Indeed, as the Jews knew well enough, the Cossacks were the natural enemy of all who were interested in liberty, and they had been so for centuries under the Tsars.

A clue to what motivated Babel to join up can be found in Colin Wilson's seminal study *The Outsider,* a work that made an enormous impact when it first appeared in the 1950s. In many respects, Babel was a typical 'man outside', a man who cannot see things as others see them, a man who finds himself excluded from the prevailing view of the world. "I see too deep and too much", Barbusse has his hero say in the classic First World War text, *Under Fire.* The outsider cannot live in a comfortable, insulated bourgeois world, accepting everything he sees and touches as reality. What he sees is not order but chaos. The world for him is not rational but irrational. It is a world with which he cannot easily come to terms. It is a world, in fact, that is fit only for destruction: "The work of the future will be to wipe out the present, to wipe it out more than we can imagine, to wipe it out like something abominable and shameful".[6]

The outsider's position is almost a pathological condition. The true outsider is not a man 'outside', excluded by others only by religious belief, social class or even race. An outsider is a man who responds to history intellectually (rather than emotionally). He finds himself at war with a world that is at war with itself.

In Wilson's book the traditional outsiders have three features in common. All three are illustrated in Babel's life: the belief that

1. salvation lies in extremes;
2. the world is full of enemies; and
3. an escape *into* history (or significance) comes in moments of great spiritual intensity.[7]

What unites all three is the idea that war had become the permanent condition of life, if the only peace worth having is peace of mind.

To begin with, it was particularly ironic, given the long history of violence between Cossacks and Jews, that Babel should have praised them as a people unaffected by civilisation. They were men of the body and the horse, witness to the truth of the aggressiveness and passion of history that was at odds with the dull conformity of bourgeois, Jewish life. For Babel the Cossack was a noble savage—not noble, perhaps, very often, yet having in his savagery some quality that contrasted markedly with the distinct lack of noble bearing of his own people.

Babel portrayed the life of the Cossacks in stirring terms. Take, for example, a passage from his diary dated 9 August 1920:

They are all more or less peasants. In the evening they sing songs that sound like church music in lusty voices, their devotion to horses, beside each man a little heap—saddle, bridle, ornamented sabre, greatcoat, I sleep in the midst of them. . . . The cavalry and its horses recuperate after their inhuman toil, men take a healing rest from cruelty, living together, singing quietly, telling each other stories.[8]

There is no doubt that like Tolstoy before him Babel admired such men. In his description of the First Brigade commander, Zevitsky, a man of whom he clearly thinks highly, we hear of his "youthfulness" in terms of "iron and fire". What he recognised in the Cossacks was a man untrammelled by the constraints of civilisation, a man of simple virtues, a "man who moved with speed and grace".[9] Zevitsky's grace is the real thing. Babel does not compare it, for example, with the pathos of human beings who are either less physically strong or morally less self-assured than his hero.

His main contribution to the revolutionary literature of the period are the stories that make up the collection called *Red Cavalry*. It is his most important work. His tales were based very closely on his insights and recollections of his time at the front. Without its becoming immediately obvious, they are told by two narrators: one, the Jewish war correspondent, bespectacled, bookish and sensitive; the other, the character the correspondent would like to become and constantly strives to be, a true revolutionary with no fear of killing.

The strain of Babel's life was a consequence of his having to live two intensely demanding lives. The humanitarian in him would not be silenced, but his relationship with the irrepressible force of history was deeply ambiguous. The duality accounts, perhaps, for the extreme violence of his stories. Babel was too gifted a writer to omit mentioning the Cossacks' acts of cruelty. After a particularly vicious and gruelling stretch of fighting that ended in the massacre of many of the prisoners in their care, he admitted that further analysis was beyond his strength: "I must look deeply into the soul of the fighting man, I am trying to, but it is all so horrible, wild beasts with principles".

That bestiality was not something he could regard as entirely external to himself. Grieved by his inclusion in the destructive force that moved "like a whirlwind, like a stream of lava, hated by everyone", he sometimes used the first person plural in describing the troops' transgressions. "Our way of bringing freedom", he wrote on 18 August, "horrible".[10]

Why did he join up? He claimed that it was to expiate his father's shame. According to his own version of events he had been born in the Jewish community of Odessa and never forgot the day on which his father had gone on his knees before a Cossack captain on a horse and said: "At your service", touching his fur cap with his yellow gloved hands, paying no attention to the mob looting his store.

In fact, he was the son of a prosperous family that owned a warehouse in the business section of Odessa. The city itself was also a modern, cos-

mopolitan town where Jewish children were taught music and read continental literature, in Babel's case the works of Maupassant and Flaubert.
The grim experiences that he accredited to his youth were no more than an
expression of his personal distaste for the life led by the majority of his co-
religionists. What drew him to Bolshevism was his hope that it represented
an historical force that would redeem Jewish life. It was a hope shared by
several non-Jewish authors such as Maksim Gorky, who wrote to H. G.
Wells to assure him that what he and others read about the Bolshevik Revolution in the Western press was not necessarily untrue, but it was not important. "I do not close my eyes to the negative result of war or revolution,
but I see, on the other side, how the people gradually becomes an active
force".[11] Babel hoped that his own people would be similarly transformed.
For him the real enemy was to be found within—in their attachment to a
medieval way of life. His hatred of the traditional *shtetl* life is a particularly
strong theme in his writings. He had nothing but a profound loathing for
the medieval ghettos into which the Jews had been locked for centuries.

So too did many Western commentators who stumbled across them for the
first time during the First World War. One, the American war correspondent
John Reed, who crossed into Russia with the German army in 1915, found in
the Jewish quarter of Rovno "a pale, stooping, inbred race" living in the
most degrading of conditions. He was acquainted with poverty at home. The
teeming numbers in the squalid environment of the lower East Side in New
York had appalled him on encountering it for the first time. But nothing had
prepared him for what he found in the ghettos of Russia:

> Jews, always Jews [he wrote with a lack of sentimentality that should not be mis-
> taken for anti-Semitism] bowed, thin men in rusty derbies and greasy long coats
> with stringy beards and crafty, desperate eyes, cringing from police, soldiers and
> priests and snarling at the peasants—a hunted people made hateful by extortion
> and abuse, by murderous competition in the foul, overcrowded cities. . . . Vener-
> able ravs and great scholars bent under the weight of virtuous years. . . . Sensi-
> tive-faced boys who pass repeating the lessons on the way to the *heder*—a race
> inbred and poisoned, with its narrow learning because it had been persecuted
> 'for righteousness' sake' and butchered in the streets by men whose banner was
> the Cross, . . . Jews impregnated the mass—the air smelled [of them].[12]

When encountering such a passage, of course, one cannot help but be reminded of their fate twenty years later, when another German army
marched into Russia determined to rid Eastern Europe of the *Ostjuden*.
Even without that knowledge, the picture Reed painted of Jewish life helps
us to appreciate how tempting it was for Babel to embrace any political
movement that promised the Jews an escape from the past. That is why he
was ready enough to accept revolutionary violence as the price that the
Jews would have to pay for their own redemption.

In return, he tried to transform the violence he saw into the poetry of war or revolution. As the correspondent remonstrates in one of his tales: "'The International, *panie*, comrade, one does not know what to eat it with. 'One eats it with gunpowder', I replied to the old man, 'And seasons it with finest blood'".[13]

Secondly, what makes Babel so ambiguous a figure was his acceptance of the need for a society to be in conflict with someone. A society had to have enemies both internal and external if it was to amount to anything:

> "I understand you", the commander interrupted. "I understand you completely. . . . Your aim is to live without making enemies. . . . Everything you do is aimed that way—so you won't have any enemies."
>
> "Give him a triple kiss", muttered Bizykov, turning away.
>
> On Boulin's forehead a fiery spot was imprinted. His cheek twitched. "Do you know what the end of this is?", he said, unable to control his breathing properly. "The end of it is . . . boredom."[14]

As a party, the Bolsheviks put an especially heavy emphasis on struggle. Marx's debt to Hegel, after all, stemmed from the fact that Hegel's thinking was conflictual. Whereas Plato had regarded the contradictions of life as obstacles to assessing the truth, Hegel had insisted that they were crucial. It was only through their opposition, through the dialectic, which was often called "the theory of the union of opposites", that any progress towards reality or truth was possible.

Marx merely took the theory of the dialectic one step further by arguing that the force that lies behind history is the conflict between classes. Marx did not pretend to have discovered the class struggle as the basis of history, but he claimed that to have proof that it was bound up with a particular phase in the history of production.

Consider, for example, the claim in the *Communist Manifesto* that life is "more or less veiled civil war" raging within an existing society up to the point where it would end in violent revolution. It followed that there could be no genuine peace in a society—if, that is, the working class was to be victorious, to see its victory as the meaning of history and through the class struggle to give its own existence historical meaning for the first time.

In Lenin's Russia this message became even more pronounced. It is the essence of all totalitarian creeds that the political realm is largely shaped by conflict against adversaries, real or imagined. Enemies were understood in their concrete, existential meaning, rather than as metaphors or symbols. It followed that one could talk about politics only when the real possibility of conflict was present. The essence of political life was struggle.

As a Jew, Babel saw for himself the need the Cossacks had for "the uses of adversity". One of the striking features of Cossack life, writes Neal Ascherson, was fear of the 'other,' a fear that stemmed from an excruciating crisis of identity.[15] The Cossacks, after all, were an 'outpost' people too, faithful defendants of a tradition whose centre, Moscow, was far away.

That fear was reinforced by their numbers. Like the Bolsheviks themselves, they were in a minority in a country largely indifferent to their own concerns. Because their numbers were small they always had to impose their dominance, to display their power. Their sense of collective identity, indeed, depended on the enactment of that dominance as if they feared that if they could no longer demonstrate power they would feel, in their own eyes at least, no longer entirely themselves. The Cossacks were distinct from the settled Russians but at the same time were appointed the custodians of Russian virtue. In the past they had emerged from the steppe. They now impressed Russian values upon it. A Russian in their eyes was someone who subdued the Tsar's enemies, especially non-Russians, above all the Jews.[16]

Babel shared some similarities to the Cossacks. He too was a member of a minority in a country that rejected the right of the Jews to become 'Russian.' Assimilation, the path that many Jews took in Western Europe, was impossible in the East. The only possibility after 1917 was to become a citizen of the new Soviet state, to take part in a unique experiment in social engineering, to seize the chance to join the human race. Babel tried to play a role in that transition. It was not for nothing that Stalin called the intellectuals "the engineers of human souls".

Thirdly, the wish of the outsider to be inside history, to make his future himself rather than have it made for him, was also a common theme of Russian literature. Take the character of Volodia Kozel'tsov in Tolstoy's *Sketches of Sebastopol*. Kozel'tsov knows nothing of the reasons for the Crimean War, in which he finds himself engaged. All he wants is to take part in a significant event. He does not ask any serious questions about the purpose of the war; he does not ask any questions at all. All he wants is to be in step with history so that he will be remembered after his death, for memory is an important part of a person's identity. His image of history as an epic struggle (a war in all but name) offers him the unique possibility of self-realised action, one that does not exist in the outsider's world.[17]

The historical moment that the revolution represented was for Babel too an "empathic time" that offered even the traditional outsider a role in publicly recorded history. He was convinced that for life to have any meaning, his private and personal life had to take second place to his public life, for the latter offered him a unique opportunity to become part of the wider "meaning of history".[18]

His real moment of epiphany, alas, came after his arrest by the KGB in 1940. When he asked how he should behave, he was told to deny everything. In fact, he confessed to everything and liberally betrayed his friends until the end was inevitable. At this point he recovered himself, including his courage, and retracted everything he had previously confessed. While he was in prison his wife sent him shirts and handkerchiefs sprinkled with her perfume so that he would remember her. She had no idea that her husband had betrayed her as well as his friends by entering into a liaison with the wife-to-be of the KGB head, Yezhov, who was himself later liquidated by Stalin.

Perhaps his betrayal of his friends was induced by a disintegration of his personality of the kind that we used to call a nervous breakdown. We who have had the misfortune to have lived in the brainwashed twentieth century can accept that Babel tried to save his life, even while he was losing his identity; and at the eleventh hour he regained the second at the expense of the first.

All his life he had to compromise to live in the new socialist world. He claimed that he was the son of a Jewish storekeeper in order to disavow his bourgeois background and satisfy Marxist dogma. When he wrote of his time before the Great War in St. Petersburg, to which he had moved in order to be near to Maksim Gorky, he claimed the friendship of proletarian friends, rather than the members of the middle-class circle in which he had lived. The writer Georgy Munblit knew him as a "sly, unfaithful, eternally evasive" man.[19] What was he evading? From whom was he hiding? Perhaps he was hiding from himself. "Superior craftsmanship", he told Munblit, "is the art of making your writing as unobtrusive as possible". In Stalinist Russia survival required the writer as well as his writing to be unobtrusive as well.

Ultimately, of course, Babel was complicit in the horror of the early Bolshevik years. He saw at first hand the evil of the Bolshevik experiment. But he would not denounce it. He did not leave for France, as he might have before his passport was rescinded in 1935. He would not even remain detached. He had the desperate need of the outsider to believe in anything.

His fate in the end was to lose touch with himself. Perhaps he was trying to rediscover himself, especially his Jewish roots, at the end of his life. When he was finally arrested he was translating the work of Shalom Aleichem, the first writer of note to write in Yiddish, a dialect spoken by most Jews from Warsaw to Odessa, a mixture of Middle High German and accretions from Hebrew and Aramaic. It was a language espoused by a marginal people, a language of outsiders, a language of exile in a gentile world. It was the language of an oppressed people whose only hope was that one day they would be insiders in a country of their own.

Ernst Jünger and the War Machine

The final aim of natural science is to discover the motions underlying all changes and the motive forces thereof: that is, to resolve itself into Mechanics.
—Hermann von Helmholtz, in Oswald Spengler,
The Decline of the West (1918)

Perhaps one of the best ways to encounter the writer Ernst Jünger, who was one of the most influential illiberal writers of the century, is through the

pages of Thomas Mann's last novel, *Doctor Faustus*. Composed after the
Second World War, the novel is the imaginary biography of a German composer, Adrian Leverkuhn, as told by his friend, Serenus Zeitblom. Written
between 1943 and 1947 while Mann was living in exile in the United
States, *Faustus* is not merely a novel about music (which Mann believed
brought out the best and the worst in the German spirit); it is also an indictment of an entire culture.

The twofold indictment of the century's "bloody barbarism" and
"bloodless intellectualism" levelled by Zeitblom at Leverkuhn's penultimate composition, stands for Mann's own criticism of the Third Reich. The
notion of aestheticism, nihilism and political barbarism captured in the
Kridwiss Circle, a group of protofascist conservatives who champion Sorel
in the name of Germany's "deliberate rebarbarisation", are some of the
most disturbing aspects of the book.

One of the main features of barbarians, of course, is that they rarely consider themselves to be barbarous. The description is usually applied by outsiders looking in. What distinguished the twentieth century was that in its
climate of hatred for all things bourgeois, many intellectuals were happy
enough to champion barbarism as a superior way of life. Mann's narrator
draws a picture of a character who is indistinguishable from Jünger's frontline hero. "Their world was at once old and new, revolutionary and regressive", no more or less reactionary than "the path that leads back round a
sphere". In the image of the sphere progress and regression, left and right,
pre- and postwar are all interlinked. One leads to the other in the same vicious circle—a return from civilisation to the barbarism that preceded it.[20]

What we have here is not so much Nietzsche's transvaluation of values but
rather a transitional stage, the inversion of previously accepted values, a stage
recognised by Nietzsche himself when he wrote, "I have the gift of reversing
perspectives".[21] For Nietzsche, 'reversed perspectives' were based on instinct
not reason, on the subjective rather than the objective in life.

"Has your music been inhuman up to now?" asks the violinist Rudi
Schwerdtfeter of Leverkuhn. "Then it owes its greatness to its inhumanity".[22] In the composer's later life we see barbarism triumphant. Particularly vivid is Zeitblom's shocked reaction to the Kritwiss Circle's claim that
the First World War had demolished bourgeois conventions. What alarms
him most is that its members should welcome the prospect with such enthusiasm. What appals Zeitblom most is the existence of a cultural avant-
garde denouncing the culture it feeds on "and cheerfully at that". He can
only interpret such behaviour as "an act of self-denial".

The German people, adds Zeitblom, "are rather too fond" of catastrophe. "We are a people quite different from all the others, scornful of everything sober and normal, with a mightily 'tragic' soul". Zeitblom's use of the
word 'we' is important. On the one hand, he has as clear a perspective as

one could wish of the self-destructive folly of national socialism. On the other, he feels within himself the pull of the mentality he describes. In all honesty he feels that he must associate himself with the self-destructiveness he decries so eloquently.

Mann's novel is all the more important because he himself only renounced the romantic nationalism of his youth after the First World War. In one of his most notorious works, *Reflections of a Nonpolitical Man* (1918), he had written that the German people had no time for the political element in their lives, for the parliamentary horse trading that he held responsible for poisoning national life. "I don't want politics", he insisted. He wanted order and decency instead. "If that is philistine", he added, "then I want to be a philistine".[23]

What distinguished Jünger as a writer from many of his peers was a similar antibourgeois sensibility that when taken to extremes could find only in war the justification for life. He refused to accept that the ambiguities of bourgeois life, including its losses, were the price to be paid for its gains.

The twentieth century was indeed the bourgeois century: it was the first era in which its members could claim a large share of political power and cultural authority. If the *embourgeoisement* of culture might, in the short term, seem to have been a victory for caution and convention, it was equally an assault on the old fortresses of aristocratic life, on the ancient certainties of class privilege and traditional faith. It made a breach in the walls that could not be closed easily. It opened everything up to question and produced as a response a desperate craving for certainty. The bourgeois era was the most radical in history.

This was not the understanding, of course, of Jünger's generation. Looking back at their service on the western front, they concluded that because of—not in spite of—the privations and boredom of army life, they had experienced life more intensely than they could within the stifling social conventions at home. For that reason, Jünger criticised the "typically shallow French attitude" expressed in Barbusse's highly successful antiwar novel *Under Fire* (1916), in which he had stressed the material aspects of war and lamented its destructiveness. The author, Jünger complained, had no "mind to accept the responsibilities that demand sacrifice". As he wrote in his most celebrated book, *The Storm of Steel*, German youth found an intensity of meaning in the national idea, in their country's destiny, in Germany's future. That is what they were prepared to die for, and nearly 3 million had.

It would be wrong, of course, to conclude that what distinguished Jünger's idea from those of more liberal writers was merely their attitude to war. There were many liberals who did not find war entirely unredeeming. There were many who were prepared to acknowledge, for example, the camaraderie they had found at the front, particularly between officers and men, one that had bridged the class barrier, however briefly. Where they parted company with Jünger was in their refusal to conclude that it was only through war that a man could become a more authentic human being.

This difference is thrown into particularly stark relief if we compare the responses of Jünger and Siegfried Sassoon, two men who in their initial enthusiasm for the war, and in their personal bravery, shared at least something in common. Sassoon's trilogy *The Memoirs of George Sherston* describes Sassoon's own development from a self-centred but eager soldier to a man who became more critical of the war as it continued. Sherston is a man who begins to doubt whether intellectuals should think about war at all. Sassoon shows the gradual process of his hero's education and, very importantly, its accidental nature. Sherston's kindness and shrewdness are gained at great cost: the recognition of his own limitations.[24]

Sassoon's war poems also convey a sense of urgent awareness of the reality of the human body and the vulnerability of life. After the war he did not look for a 'new man' but for a peace in which men and women could understand what had happened to the old one. In the words of one historian: "Reconstructing a world in which many wrong choices had been made by many different people in very different social roles he was able to tolerate the social complexity of the act of choosing, insisting on individual responsibility for the choice".[25]

By comparison, Jünger's response to the war was entirely intellectual. He conceded that the war had dwarfed the heroic individual, that the soldiers had died fighting for smaller and smaller scraps of land. But in the summer of 1918 the war was not without meaning, for meaning was "the shaping of a world still hidden in the future".[26] The humblest soldier's sacrifice had been of historical importance, for it had witnessed a new stage of human evolution, the metamorphosis of man into a machine, the idealisation not of the heroic but of the mechanical. In Jünger's eyes the soldier had been reduced to "a single accentuated determined release of energy".

This vision was particularly appealing to an intellectual class that was haunted by the fear of civil discord or class war in its most unadulterated form. It was Nietzsche who had been the first to note that modern states were most powerful when they were at war. Not only could they mobilise all their resources, but also they could succeed in nullifying social dissent at home. The process of war, he observed, produced a "chemical transformation" that brought the entire nation, regardless of class, "into affinity with that purpose" for the first time.[27]

Invoking a similar metaphor, Clausewitz had written that war is a "pulsation of violence which is variable in strength and therefore variable in the speed at which it explodes and discharges its energy". Energy was one of the principal motifs of twentieth-century life—energy as the exponential mobilisation of an entire people's 'will to power.' Like Hitler, Paul von Hindenburg's old quartermaster Erich Ludendorff wanted to mould society into a war machine so powerful that it would make the impossible possible. Ludendorff wanted to use violence in such a way that it would explode "in a single discharge". He was critical of Clausewitz for distinguishing between two states: war and peace. In his own book, *On Total War* (1936), he insisted that if Germany was ever to win its next engagement, there could be no distinction between the state, the army and the people (Clausewitz's trinitarian principle). Peace demanded that a society be permanently mobilised for war. The entire nation should constitute a great army, with every man, woman and child serving at their posts.

Jünger's concept, in other words, was very much in tune with the spirit of the age. War and peace could not be distinguished if the aim was to create a homogeneous society that would, for once, be at peace with itself. Where this idea gained an intellectual gloss was in Jünger's treatment of the individual, both in his fiction and in his writings about his experience at the front. In many of the great works of the century, such as Sartre's *Nausea,* or Kafka's *Trial,* or Camus's *The Stranger,* we find not an individual but a condition. Musil confessed that he was interested, for his part, not in human beings so much as the human situation.[28] Everything was reduced to a theme. The characters of twentieth-century fiction are representatives of mass society, a society denoted not by its people but by its problems.[29]

Much of this can be dated to the death of individualism on the western front, the death of the heroic individual in the mechanised, industrialised slaughterhouse that war had become. But it was also the experience of a larger consciousness still. What the modern novel often represents, in the words of Alain Robbe-Grillet, is the desire to move "beyond the anthropocentric". In the course of the twentieth century this took the form of a rejection of anthropomorphism, or the projection of human meaning onto the nonhuman world.

Human beings were understood increasingly in nonanthropomorphic terms, as bits of nature like any other. It was a dangerous philosophical position to adopt because it suggested that man was no different from the machines that he had invented. Like them, he was conditioned by external stimuli. Human subjectivity in the form of desires, wishes and hopes was merely a reflex action. From such a reading of history it followed that man was fated to become more of a machine, a cog in the wheel, a functioning unit. It was a totalitarian vision that enjoyed especial favour in the Soviet Union, the first scientific socialist state that set out to reengineer mankind into an unthinking, unreflective being who would be prepared to put the general will before his own.

The concept of a posthuman world was an attempt to convince men that the humanity they would all share as cogs in a machine was some compensation for the power that had been taken away from them as individuals. The attempt to deconstruct mankind was an idea that was very much in the air in the early years of the century. Jünger's expression of it was a typical example of how the modern consciousness was expressed by many other writers who were in contact not so much with each other as with the spirit of the times.

That spirit touched the English as well. One of the most influential writers of his age was H. G. Wells. *The War of the Worlds* is still his most popular tale. It tells of the invasion of Earth by a race of Martians more intelligent than the human race. While clearly more intelligent, however, they are more deadly, because more calculating. Their weapons are more deadly still. Physically feeble as a result of their extreme evolution and unaccustomed to the gravity of the Earth, their strength comes from their machines, from the lethal use of poison gas and death rays, the depersonalised instruments of mass destruction.

Wells's novel is profoundly important as the expression of an era, not only because he anticipated the use of poison gas on the battlefields of the western front. In a brilliant note towards the end of the book, when the Martians are unexpectedly destroyed by human bacteria against which they have no immunity, the text casts doubt upon the appropriateness of drawing any absolute distinction between a human being and a Martian.

Man too possesses the potential for the inhuman slaughter of his own species. As the artillery man declares after looking into one of the Martians' abandoned machines: "Just imagine this: four or five of their fighting machines suddenly starting off—heat rays, right and left, and not a Martian in 'em. Not a Martian in 'em but men—men who have learned the way how."[30]

The triumph that the artillery man envisages is sobering indeed. He anticipates the coming of an age in which the most advanced stage of human evolution would be marked by the transformation of man not into a more 'authentic' human being but into a machine—or, in effect, a Martian.

Curzio Malaparte on the Eastern Front

The year 1943 saw the centennial anniversary of the poet Friedrich Hölderlin's death. The philosopher Hans Gadamer commemorated the event in a lecture he gave at the Technical University in Darmstadt. Hölderlin's reputation in modern Germany, like Novalis's, was extensive. He had long been honoured as the formulator of a special Christian-Germanic conception of history.

The Germans were awakened to him in the twentieth century because of the convergence of his poetry and the course of contemporary German history. The age of Hölderlin too had been the beginning of a century of revolution. "Our own time", observed Gadamer, "looked like a realisation of everything implicit in 1789".[31] Hölderlin's work, he added, was stamped with the immediacy of those forces, far more than the work of Schiller or

Goethe. The fact that he felt his love of Germany to be "the final and highest poetic expression" gave him a sense of added significance in the year 1943.

At the core of Hölderlin's poetic vision was an acute consciousness of history, a history in which the future is all-important—the future to which the present bears witness. His prophetic gift was the ability to recognise that Germany lived in a godless age, that a God surrogate, the nation-state, had yet to be created. The national spirit was not a joy that wished to be shared, but rather it became a joy at the moment of being shared. Only when shared was it "a joy with a spirit". "No one was able to bear life alone; being shared, such things rejoiced the heart and shared with friends, become an exultation". In the eyes of Fascism, the most ecstatic moment of all was war.

It was the peculiar misfortune of the Italian writer Curzio Malaparte to witness the attempted realisation of Hölderlin's spirit in the Third Reich, to see the apotheosis of the German spirit in the steppes of Russia, in the vast Russian wastes in which Hitler's hope of creating a Greater Germany met its end.

As an Italian journalist attached to the German forces, Malaparte recounted a day on which he had found himself motoring in the company of a friendly German officer through the deep forest near Oranienbaum on the Leningrad Front. Lieutenant Schultz had been born in the valley of the Neckar, "Hölderlin's valley", the officer called it. Schultz was a cultured man who could quote the poet and did so in a few lines:

On the Rhine, where the Neckar's lawns grow
They think that to abide
There is no better spot in the world
But let me to the Caucasus go.

For Hölderlin the voyage of the forefathers of the German people along the Danube was the movement towards the days of summer, towards the Caucasus, the land of the sun. In 1942 the Germany army came close to planting its flag on Mount Elbrus, the Caucasus's highest peak.

All that, however, lay in the future. Continuing his story, Malaparte records how they arrived at a spot where the forest was thickest and deepest. Looming out of the mist was a soldier sunk to his belly in snow, standing motionless, his right arm outstretched, pointing the way to the front. "There", Schultz observed, "is another one who would like to go to the Caucasus". Malaparte asked who the soldier was. Wouldn't the poor devil die of cold if he continued to direct military traffic in such weather? "There is no danger of that", he was told, "you can ask him whether he is cold or not".

By the time both men had walked up to him, it was clear that he was dead. He was, Malaparte was told, one of many "traffic police". As a Russian prisoner he had been killed with a bullet in the temple prior to being placed in the snow, a victim of war who had been put to some use so that even in death the bullet would not be wasted.[32]

Malaparte was an unusual critic of the war. In his youth he had been a committed Fascist, perhaps the most famous of its intellectual supporters, though too idiosyncratic for the regime, which imprisoned him for a short period. Malaparte had demanded war in the 1920s, critical as he was of the Italian people's impassivity. If they were ever to amount to anything in history they would have to be taught the necessity of suffering. As a sensationalist Malaparte craved action. He was fascinated more by the destructive processes of revolution than its results. In Mussolini he had even seen a man outside the race but in tune with the times, "a proof of what our people can be but have not yet become".

Mussolini's historical function, he had insisted, would be to give back to the nation a sense of destiny of the kind that Hölderlin had given to the Germans (in a different time, of course, and in very different terms). War, added Mussolini, set a seal of nobility on a people who have the virtue to face it".[33] If a nation was to be at peace with itself it would have to be permanently at war with the world.

What made Fascism unique was its belief in the need for national vitality, without which a people would decline or become terminally senescent. This was not an idea that was unique to Fascism. In his seminal book *The Great Transformation* even a liberal writer like Karl Polanyi could describe Fascism as a force that had turned the Italian people into a formidable life force. In support of that proposition he quoted an English anthropologist who had claimed that the imperial peace the British had established in much of Africa at the end of the previous century had been catastrophic for its subject peoples, for it had reduced them to a permanent state of listlessness. War had given them life; peace had emasculated them. From cultural maturity they had descended into a state of cultural infancy. Their most likely fate would be to die of boredom.[34]

Mussolini's views had their origin in two very different intellectual camps: nationalism and revolutionary syndicalism. By the 1890s many nationalists were concerned about the fragmentation of their communities by class divisions that manifested themselves in divisive party politics. They wanted to reinvigorate their communities, to win the working classes back from socialist internationalism. It was internationalism, not socialism, that they found most threatening, precisely because of its popular appeal.

For their part, many syndicalists yearned for an apocalyptic act, a general strike in which the labour unions would destroy bourgeois values. They scorned parliamentary socialists for their timidity, for their insistence that capitalism must evolve into its final form before the proletariat could aspire to replace it. The syndicalists offered instead an activist, revolutionary programme through which, in the words of Georges Sorel, the most important syndicalist thinker, the masses could be saved by "a transforming myth", a call to arms, a sudden redeeming blow that would presage the end of the bourgeois era.

Later, despairing that the proletariat would ever become heroic, that it would ever find the courage to launch a general strike, the syndicalists in Italy went a step further, finding in nationalism the transforming myth that would save the nation. By 1910 Sorel's followers in Italy had transformed the apocalyptic class war into a war between nations. These ideas won the approval of the Futurists, who depicted in their paintings highly stylised scenes of mass violence in the hope of awakening the revolutionary consciousness of their proletarian audience.

The Sorelian celebration of violence became a key ideological platform in Mussolini's mythic mission of a regenerated Italy that had a specific task to perform and a noble destiny to fulfil. For fascist intellectuals like Malaparte it offered an alternative to political life, the chance to create what Hitler once called "a new antihistoric order". Sorel's transforming myth was to be replaced by another—an order that would reverse the postrevolutionary tradition of the previous century.

It was, of course, a ruthless doctrine, but one by which Fascism was fully prepared to live. If the First World War helped to bring Mussolini and Hitler to power, the Second destroyed both of them. One of the ironies of the twentieth century was that both were both defeated on ground of their own choosing, in a war that the democracies had tried so hard to avoid.

Long before then, however, Malaparte had lost all enthusiasm for war as a means of redeeming humanity. He did not think that the Italian people could be enthused with a spirit of heroism, any more than he believed that the imperfections of the Aryan race could be bred out in Hitler's New Order. Nor did he have much time for Babel's heroising of the Cossack way of warfare, which he recognised had long since exhausted its possibilities. By 1941 war had lost its romantic appeal, as he discovered for himself one afternoon while travelling among the overturned cars, burnt trucks and abandoned guns of a recent military engagement. For miles around he saw only dead iron, the dead bodies of machines, hundreds upon hundreds of miserable steel carcasses, "the stench of putrefying iron", a stale, sour stench that quite overwhelmed the smell of men and horses—"the smell of old wars".

Malaparte was even more struck by the fate of the Tartars he came across as the Wehrmacht marched east. Like the Cossacks they were descendants of the horsemen who had swept across Europe 700 years earlier. He had seen the face of a Tartar tankman in a tank buried in the mud. He had met up with a Tartar prisoner of war while en route to Kiev. The Tartars were the most adept of horsemen, a tireless, cruel race of men who had been born and lived with horses, who had fed on horseflesh and mare's milk, who had dressed in horse skins, slept under tents made of horse hides and had been buried in deep graves astride the horses they had ridden in life.

Now they had been transformed by executive fiat into the best mechanical workers in the Soviet Union, the best storm troopers among the workers, the best drivers of tanks, the best engineers in the armoured divisions. In three successive five-year plans they had been transformed from horsemen into an industrial workforce, from horse breeders into the *udarniki* in the ironworks of Stalingrad and Magnitogorsk.

That is why Malaparte pitied the poor Romanian soldiers he encountered when reporting the drive on Stalingrad in the second summer of the war. They did not understand that they were fighting not a country, but a machine that could not be defeated. They did not recognise that they were fighting a country that could turn the most warlike people of one age into the most industrially proficient of the next. Communism had transformed the Tartars of the Don and the Volga, of the Kirghiz steppe and the shores of the Caspian and Aral Seas, from the nomads of the steppe into specialists of the five-year plan.[35]

The war that Malaparte witnessed at first hand on the eastern front was not so much a protagonist as a spectator, in the same sense that a landscape is a spectator. War was the objective landscape of his book. Its chief character was the grey and gruesome monster, *Kaputt*, a mysterious German word that meant "gone to pieces, gone to ruin", a word that expressed, as perhaps no other could, what Europe had become by 1945—a pile of rubble.

In the late 1940s the Pulitzer Prize–winning novelist John Steinbeck visited the Soviet Union in the company of the photographer Robert Cappa. As they retraced Malaparte's steps, they reported on and photographed the lives of ordinary Soviet citizens. *A Russian Journal* was the extraordinary result. Spurning the empty and dangerous polemics of the Cold War in these early years, it offered a testament to a country that, although it had suffered egregiously, was still enthused with a sense of a better future, that was eager to get there quickly.

Of all the cities they visited, Stalingrad etched itself most vividly in their consciousness:

Directly behind the hotel and in a place overlooked by our windows, there was a little garbage pile where melon rinds, bones, potato peels and such things were thrown out. And a few yards further on, there was a little hummock like the entrance to a gopher hole. And every morning, early, out of this hole a young girl crawled. She had long legs and bare feet and her arms were thin and stringy, and her hair was matted and filthy. She was covered with years of dirt, so that she looked very brown. And when she raised her face, it was one of the most beautiful faces we had ever seen. . . . The face was well developed and not moronic. Somewhere in the terror of the fighting in the city, something had snapped, and she had retired to some comfort of forgetfulness.

She squatted on her hams and ate watermelon rinds and sucked the bones of other people's soup. She usually stayed there for about two hours before she got her stomach full. And then she went out in the weeds, and lay down, and went to sleep in the sun. . . .

We wondered how many there might be like this, minds that could not tolerate living in the twentieth century. [36]

Unfortunately, the Soviet system too believed almost to the end of its existence that war had become the defining theme of life in the advanced industrial world. It was considered to be a historically determined one. The Soviet Union, in other words, was prepared to accept the price it believed had to be paid for living in the twentieth century. It remained on a war footing until the very end. For fifty years it remained locked with the United States in a deadly strategic embrace. As in the simulated duel of a Hindu Dashera god, the two powers were inextricably interlinked in each other's fate. A war between them promised to reduce the world to rubble on a scale much more vast than that of the devastation Steinbeck witnessed at first hand in the 1940s.

Against all odds, of course, man survived. A nuclear war did not break out. The bombers and missiles were not despatched to their programmed destinations. Looking back on that period of history, however, we can appreciate how close the world came to destruction. Indeed, in terms of odds defeated and probabilities denied, its escape verges on the miraculous.

Conclusion

Let me return to Hölderlin's Germany. He remains to this day, perhaps, the most German of the country's poets. What he created was a poetics of history whose terms for the incarnation of Germanness were essentially aesthetic categories that had no place at all in the Anglo-American imagination. The nation became a fictional device with a fictional myth and history. As Sartre once said, it became "a novel that is true".

Regrettably, as Gadamer later recognised, the problem of turning politics into poetry was that it forced one to engage in a flight from the real to the imaginary; or perhaps it would be more fair to say that the attempt to create a political aesthetic involved devaluing the real in favour of the imaginary. What was the Third Reich, Gadamer had asked, but "the story of a poetic production, the appearance of which was delayed by a full century after Hölderlin's death"? What poetry did, he added, was to put a nation in touch with God (or Being). That had been the theme of Hölderlin's poetry. "To be unpoetic", he wrote, "means to claim to know nothing about the divine".

The problem of being loved by the gods, of course, is being called to heaven early. By the age of thirty-eight Hölderlin had accomplished nearly all his work. A few years later he entered into a quiet madness that lasted another thirty-six years, a madness that speaks of something else in his writing, the terrible price paid for thinking too intensely or seeing too much.

His madness was the inevitable upshot of trying to understand the nature of God, or in the post-1789 world the nature of history or being. In his prose fragment 'In Lieblicher Blaue', he was doubtless thinking of his own condition when he wrote: "If a man looks into a mirror and finds his image there as though it were a painted likeness, then he recognises himself. Man's image is possessed of eyes. . . . Oedipus had an eye too many. The suffering of this man appears unrelatable, inexpressible and without language." Oedipus suffered because he was possessed of a third or inner eye that could dispense with an outer vision. "To wrestle with God . . . is to suffer. Madness perhaps is the price of self-knowledge".[37]

Hölderlin's own mental breakdown was reflected in the breakdown of his language, the disintegration of his speech, which reflected in turn the disintegration of his personality. A doctor who examined him in 1805 reported that it had become impossible to understand him, that his speech seemed "to be composed partly of German, partly of Greek, partly of Latin sounds".[38]

A century later the country that produced Hölderlin dishonoured itself in the madness of the Holocaust. After Auschwitz, many writers who had experienced it at first hand, and others who had not, found themselves locked in a silence that precluded them from speaking.

One was the German expressionist poet Armin Wegner, who survived into the postwar world in self-imposed exile in Italy. "For two decades", he remarked in his old age, his "tongue had been lying in his mouth as though paralysed".[39] Another survivor, Jean Amery, found Auschwitz a linguistic hell as well as a human one. As a philosopher he was horrified by the corruption of the German language to be found in the euphemisms of the Final Solution—in the code words for killing such as 'pacification' and 'special treatment'. In the camps, wrote Primo Levi, the German language "scorched his mouth when he tried to speak it".[40]

When the poets did record their experiences or feelings they often did so in fractured German. Paul Celan continued to write in German while in self-exile in France. The fragmentary, idiosyncratic dialect that he invented, whose grammar was as tortured as his prose, was a response to the alienation he felt from his country of birth. Even non-German-speaking victims like the poet Eugenio Montale wrote in a difficult, highly subjective verse that was described by a fellow exile, Joseph Brodsky, as an act "of cultural self-defence . . . against fascism".[41]

As the novelist Günter Grass recognised, language itself had betrayed Europe, the language of German illiberalism, especially that of Heidegger, whose obscurity of thought, leviathan sentences, atrocious grammar and density of thinking portrayed an embarrassment about stating things too clearly. Grass's pastiche of Heidegger's metaphysical jargon in *The Dog Years* is an impressive indictment of the damage that the obscurity of the German language had done to the German mind, to its ability to think clearly.

The victims were not the only ones who fell silent. So too did the former apologists of Nazism, or those who had toed the party line, of whom by far the most important was Heidegger himself. After the war the philosophers fell silent. After 1945 it had become impossible for them to make the history of the German nation. That is why Heidegger insisted in his last years that philosophy was dead. That is why he accused it of failing in its primary task. It had failed to put Germany in tune with Being. If it could not do that, what was the purpose of studying it?

Chapter Three

A People Without a History

If you considered what the historical memory of mankind would re-tain, it would not bother to retain . . . the Sammlers. Sammler did not mind his oblivion. . . . He thought he had found out the misanthropy of the whole idea of "the most memorable". It was certainly possible that the historical outlook made it easier to dismiss the majority of in-stances. In other words, to jettison most of us.
—Saul Bellow, *Mr. Sammler's Planet* (1970)

We will not be able to construe history without being construed ourselves.
—Hugo Ball, *Flight out of Time: A Dada Diary* (19 June 1919)

At the end of Thomas Mann's novel *The Magic Mountain* the life of the members of the sanatorium is rudely awakened by history in the form of the Great War. Mann's novel is about time, a fact carefully underscored by the contrast between those who live a timeless life in the sanatorium and those who live at the bottom of the mountain where life follows the rhythm of the seasons. The hero, Hans Castorp, a young engineer from Hamburg, visits the Berghof and stays seven years until 'the thunderbolt' of war in 1914 tears him away from the bewitchment of his mountain retreat.

At the Berghof none of the patients confronts the passage of time, the time of calendars and clocks, historical time or modernity. At the Berghof time is divested of any measurable character or even interest in measurement. Then the thunderbolt strikes, the deafening "shock that fired the mine beneath the magic mountain [which is named for the first time] and set our sleeper urgently outside the gate". It is the eruption of historical time that breaks into the enchanted prison from outside. Castorp leaves the sanatorium to fight in the Great War. The final glimpse we have of him is in the trenches "and thus in the tumult, in the rain, in the dusk [he] vanishes out of our sight". His fate as a soldier now belongs to another story—to world history.[1]

Castorp's disappearance, in this respect, is very similar to the fate of Antoine in Roger Martin du Gard's masterpiece *Les Thibaut*. Gassed and crippled in the war, certain that he is going to die, he is still victorious. As Camus added in a review of the book, Antoine "vanish[es] into the very stuff of history of which men's hopes are made and whose roots are human misfortune".[2]

At the end of Mann's book, as we are reminded by Paul Ricoeur, the reader must have doubts about the years the young Castorp has spent "in the past" represented by the "timeless" Berghof, which is part of time but not of history. Was it possible to free himself from the bewitchment of the mountain, from its magic spell, without being torn out of the enchanted circle? Could the hero have learned anything from the experience of the sanatorium, educative, even spiritually rewarding though the years he spent there were, without descending to the world below to make sense of them by putting them to the test of action? Is not the confusion of world history the crucible in which Castorp finally recognises himself as a person, a man who is able to survive in the flesh as well as the spirit, even if death on the battlefield is the price of self-understanding?[3]

This was the heroic version of history, the idea that man could heroise the present by stamping his imprimatur on it, that a people could leave more than its traces behind after its passing. In this chapter I shall discuss three features of this understanding of History.

1. The first was that history involved the continuous action of a protagonist, not humanity but its representatives. Its subject had to be either a nation, a class or a civilisation, rather than an abstract entity, humanity. As the subject of history, humanity lacked substance. It was never present in its own person. It acted by means of its representatives. History was a theme in which humanity became many: slaves and masters, workers and the bourgeoisie, peasants and the state. History was a discourse between them, a dialectic that would be resolved in favour of the stronger of the two protagonists.

The protagonist I shall look at was the nation-state. It was the received wisdom that at certain times in history a people came into its own. On the eve of the twentieth century it was clear that the next hundred years were going to be the German, the Russian or the American century. In the event, the United States saw the other two off.

Hegel once called the United States "a happy country without a history". History and happiness, in the German mind, were incompatible; it was the great good fortune of the Americans to discover that they were not. The Americans may have been rendered unhappy by their attempt to make history on their own terms, to colonise the future themselves, but unlike the

Germans or the Russians they were not ruined in the attempt. They were not rendered 'historyless'.

2. The idea that a century could be patented by a single nation required that it also involve a single theme. For the Europeans history was progress, or one of its synonyms. As such it could take no account of stragglers, of those who failed to keep up.

The Europeans, in fact, showed little compassion for the peoples of the non-European world. The French explorer Baudin, while planning his voyage to the South Pacific at the dawn of the nineteenth century, received the following advice from his government: "The philosophical traveller, sailing to the ends of the earth, is in fact travelling in time; he is exploring the past; every step he makes is the passage of an age".[4] In discovering the Polynesian people the Europeans reencountered themselves, or their own prehistory. It followed that the peoples of the Pacific had no history of their own. Their fate was to become part of the history of those who had (re)discovered them.

As late as the 1830s parts of the non-Western world were still regarded as a human museum in which Europe might study its own prehistory. One of Tocqueville's hopes when he visited the United States was that he would be able to study at first hand "a social condition" that had once played an important part in European history but that now survived chiefly in the Americas. François Guizot's lecture series *The History of Civilisation in Europe* inspired him to study the original barbarian tribes who had overwhelmed the later Roman Empire. He chose to study them, however, not as Guizot suggested, by reading James Fenimore Cooper's romances "upon the savages of America", but by going to the New World to see the Indians for himself.[5] By the time he arrived, of course, they were already on their way out of history: they were about to be dispossessed of their lands and religion.

3. That in the following century, fate was nearly visited on the Europeans themselves who discovered that a third theme of the heroic version of history was its apocalyptic nature.

The twentieth century perspective included an obsession with living in what Walter Benjamin called the *Jetzzeit, the* most important moment of all, in which history would come to a stop, "a messianic cessation of happening . . . a revolutionary chance in the fight for the oppressed". It was a moment of awakening that would ignite "the explosives that lie in the past", and "blast the epoch out" of the continuity of homogeneous time. The *Jetzzeit* would constitute a "flash of lightning" that would illuminate "the birth of authentic historical time".[6] The *Jetzzeit,* in other words, was the point of intersection between two radically different moments in time— the messianic and the immanently historical that would open up modernity to the promise of fulfilment.

It was important that the words Benjamin used were drawn from the scriptures, for they offered an image of redemption. There was no redemption within historical time, of course, but there was the redeeming power of history itself. In that sense, the *Jetzzeit* was akin to a religious experience, or what Benjamin called "an unveiling of the face of God".[7]

Invoking the same language, no doubt unconsciously, Spengler too depicted his own time as the "years of decision". "The world war was for us only the first *lightning* and thunder from a cloud passing across our century heavy with destiny".[8] In a reference to Spengler's claim that "the form of the world today is being recreated from the ground up," Benjamin contrasted the logic of Jewish messianism to the Tower of Babel, where the attempt to glimpse the face of God had foundered on the misunderstanding of the builders. "The Jews handle ideas like quarry stones," Benjamin once remarked; "they build from above without reaching the ground".[9] That was the problem of trying to make History. It challenged God. The result was the fate of the builders of Babel.

The problem was that the master builders of the twentieth century who tended to treat humanity as the material out of which the future was made, were not beyond turning on their own citizens in their moment of failure. In 1912 the French mystic Léon Bloy wrote: "For he who sees into the Absolute war makes no sense unless it exterminates, and the very near future will demonstrate this to us. It is foolish or hypocritical to take prisoners."

Napoleon, Bloy added, had not been sufficiently in tune with history. He had wanted to pardon his enemies, to show mercy, to be magnanimous. "He was not, therefore, the monster required for total apocalyptic war with all its consequences".[10] In 1912, alas, the monsters were waiting in the wings in the persons of Stalin and Hitler, the two master narrators with their privileged insight into the meaning of History, a story in which ordinary men and women found themselves caught up.

A People with a History: Hegel and the German Nation

Hegel seems to say, Look, I have sat long gazing at the all but imperceptible transitions of thought to thought until I have seen with the eye the true boundary. . . . I know that all observation will justify me, and to the future metaphysician I say, that he may measure the power of his perception by the degree of his accord with mine. This is the twilight of the Gods, predicted in the Scandinavian mythology.
—Ralph Waldo Emerson, *Journals* (1866)

To understand why Hegel looked forward to "a German century", why he considered the Germans to be the only people in the vanguard of history, we must look more closely at his interpretation of history itself. It was, in the event, one that was to profoundly determine German thinking in the run-up to two world wars.

History for Hegel had a meaning that could be decoded. It had a message, in other words, with which it behoved the most advanced nations to keep in step. In the *Philosophy of History* he defined history as "the Spirit's effort to obtain knowledge of what is in itself". What he was arguing, in effect, was that only those events that are self-consciously brought about, that had been 'willed' or self-consciously acted upon, could really be considered of historical interest. That is why he saw Napoleon at Jena as the spirit of the age, the World Spirit conscious of itself. Napoleon had set out to refashion Europe in the name of the revolutionary principles that had been put forward in the Declaration of the Rights of Man.[11]

Nor did Hegel have any doubt that self-conscious ends were likely to prove more decisive when pursued not in the name of dynastic advantage but for purposes defined and articulated by states. In the state he saw an institution that he considered, at this point in history, to be the highest stage of political life, precisely because it constituted in its own person the social and political identity of an entire people.

It was because the English were the most nationally conscious people in the world, he wrote, that they had become the most powerful nation:

> If he is asked, any Englishman will say of himself and his fellow citizens that it is they who rule the East Indies and the oceans of the world, who dominate world trade, who have a parliament and trial by jury, etc. It is *deeds* such as these which give the nation its state of identity. This spiritual totality constitutes a *single being*, the spirit of the nation.[12]

In this respect, the difference between Europe and Asia was marked. Later in the century the French traveller Gustave Le Bon added:

> England is the Western world with its complex civilisation developing itself according to a geometric progression and marching rapidly on the basis of new forces towards an uncertain future. India is the East immobilised in an eternal dream, its eyes fixed not on the future but on the past, relentlessly probing the thought of its ancestors and its gods.[13]

This Hegelian gloss on history was especially significant in the European encounter with China, a civilisation, of course, that was more emeritus than Le Bon's.

Take the work of one of his compatriots, Pierre Loti, a prolific and popular writer at the end of the nineteenth century who spent a considerable amount of time in China as an officer in the French navy. His book *The Last Days of Peking* was one of the most successful ever published, going into fifty-two printings between 1902 and 1914. The book grew out of the pieces he had written for newspapers while serving in the International force that was despatched to put down the Boxer rebellion. On the surface, it is a conventional example of the adventure memoir; but Loti gave it an emotional intensity that transformed it into a quintessential Western view of China. It was not enough for its author to describe the city wall of Peking. He had to evoke a mood that stood for China as a whole. Thus on its first appearance the wall appeared to him "as the colour of mourning", a colour fitting for a society that was in terminal decline, that constantly mourned its descent from power, a civilisation that was in despair of itself.

In due course this portrayal of China entered the Chinese consciousness as well. In Ts'ao Yu's play *Peking Man*, which was written in 1942, the ultimate symbol of the Chinese people is a mute workman who poses for a Western anthropologist studying prehistoric Peking. The play ultimately portrays the incapacity of an entire nation to live up to its own magnificent past, a nation that as a result cannot deal with the challenges of the modern era.[14]

The main reason why the oriental societies were dismissed as being historyless was the general belief that only a people who were part of universal history could consider themselves to be reflective historical actors. Other societies, even those older than the West, would not long survive if they had nothing to say to anyone else. In that sense, there was no appeal against history, however unjust might be its final verdict. As one writer observed, "Even Kant did not dream of charging the sans-culottes with infractions of common law nor Hegel the soldiers of Jena".[15]

Hegel did not restrict his list of historically obsolescent people to Asia. He included in the list the Slavic peoples of Eastern Europe. It was true that they had founded kingdoms and sustained themselves over the centuries, sometimes as an advance guard in the centuries-old struggle between the Christian and Islamic worlds. The Poles had even saved Vienna from the Turks in 1683. But that had been their last moment in history. They could not save themselves a century later when an ungrateful Austria joined with Prussia and Russia in dismembering their kingdom. As for the Slavs in general, they were excluded from any further consideration because hitherto they had not appeared "as an independent element in a series of phases that Reason has assumed in the world".[16]

What is significant is that the intellectuals of Eastern Europe agreed with him in their deepest moments of gloom and self-reflection. As Mr. Nagy tells the hero of Zsigmond Moricz's novel *Be Faithful unto Death* (1921), the Hungarians had always been sidelined by history, although on two occasions they had saved the West from Asiatic invasions. It took the Magyar tribes a millennium to leave the depths of Asia and migrate to Europe, where they had settled in the Carpathian Valley. As for the second thousand years, the first great calamity was the Mongol invasion of 1241:

> The Mongols didn't get past Hungary. That was always our destiny: we were the ones who had to stop the hordes from the east. Hungary was always the last battleground. It was the bastion where the Asiatic hordes had to stop. Isn't

that amazing, that the Hungarians should have come here from the east to
protect the west from the easterners? We held sway at that, fighting our eastern
relatives to defend the alien westerners who have remained strangers through a
thousand years and have despised us.

What was true of the Mongol invaders was equally true of the Turks, who
inflicted a decisive defeat on the Hungarians at the Battle of Mohacs in
1526, leaving the middle third of the country to be ruled by the foreign invaders for the next century and a half. "Isn't it terrible", Nagy tells Misi,
"that we are here in the middle of Europe . . . and there isn't a single other
nation . . . who understands our language. We are condemned to be on our
own."[17]

It is ironic that the novel from which I have just quoted, with its deeply
felt reference to "alien westerners . . . who have always despised us", was
serialised in *West (Nyugat)*, which was both the title and the political credo
of the country's most significant literary and intellectual magazine in the
1920s. It was also an aspiration for Hungarians to be included in the history of Western Europe, where the history of others as well as its own was
consciously forged. In short, the Hungarians had failed to impress themselves on the imagination of the outside world. Their own national story
did not constitute one of the four stages that Hegel had identified on the
road to human consciousness.

The first had taken place in the East and involved the history of China and
India. Hegel was one of the first European thinkers to incorporate Asia into
his conceptual world and thus rescue it from historical marginality in the European imagination. The East nevertheless represented for him an "unre-
flected consciousness". Nothing happened. Its history, in consequence, was
"really unhistorical, for it is only the repetition of the same majestic ruin".[18]
China lacked an objective history, being "at first the oldest and the newest
realm". Nothing happened for centuries. It repeated its history in cycles.
Marx said much the same when describing it as "a giant empire containing
almost one third of the human race vegetating in the teeth of time".[19]

The second stage of history had been represented by the Greek city-state.
Greece was not a single society but made up of diverse states. It was their
diversity that made the Greeks different, in their own eyes, from the unchanging barbarian societies beyond the frontiers. But the Greeks lived in
an unmediated political community. They did not live with the conflicting
demands of the private and public spheres that were at the core of modern
political life. They lived for their city without further reflection. In that
sense they had no concept of individuality. They *were* the state. And in that
sense they were a profoundly unmodern people.

It was the rise of Christianity that Hegel deemed to have initiated the third
stage of historical consciousness. The Christian Church was able to mediate

between the subject and the political power. Christianity, indeed, introduced the element of subjective consciousness into the world. If the oriental phase of history knew that only one man was free (the despot), and the city-state knew that only some were (the free male citizen, as opposed, of course, to women or slaves), Christianity preached that before God all men were equal.

The historical context within which the Christian faith became dominant was unique since it was carried by a historical agent, the German people, who had never been subdued by the Romans or brought through conquest into the Roman world. That is why Hegel called the fourth stage of history "the Germanic world", by which he meant Western Christendom, a world that had been founded in the ruins of the later Roman Empire. He did not argue (contrary to what is often claimed) in favour of the supremacy of the German nation, only in favour of the defining importance of German ideas. Unfortunately, it was not long before nations began to appropriate history in their own name, a process that led Hegel's followers to misread his phrase *"Die Germansiche Welt"* as "the German world" rather than the "Germanic".[20]

In short, Hegel believed that the future would be determined by a state that was conscious of itself and its destiny. Although he attributed the power of modern states especially to their economic strength as well as the invention of technology, he remained convinced that history was political history, the history of ideas realised through political action. The course of history was determined not by technology, or even economic growth, but by a people growing conscious of its power and freedom of self-determination. History would be increasingly determined by whether a people had the will to use its power, whether, in the quasi-Hegelian vernacular of one German writer in the 1920s, "it had the will to assert itself historically".

The problem with the Hegelian interpretation of history was that it was hijacked by the nation-state. Hegel himself was one of the first philosophers to write about the force of nationalism. He welcomed it as an idea that offered a unique opportunity for men to live together in harmony rather than against one another in a quasi-Hobbesian state of nature. For Hegel, the nation-state was an entirely 'ethical' phenomenon or it was nothing at all. Freedom, after all, could not be realised unless individuals found freedom in the sense of the whole, in the community in which they lived. Freedom could be fully expressed only if the freedom of one was the freedom of all, if the citizen recognised that his own well-being depended on the well-being of others.

A healthy state, he wrote, would be able to draw upon a powerful constituting force, the "consciousness that my interest, both substantive and particular, is contained and preserved in another's interest in the end". Such a society would be able to realise the common good. In wartime courage would be less a personal than a social attribute. In *The Philosophy of Right* he added: "The true courage of civilised states is readiness to sacrifice in the service of the state, so that the individual counts as only one amongst many. . . . In India 500 men [under the British] conquered 20,000 who were not cowards but who only lacked the disposition to work together".[21]

What Hegel was claiming was that only a state in which the citizen acknowledged obligations and duties could survive in the modern era. Citizenship must be earned and the responsibilities of each citizen acknowledged. Where rights were claimed in isolation, they would lead to competing claims, which would give rise to class conflict or social alienation. Such a state, far from being able to count on the loyalty of its citizens, would become something against which its citizens would make claims. In that respect, Hegel thought of 'rights' as similar in nature to cheques. The rights a citizen enjoyed had value only if there was money in the bank. They presupposed a society in which everyone was collectively willing to pay the price of the claims made upon them.

A country's 'ethical health', as well as its will to win, was very much a theme of nineteenth-century views of warfare. It confronted the individual with death and, in teaching him the contingency of life, taught him the importance of the 'social' in life, the fact that history does not come to an end when an individual dies. The most extreme version of this theory is to be found in *The Philosophy of Right* in which Hegel argued that war mitigated what he called "the vanity of temporal goods and concerns," that is, the materialism of modern liberal societies: "Just as the blowing of the winds preserves the sea from the foulness which would be the result of prolonged calm, so also corruption in nations would be a product of prolonged, let alone, 'perpetual peace'".[22]

It should always be remembered, however, that Hegel did not argue that war was the health of the nation, only that it constituted a state in which its health was put to the test. Nor had he any intimation of an age of total war, in which nations would find themselves locked in an internecine struggle against their neighbours. He assumed that wars would remain limited, both in scope and duration; that they would be fought by armies, not societies; and that they would result in only minimum loss of civilian life.

Unfortunately, armed conflict made the assertion of national vigour extremely expensive for the individual powers even before the First World War. It made it catastrophic during the Second World War, in which the cult of the national spirit was measured increasingly by its willingness to make sacrifices for the common good. It was not coincidental that in his description of the Aryan race, Hitler talked much about the absolute meaning of sacrifice. In *Mein Kampf* he wrote, "The Aryan race had attained superiority over all others by the 'measure' of its readiness to put all its capacities to the service of the community". He added, "Posterity forgets men who have only served their own interests and celebrates heroes who have renounced their own happiness". The measure of any race in history was its readiness to "voluntarily submit to the collectivity and, when the hour demands it, to go so far as to sacrifice itself".[23]

When Goebbels toured the bombed-out cities of the Reich after 1943 he reminded the German people that they shared "the common fate" of the soldiers at the front. The apotheosis of this idea can be seen in the Third Reich's last propaganda film, *Kolberg,* which told the story of the heroic defence of the city against Napoleon in 1807. The film was Goebbels's testimony to the self-sacrifice endured by the German people, with its offer of redemption for the generations to come.

In the film, when Gneisnau, the garrison commander, utters the stirring lines from a poem by Karl Theodor Körner, "Now rise up nation and let the storm rage", he was employing the exact reference that Goebbels himself had used at the climax of his famous Sportpalast speech after Stalingrad, in which he first called for a commitment to total war.[24] When Kolberg is put to the flame and flooded to stem the advance of the French army, the clear reference is to the suffering undergone at home in the daytime and nighttime bombing by the allies.

By then the only consolation Goebbels had to offer his fellow citizens was Gneisnau's own benediction: "A regenerated people will arise from the ashes".[25] Like the citizens of Kolberg, the German people would generate the rebirth of the nation. He might well have also quoted Gneisnau's farewell message to his fellow citizens: "I leave you with a heavy heart. I will do everything possible for a city where virtue still lives. . . . Pass this spirit on to your children".[26]

Fortunately for Germany, that spirit was not passed on, or not in the form Hitler would have wanted. As he once said of himself, "the trick of the Pied Piper of Hamlin can only be played once".[27] Nations do not follow their leaders to perdition twice, certainly not in the same century. By his actions Hitler almost left Germany historically intestate. But for the reconstruction of the country by the victors, *Kolberg* might have become a final codicil to its contract with history.

A People Without a History: Liberal America and the Winning of the West

I saw no wild or independent Indian but now and again at way stations, a husband and a wife and a few children, disgracefully dressed out with the sweepings of civilisation came forth and stared upon the emigrants.
—Robert Louis Stevenson, 'The Amateur Emigrant' (1883)

In his account of his travels in America Alexis de Tocqueville recorded the fate of the Indian nation. None of the tribes that had formerly inhabited the territory of New England—the Mohicans, the Pequots, the Lenapes—had any existence but in the recollection of men. He himself met with the last of the Iroquois, a once proud people who had been reduced to begging alms. There was no instance on record, he added, of so rapid a disappearance from history. He was at hand to witness one of the means by which it was accomplished, forced migration.

While travelling along the west bank of the Mississippi at the end of 1831 he witnessed the arrival of a large band of Choctaws. It was the middle of winter and the cold was unusually severe. Snow had fallen heavily a few nights before and the river was now frozen. The Indians possessed neither tents nor wagons. They were driven by despair, but also by promises of better grazing land and offers of assistance in the West. Commenting on their distress, Tocqueville predicted that the Indians were doomed to perish from their inability to keep in step with history.

Tocqueville had no doubt that history alone should be held accountable for their fate. It was history, not the Americans, who had condemned them to the status of victims: "a happy distinction which had escaped the casuists of former times and for which we are indebted to modern discovery".[28] From the perspective of history their extinction seemed inevitable. If they continued to live their own life they would perish completely. If they attempted to adapt, contact with a more powerful community would devalue their cultural life and lead to even greater spiritual destitution.

In Latin America the Spanish had sacked the New World like a city taken by storm, destroying everything and everyone in their wake. In the United States the destruction had been very modern: "The purpose had been accomplished with singular felicity, tranquillity, legally, philanthropically, without shedding blood and without violating a single great principle of morality in the eyes of the world". In the end, Tocqueville came to a damning conclusion: "It is impossible to destroy men with more respect for the laws of humanity".[29]

Tocqueville's account was definingly Hegelian in tone. He could, for example, have employed another modern idea—that of biological determinism, and explained the fate of the Indians as the inevitable result of a weaker race making way for a stronger. He chose to attribute their misfortunes instead to the fact that, from the beginning, they had a separate destiny that was not that of the white settlers. "Chance had brought them together on the same soil", he observed, "but they had mixed without combining". They had been unable to join the settlers in their line of advance into the future.

The separate treatment that he accorded both Indians and whites in his study is a reflection of his view that each race followed a separate destiny. The whites knew it from the beginning; the Indians had begun to suspect it far too late. The problem was "their childish carelessness of tomorrow", which was a marked "characteristic of their savage nature". As a very modern man Tocqueville had no hesitation in concluding: "Only two roads to safety were open to the North American Indians: war or civilisation. In other words, they had either to destroy the Europeans or become their equals".

Unfortunately for them, the Indians had waited far too long to wage a war of annihilation against the whites. At the time Tocqueville wrote they were far too few in number to pose a formidable threat. At the same time they could not be assimilated into white society. Their fate was clear enough to anyone honest enough to admit it: to disappear from history altogether.

When Tocqueville returned to France he turned his attention to Algeria, which had just been incorporated into the French empire. He recognised that the methods used by his own countrymen had been very different from those he had witnessed in the New World. The resistance of the Algerians had been broken not by 'resettlement' but by a war of extermination. Despite the different experiences of the two societies, however, he also recognised that they shared one thing in common. In their dealings with a non-Western people both had studied them "with a weapon in hand"; both had overwhelmed them "before [getting] to know them".[30]

Tocqueville's account shows how a liberal society could subscribe to Hegel's ideas when it came to dealing with problems in its own midst. There were dissenters in their ranks, to be sure, those who questioned the cost of winning the West, critics like Mark Twain and Herman Melville who warned that the fate of the Indian might one day be visited on the whites. But for the most part their warnings went unheeded. "We can't stop history in full course", remarks a British politician in Joyce Cary's novel *Prisoner of Grace*, "and history is going all against the primitive—it always did". Tocqueville himself compared the European to a force of nature. If other races could not serve him indirectly they were likely to "disappear before him" little by little until they were no longer present even in the imagination of the superior race.

It was originally hoped, of course, that the Indians could be brought in from the 'outside' or forcibly 'modernised' through assimilation; that they could be rendered modern by becoming American. In that respect Stephen Ambrose rejects the word 'genocide' when talking of their fate, preferring the word 'ethnocide' instead. Perhaps the distinction is academic. As Robert Wiebe asserts, the whites did indeed want the Indians to be incorporated into their own culture, but the means they used were not only counterproductive, but genocidal.[31] When the United States despaired of success it tacitly sanctioned the massive dispossession of land from which the Indians derived their very identity. If in that sense the republic was complicit in their destruction, it did not sanction their extermination. It largely stood by in the wings in a position of mute accommodation with history.

The systematic displacement of the Indians that was pursued after 1840 cannot be explained by the dangers they posed to white immigration, to the future of America itself defined in terms of its westward expansion, or its 'manifest destiny'. Contrary to Hollywood versions of the tale, few settlers tracking across the plains to Oregon or California were attacked by Indians. The historian John Unruh's careful analysis shows that of the approximately 250,000 overlanders who went west between 1840 and 1860, fewer than 400 were killed. And of these, 90 percent lost their lives in a comparatively small area of the country.[32]

Because the development of the land was continuous, however, it was bound ultimately to require a military solution to deal with what was euphemistically called 'the Indian problem'. The government pursued successive policies towards the Indians—building military forts in the Mississippi Valley in the 1820s, physically removing the Eastern Indians to present day Oklahoma and Kansas; and subduing the Plains and Southwestern Indians by removing them to reservations. The premeditated massacre of 300 Plains Indians at Sand Creek in November 1864 alerted the Indian tribes to their peril and initiated the most violent period of all in the confrontation between the two societies. It culminated in the great Sioux War (1876–1877) and the annihilation of General Custer's 212 men at the battle of Little Big Horn. The engagement was particularly embarrassing because it became national news on 4 July, just as the United States was preparing to celebrate the centennial of the Declaration of Independence.

The Indians' most dramatic victory sealed their fate. In little more than ten years all tribes were settled on reservations, where the land was so poor that they were invariably reduced to welfare dependence on the federal government. According to the census of 1890, when the frontier was officially closed, only 248,253 Indians were still alive. About 250,000, in other words, had died in the most frenetic phase of American expansion in the forty-year period from 1850 to 1890.

As a "people without history" their fate can be seen from three perspectives:

1. It confirmed the savage as 'inferior', as an 'outsider', as one who had been sidelined by history.
2. It confirmed the whites in their belief that the fate of a primitive society was largely of its own making.
3. It confirmed the successful culture in its own view, that it had earned its success because it had had an inkling of what history demanded.

I shall look at each of these themes in turn. If they were all what Peter Gay would call 'alibis of aggression', it is important to recognise that none of them constituted a consciously thought-out strategy or philosophy that could be deemed to justify the dispossession of an entire people. That is what makes the example of the American West very different from most others, which were justified in highly historicist or ideological terms.

Most of the books that justified ex post facto what had happened, such as Theodore Roosevelt's *The Winning of the West,* were written after the event. Most of the ideas that constituted the myth of westward expansion, notably Frederick Jackson Turner's theory of manifest destiny, were formulated after the frontier had been settled. The immigrants who made the painful and dangerous Atlantic crossing had not been inspired to emigrate to the New World by a reading of the Declaration of Independence or the Constitution. They came to find land. The Indians fell victim not to an ideology but to a historical phenomenon, mass migration from Europe. Only a later generation would choose to locate their displacement in the larger context of genocide, with the fate of the Armenians, the Cambodians or the Jews, a litany of the damned, the dispossessed and the displaced, the victims of the twentieth-century pursuit of a very different form of social regeneration.

What was particularly modern about the Indian wars, what made their displacement different from previous land dispossessions stemming from the right of conquest, was that the victims themselves recognised that they had fallen foul of a historical process. As the chief of the Cree Nation told a Senate committee at the turn of the century: "The Indians didn't have time to grow up that individuality which is necessary to merge them with the American citizen. The change came too soon for them".[33] In an address to Governor Isaac Stevens's Commission of Indian Affairs fifty years earlier, the great Indian Chief Seattle, after whom today's city is named, remarked: "We are two distinct races and must ever remain so, with separate origins and separate destinies . . . there is little in common between us".[34]

In fact the two peoples shared in common one very important thing: land. The Indians were unswervingly ruled by the march of the seasons and the demands of the land. After 1840 they lost control of their destiny by failing to make the land their own, at least in the modern understanding of the term, by failing to tame or possess it.

The settlers who arrived on the Great Plains in the 1830s were also driven by a destiny that was inherent in their origins. As Robert Frost wrote in 1942, a few months into the Second World War, a struggle that challenged the Americans to define themselves as never before in their history, the first Puritan settlers "were the land before the land was ours". It was the land that had forged America: "She was our land more than a hundred years before we were her people". The American people had allowed themselves to be 'possessed' by it:

> It was ourselves
> we were withholding from our land of living
> and forthwith found salvation in surrender.

In short, the land that was the Indians' birthright was the immigrants' future. It also allowed them to conduct a unique experiment in human engineering: the forging of a new type of man. The immigrants from the old world were prepared to use the power they had, including military power, to build their own world according to a design of their own making.

By then the Indians had discovered the dreadful truth that the land for the whites was not only a physical as well as moral symbol of their freedom. It was more. It confirmed that they had a future in a way the Indians did not. In other societies, writes Octavio Paz, the future was a human attribute. Because we are men we know we have a future. In the course of the nineteenth century, however, this view was inverted in the one region in which the future seemed to be its chief attribute, the New World. The Americans were men because they had a future. Whoever were historyless like the Indians were not. Instead of man determining the future, the future had begun to determine who could call himself with any confidence a member of the human race.[35]

In recent years, of course, in our environmentally conscious times, a number of writers have seen the westward expansion only in terms of territorial appropriation. They have tried to project the Indians' plight into their own experience and to transfigure it at the same time. They have tried to create a new American consciousness, one close to the land, to the continent's 'spirit of place.' They have tried to render the whites accountable for the 'great sin' of the European settlement, the murder of the Indian nation.

It is a false consciousness, however, because it is based on little knowledge of Indian history. It paints a picture of the past that many Indians themselves would find false, in projecting an image of an environmentally conscious race in tune with nature. In fact the Indians expressed more concern for the lack of game on the prairies, together with the inadequate supply of water. The white man's concern was with the ability of the prairies to support livestock and with the availability of potential agricultural markets in the east. Both groups bitterly complained of the absence of timber for housing; both came from cultures whose origins were in the woodlands— the Indians from the East, the whites from a still heavily forested Europe. Significantly, they shared a common dislike of the barren soil, the poor climate and the often appallingly harsh winters that distinguished life in the West from the comparatively easy existence in the East on which both societies had turned their backs.[36]

Confronted with the same environment, the two groups' *initial* response had been remarkably similar. The difference between them was that the whites did not accept the conditions they found. They had the technology to master the wilderness as well as the will to do so. Towards the end of the nineteenth century the settlers began fencing in the land: the mark of a settled rather than nomadic people. By 1880 one factory alone was turning out 600 miles of fencing every ten hours. In the end the Indians paid dearly for not making more of the fact that they had been the first settlers on the prairies. They missed the one advantage history had given them—that of getting there first.

Secondly, the popular myth that the Indians were killed off by capitalism, by cattle barons in the West and railway contractors and venal Congressmen in Washington is just that—a myth. Instead, the Indians were displaced by a generation of settlers who engaged in a unique dialogue with the land, one from which the Indians were necessarily excluded. Their 'heaven' was to be created in life, their destiny was to be seized, not merely dreamed of. Both people dreamed, of course, but there was one crucial difference: the whites were inspired by their dreams to act, not to remain sedentary.

The people who displaced the Indians *were* the dreamers, even if in the short term, they paid a high price for realising their dreams. In the act of displacement the first settlers often became 'white Indians'. Life on the frontier was unimaginably harsh. Early death and high infant mortality were commonplace. Women in particular were reduced to the status of hired hands. Frequently it was they who had to drive teams of oxen, or trudge behind the wagons in great clouds of dust, collecting the buffalo 'chips' that were needed to cook the evening meal. Their diaries, writes Lilian Schlissel, convey what purely demographic information cannot, the complexities of a life that had sundered them from the more feminine society into which they had been born.

One such woman, Miriam Davies, who settled with her family in Kansas in 1853, complained:

> I have cooked so much out in the sun and smoke that I hardly know who I am and when I look into the little looking glass I ask "Can this be me?"
> Put a blanket over my head and I would pass well for an Osago squaw.[37]

The wilderness transformed Davies into a white Indian. She and her family had moved to Kansas to transcend their former condition. The land was their present, but it was also their children's future. Davies did not become a squaw, she became a 'man', working in the harshest conditions imaginable, digging the ground, building cabins, as well as ploughing and planting the land.

In the West differences of gender meant very little. Although a later feminist generation would regard domesticity as worse than a prison, not an escape but a form of semipermanent confinement that kept women permanently in submission, domesticity was a goal to which the early frontier women aspired—the promise of a day when they might escape a life of backbreaking drudgery.

That is one reason they showed no real interest in the Indians' plight. They did not have time. Only in retrospect, long after the Indian tribes had been corralled into their reservations, only after a new generation of Americans had discovered an environmental agenda, did the Indians seem to have been doubly betrayed: not only to have forfeited their land in the face of a relentless, almost elemental invasion, but to have been dispossessed by a people whose *grandchildren* no longer 'honoured' it.

In the end the settling of the frontier was not a history of great men and great deeds. Instead we should focus on the transformation of two cultures colliding on an ever advancing frontier. In this conception of how the American West was won, heroism is to be found not in dramatic set-piece battles with Indian tribes, but the continual striving and struggle of ordinary men and women, leading quite extraordinary lives.

Thirdly, if the Americans were aware that they were part of a *historical* phenomenon that they themselves did not fully understand, they never doubted that they had earned their success by keeping in step with history.

James Fenimore Cooper's *The Last of the Mohicans* (1826) was one of the first popular works to capture an awareness that the whites were in at the "death of a race". The catastrophe that was about to unfold was stated more vividly still by the painter George Catlin a few years later—from the artist's point of view:

> Nature has nowhere presented more beautiful and lovely scenes than those of the vast prairies of the west, and of man and beast no nobler specimens than those who inhabit them—the Indian and the buffalo—joint and original tenants of the soil and fugitives together from the approach of civilised man. They have fled to the Great Plains of the west and under an equal doom they have taken up their last abode where their race will expire and their bones will bleach together.[38]

The 'inevitable' disappearance of the Indians prompted Robert Halsey to develop a collection of Native Americana for the Metropolitan Museum of Art, to preserve at the eleventh hour what cultural artefacts had survived the dispossession of the Indian nation. By the turn of the century the Indians had become objects of anthropological or archaeological interest. It was tragically fitting that when the last 'wild' Indian who had taken to the hills rather than be confined to a reservation was finally captured in 1911, he was sent off to spend the last years of his life at the University of California's Museum of Anthropology.[39]

The land rush of the nineteenth century offered the settlers the chance to secure the freedom that they came to America to find. Very few emigrated from Europe to forge a land 'better' than their country of origin. Most expected, however, to be redeemed by their emigration. As a Yiddish memorialist wrote in the late nineteenth century, the Atlantic crossing was "a kind of hell that cleanses a man of his sins before coming to the land of Columbus." The journey from Bremerhaven or Liverpool was a grim rite of passage. Those who made it were treated to a symbolic death "in a stinking wooden coffin with the promise of an uncertain and hazardous resurrection" inspired by the idea of "the wild and boundless licence of the new regions".[40] Most entertained the hope of finding in a new country a chance to create themselves anew, an opportunity that they knew they could never find in the Old World they had left.

Given adequate climatic conditions and a welcoming rather than a hostile environment, they were bound to succeed—at the expense, unfortunately, of anyone standing in their way. The Indians were not an enemy to be exterminated. They were part of the landscape to be pushed back. The absence of any serious questioning about the moral cost of America's westward expansion was due neither to ignorance nor to indifference, disingenuousness or lack of imagination. It was sanctioned by history. The European settlers could not turn back in 1800. They had to advance into the wilderness or abandon the American experiment altogether. In that sense they were inspired not only by greed but also by intellectual curiosity. "Opening doors", George Steiner reminds us, "is the tragic merit of our identity".[41]

In terms of the dispossession of a native people the experience of liberal America may not seem to have contrasted notably with that of other, more illiberal societies, but the contrast was marked in the *attitude* of the settlers nonetheless. In southern Africa, by contrast, the outcome was very different. Here the natives could not be conjured away. Their very presence, mute but ineradicable, was a constant reminder to the white settlers of their own tenuous hold on the future. Although they put the natives to work on the farms and later dragooned them into the mines, they could not break their spirit or racial identity. In the process they corrupted themselves; they devalued their own spirit of freedom, which they had once considered their birthright.

One of the first people to suspect as much was Frederick Courteney Selous, the founder of Rhodesia, an eponymous Calvinist committed to bringing Africa into the modern world. Long before his death he had begun to have doubts about the whole venture of white settlement in southern Africa, in part because of his concern about the low quality of the settlers coming from Britain.

Interestingly, his doubts were first raised after he had visited the American West in the late 1890s. There land, with far less agricultural potential than Rhodesia's, had been settled by men "of a stamp such as one does not encounter . . . in any country where there is a large black population and where, consequently, in the matter of manual labour, white men usually only act as overseers".[42]

In America the settlers were fortunate that the Indians were nomadic, that they could not be forced to work in the plantations or the mines. The encounter with modernity in Africa was very different. In what became South Africa it was different again. There the Boers had arrived at much the same time as the settlers in America. They had been encouraged to migrate by the Dutch East India Company. As the frontier was pushed northwards their ties with the company, to whom they nominally owed allegiance, greatly diminished. The Boers were a farming community. Their average holding was a block of land comprising about 6,000 acres. Each Boer farm was self-sufficient. The Boers demanded only one thing from the company: protection against the natives. It was something that no company governor was prepared to offer.

During the course of the eighteenth century they gradually pushed northwards, leapfrogging one farm to the next, until in the 1770s they came across a people, the Bantu, who were far more formidable militarily than the Hottentots in the Cape. The British occupation of the Cape in 1806 created additional tensions. The two societies were mutually antagonistic. The main point of division between them was their attitude towards the Bantu. The British frequently brought Boer farmers to trial for the maltreatment of natives. When the Boers eventually broke with the British, they did so not over slavery (as often thought), but over equality.

In the 1830s they decided to trek north, to escape colonial jurisdiction. It was a secession rather than a revolt. The first parties moved out in November 1835. Eventually 14,000 Boers in all trekked northwards, disposing of their homesteads, gathering their herds, putting their household goods in ox-drawn wagons and quietly moving north, away from British rule.

To the British the Great Trek was final confirmation that the Boers had transformed themselves into a tribe. Indeed, what surprised them most was the degree to which they had remained unchanged since their arrival in 1652, in some cases living on the same level (in terms of the scope of their ambition) as the black tribesmen they had put to work. The Great Trek merely confirmed them in this suspicion. It was considered very un-European—they had trekked into the wilderness, leaving behind them the homes and farms they had occupied for nearly 200 years. They were the first European people "to become completely alienated from the pride which Western man felt in living in a world created and fabricated by himself".[43] In British eyes the Boers differed from indigenous Africans only in the colour of their skin.

The Boers were a tragic people, for they fell victim to their own inability to confront modernity. In the face of Britain's civilising mission they went 'native'. Other Europeans went mad. Joseph Conrad's novella *Heart of Darkness* is the story of how even the most civilised Europeans might take an evolutionary step backwards in their confrontation with the wilderness. What made the story so compelling was the insight it offered into one of the fears that haunted modern man after 1870—the possibility of a culture reverting back to its original state, the possibility of a reversion to barbarism. Kurtz's fate is indicative of an entire culture slipping back towards its origins. It is a grim parable of a 'higher' form of mankind reverting to its 'lower' antecedents.

Jung and the Reversion to Barbarism

In the case of the United States this fear took an ironic form—after the fact, it must be conceded. In the early years of the twentieth century a few Americans began asking whether in clearing away the Indians, in making the frontier safe for civilisation, the settlers were in danger of becoming the very savages they had destroyed.

One of the first writers to make his readers aware of the 'shadow' side of their psyche was the psychologist Carl Jung. In the spring of 1957 Jung set out to tell his life story to his colleague and friend Aniela Jaffe. When visiting New Mexico he had encountered a group of Pueblo Indians, living in the twilight of their history. This was the first time he had the good fortune to talk to a nonwhite, the chief of the Taos Pueblo, an intelligent man between the ages of forty and fifty. To be sure he was caught up in his own world, as Jung was in his, but it had once been the white man's world too— one that he might reencounter at any time.

> "See", the Chief told Jung:
> "How cruel the white looks. Their lips are thin, their noses sharp, their faces furrowed and distorted by folds. Their eyes have a staring expression. They are always seeking something. What are they seeking? We don't know what they want. We do not understand them. We think they are mad".

Jung was struck by these remarks, not least because they offered an insight into what he considered the madness of the white civilising mission. "It was though until now", he wrote, "that I had seen nothing but sentimental, petrified colour prints. This Indian had . . . unveiled a truth to which we are blind".[44]

Out of the mist he saw the first Roman legions smashing their way into the cities of Gaul; St. Augustine transmitting the Christian creed at the point of a Roman lance; Cortez and the *conquistadores* with fire, sword and the message of Christ descending even upon those remote pueblos, "dreaming peacefully in the sun". The spread of Western civilisation had the face of a bird of prey. The Europeans had sought with relentless determination to enrich themselves at other people's expense: "All the eagles and other predatory creatures that adorn our coats of arms seem to be apt psychological representatives of our true nature".

Jung recounted a second story, a dream he had had on a trip to Tunis in 1920. He had found himself in an Arab city, in a citadel on the Casbah, looking back from a wooden bridge over a moat. When he was halfway across he was approached by an Arab of almost royal bearing. Within minutes they began wrestling in a struggle to see who should give way. Even when the railing collapsed and both were precipitated into the water, they continued to struggle as one attempted to drown the other.

Then the scene changed. Jung saw himself with the same Arab in a large, vaulted, octagonal room. Before him on the floor lay an open book, written not with an Arabic script but the Uigurian script of Western Turkestan with which Jung himself was familiar. He knew instinctively that this was *his* book, that he was its author. The young prince with whom he had just been wrestling was reluctant to read it but Jung forced him to do so.

In later life Jung interpreted the dream as an extraordinary experience of rediscovering several layers of consciousness that the Europeans had recently left behind them, or thought they had. He had rediscovered part of his nature that they had sought to repress. The emotional, childlike behaviour of his adversary marked him out as a shadow of himself, not a personal shadow so much as an ethnic one associated with 'self.' He found himself at odds with his own unconscious psyche. In the 'enemy' he unconsciously recognised himself.[45]

Such fears were very much part of the Western psyche in the aftermath of the First World War. As Paul Fussell writes, the Great War was important because it forged what was so strikingly modern about the twentieth century, the fear of the enemy within. In his book *The Great War and Modern Memory* he describes another dream that troubled Jung in 1926, a dream in which he saw himself driving back from the front line with shells exploding all around him. Jung interpreted the missiles coming from the "other side" as, in effect, emanating from the unconscious, from the shadow side of his own mind. "The happenings of the dream", he concluded, "suggested that the war, which in the outer world had taken place some years before, was not yet over but was continuing to be fought within the psyche".[46]

From this and other encounters with the past Fussell sees the Great War as creating a gross dichotomising, a persistent imaginative habit of modern times of distinguishing between ourselves and the enemy. Soldiers spending weeks in the trenches, often never seeing the enemy but knowing that they were always threatened by him, came back from the front unconsciously aware of the need to be on the defensive even in peacetime. 'We' have a name. The enemy does not and is all the more frightening because of his anonymity. The enemy could be a communist's capitalist or a capitalist's communist, or Ezra Pound's usurer, or Wyndham Lewis's philistine, or Roy Fuller's barbarian, or even, most graphically, Hitler's Jews. Prolonged trench warfare, Fussell asserts, with its collective isolation and obsession with the other side, helped to create a sense of permanent estrangement even in the liberal consciousness.

In the American imagination this fear took a bizarre form. In the full flush of America's self-confidence in the 1920s, at the very time that American writers were turning their backs on Europe in an existential quest to rediscover themselves, D. H. Lawrence sounded a note of warning. When visiting the Indian pueblos of New Mexico, he stumbled upon his first genuine American, the only one who was definingly non-European. The white Americans had yet to reckon with "the full force of a demon of the continent," with the Indian soul.[47]

In his essay on James Fenimore Cooper we also find the same theme. There is a trace of menace, a fear that those who pose the greatest threat to America are the Americans themselves: "When you are actually *in* America, America hurts because it has a powerful disintegrative influence upon the white psyche. It is fully of grinning, unopposed aboriginal demons. . . . America is tense with latent violence and resistance. The very common sense of white Americans has a tinge of helplessness in it and *deep fear of what might be if they were not common sensical*".[48]

One of the major anthropologists of the 1920s, Franz Boas, a first-generation German immigrant himself and a prominent member of the New York German Jewish community, went even further, stating that on the basis of his own observations the Europeans in America were beginning to resemble the Indians they had displaced. The idea of land or history reclaiming them was for Lawrence a metaphor; for Boas it was a matter of scientific observation. And what he observed was a disturbing evolutionary trend. The Americans were 'reverting' back to type. The idea would be of little interest were it not for the fact that Boas's most important research into human heredity was on "changes in the bodily form of descendants of immigrants", which he originally conducted on behalf of the U.S. Congress's Immigration Commission. Indeed, Boas spent much of his life analysing the skull measurements of first-generation Americans of Italian/Jewish descent, comparing their cephalic index (the measure of the breadth of the human head as a percentage of its front-to-back length) to that of the population in their countries of origin. His major claim was that the cephalic index was not stable—that it could change in the course of a single generation. His work on the plasticity of the skull showed, to his own satisfaction at least, that variations between first- and second-generation Americans were less marked than those between the respective European populations from which they came.

In other words, Boas claimed not only to have identified a specific American type—the Indian—but also to have discovered the disturbing fact that the white Americans were beginning to resemble the Indians whom their forefathers had displaced.[49] Here was an excellent example of a theme that ran through the modern consciousness, expressed in a bizarre form. It would even be amusing were it not for the fact that within a few years of

his published findings the Germans would begin to conduct cephalic enquiries of their own in an attempt to identify the race most fitted to survive
in the modern world.

History and Self-Victimisation

*We human beings are the only creatures who, if they have turned out
satisfactorily can cross themselves out like an unsatisfactory sentence—
whether we do so for the honour of mankind, or out of pity for it or
from displeasure at ourselves.*
            —Nietzsche, *Daybreak* (1881)

Goethe always distrusted Hegel. Far from subscribing to the main theme of
The Philosophy of History—that some people had a history while most did
not—he warned that if anyone would render the West historyless it would
be the Europeans themselves. His concern was to understand the limits of
human action in order to better understand the possibilities still open to
man. His claim that man, not the World Spirit, was at the centre of history
was tied to another central belief, that humanity could not be redeemed
from original sin by its own actions.

In the early years of the Cold War Erich Heller took up the dichotomy
that Goethe had identified between mankind's spiritual life and the world
of scientific laws, which in Heller's day included scientific socialism and the
racial hygiene experiments of the Third Reich. "He appointed himself the
kind of emissary of Being," wrote Heller, "who wanted to find out more
about man before venturing on to the task of remaking him", or redeeming
him from his own humanity and thus cutting him off from God.[50]

Of course for most of the century Goethe's warnings were ignored. Europe embarked on the task of making history on a *scale* never seen before.
Baudelaire, who was the first to coin the term 'modernity', was critical of it
for its limitless ambition. 'Vast' is one his most used terms despite the fact
that he consciously avoided words used by force of habit and took particular pains not to let his adjectives be dictated by his nouns. In his work we
find it on page after page. Daydreaming is encouraged by "the vast silence
of the country"; "the moral world opens up vast perspectives"; certain
dreams are laid on "this vast canvas of memory". Elsewhere he speaks of
"great projects oppressed by vast thoughts".[51]

No one in the modern era, of course, dreamed on a larger scale than Hegel.
Kierkegaard disliked him as much as Goethe had. Both objected to his claim
to have discovered the highest manifestation of Christianity, that there was
no beyond. Instead there was only the here and now, a world that had to be
extended always onwards if man was to be challenged to be himself.

The emphatic denial of a 'beyond' was intrinsic to Hegel's fundamental
notion of a self-determining spiritual principle that fulfilled itself in the hu-

man world and that could only come to awareness of itself through the finite species, humanity. As Hegel himself put it, "God is only God so far as he knows himself and he can only know himself through man".

Kierkegaard had no time for a philosophy or system that insisted that world history was destined to achieve its goal and final consummation within the sphere of specifically human activity and understanding. He disliked Hegelianism even more for its limitless aspirations. It treated man as an object of, not the subject of history and therefore threatened to make him its victim. The Hegelian thesis that history was the "concretion of the Idea" amounted to claiming that certain historical periods that encapsulated evolving categories of thought should be accorded primacy over others.

If this were indeed the case then man could do to his fellow men whatever he wanted as long as it was consistent with the principle that prevailed at the time. Ethics would be subordinated to the moral substance of the historical community to which a man belonged. The ethical would be determined by the objectives history had set.[52]

For Kierkegaard all attempts to objectify the ethical were inherently pernicious, for ethics was about individual conduct and conscience. The limitless world was unethical by definition. As Patrick Gardner writes, the belief that "the outward is the inward, the inward the outward, the one wholly commensurable with the other" may have a certain appeal, but it is "a temptation to be met and conquered".[53] We must accept that ethical behaviour cannot be prescribed by a goal or the spirit of an age.

One other aspect of Kierkegaard's argument is important in this connection. He notoriously found Hegel comic. "Someone who is really tested in life, who in his needs resorts to thought, will find Hegel comical despite all his greatness". The comedy of Hegel's philosophy was that he had forgotten that philosophy had to be written by human beings who necessarily must have a different kind of relation to their own lives than they have to anything else: "The only reality to which an existing individual may have a relation that is more than cognitive is his *own* reality". Living life on any other terms would be life denying and could only end in the distortion of reality or a divorce from it that would inevitably end in disaster. To live life to the full "it is essential that every trace of an objective issue should be eliminated". To live life as it was meant to be lived man could not subordinate himself to ultimate goals that it was supposed would add significance to existence itself. A limitless world would be a dangerous one.

The only true limitless world was the eternal: the relationship between Man and God. What God required of man was to live the life he had been given, "to be contemporary with himself", to live neither in anticipation of the future nor in the shadow of the past, but to live life in the present; that, he added, "is the God relationship".

Kierkegaard nevertheless qualified this position. Man must live in the present, of course, but he must also make the future consistent with his own aspirations and hopes. In making that future he should never cut humanity off from the past. Although he paid court to Hegel as a philosopher of the new, the man who had allowed the active amnesia of modernity to appear "in its most respectable form", Kierkegaard had no respect for a philosophy that paid so little respect, in turn, for tradition, that threatened the continuity of history, that challenged the organic nature of culture by cutting people off from their roots.

What "Hegelianism", as Kierkegaard called it, dishonoured most was any life but the modern. It dishonoured all previous existence by making it appear to have been merely a "life of serfdom". Similarly, Kierkegaard had little patience for Napoleon on his march to Moscow, a man who was so intent on obliterating the traditional societies against which the French revolutionaries had set themselves that he ended up almost obliterating France. As one minister of the Empire remarked, it was strange that although Napoleon's common sense amounted to genius, "he never could see where the possible left off".[54] That is why the French historian Jacques Bainville called him "an heroic comedian", echoing Kierkegaard, perhaps unconsciously.[55]

In Napoleon Hegel had seen the spirit yearning for the infinite. In Napoleon Kierkegaard saw a man who was possessed of a suicidal imperative. In invading feudal Russia revolutionary France had succumbed to vertigo: "Frenchmen on their march across the Russian steppes where the eye seeks a point on which it can rest in a time when the older men who still know what they want with pain must see individuals trickle like dry sand through the fingers".[56] The march was a metaphor for that of the Enlightenment, prefigured in the movement of French soldiers, drawn onto destruction not by the limitless Russian steppes but by their own limitless ambition. Not only had they fallen victim to the pain of continuous movement, but they had also become, at the same time, its unwilling agents. Oblivion and revolution met on the vast snow-filled Russian plains. In Russia Napoleon met his match. Feudalism triumphed because he had set out to achieve what was beyond the capacity of any man, however gifted.

The upshot of the invasion was the greatest military disaster that befell an army in modern times. In 1822 a Prussian officer visited one of the scenes of the great retreat from Moscow. Emerging from the dark forests between Borisson and Standianka he began to notice "a mass of leatherware, strips of felt, scraps of cloth, shako covers strewn on the ground. . . . As one approached the river there melancholy relics lay thicker and even in heaps mingled with the bones of human beings and animal skulls, tin fittings, bridles and such like". Close to the bank he saw an island dividing the river into two arms that had been formed, rather gruesomely, from the bodies of soldiers that had been swept downstream and covered with mud and sand.[57]

Even the disaster that befell Napoleon pales beside that of the German invasion of Russia in June 1941, the best example of all of ultimate limitless conflict. It was limitless not only in its means but also in its ends, or rather the absence of them. The war of 1941–1945 was nothing less than a *Vernichtungskampf*, or war of annihilation, a *Rassenkampf*, or war of racial extermination, directed against a Jewish-Bolshevik enemy in particular and the Slav *Untermensch* in general. Eight and a half million soldiers died, in addition to 20 million civilians. The cost, however, increases commensurably if we take into account the population deficit that followed the war made up of a wartime birth deficit (i.e., some 10 million 'not born' babies), together with a lower postwar birthrate that can be traced to the male deficit, that is the drastic alteration in age-specific sex ratios. The figures set out convincingly by one of the foremost historians of the war, John Erickson, revises the population deficit up to 48 million, or 23 percent of the Russian population.[58]

Given its sheer scope, what is most significant about the conflict was that Hitler had no other aim but destruction. Unlike Napoleon he had no objectives at all. "Wherever our success ends", he stated as early as 1928, "it will always be only the point of departure for a new struggle". In that respect, no amount of tactical success could ever bring him nearer the end because there was no end but war for its own sake. "The essential thing for the moment is to conquer", he told his generals after the successful summer campaign in 1941. As Telford Taylor once put it: "He who cannot reject, cannot select and the downfall of the Third Reich was due in no small measure to Hitler's inability to realise that in strategic terms the road to everywhere is the road to nowhere".[59]

Conclusion

In retrospect, we can see that in the illiberal world it was the fate of modern man to end up playing two roles, that of victim and executioner. In the first place, he was the executor of history, mandated to pursue its objectives to the end, even in the role of the executioner of societies that could not keep up. Secondly, the task threatened to render the executioner a victim of his own will, a man who might be reclaimed by history in the very process of victimising others.

It would be wrong to conclude, however, that liberal writers too were not drawn by the lure of history as interpreted in Hegelian terms. Hegel fascinated the Americans because of the vastness of his thoughts. The poet Walt Whitman was inclined to call him an honorary American because his vision coincided with the horizons of the United States. America was often tempted to think of itself as a historical agent rather than an actor, a country that was outside the historical process as it was understood by others.

One liberal writer who thought in such terms was the journalist Lincoln Steffens, the man who went to Soviet Russia in the 1930s and brought back the news that he had seen the future—and it worked. *Moses in Red,* a book that recounts his visit, is replete with Hegelian themes: that men can understand the laws of history and use them in turn for their own ends; that mankind would never progress unless it was willing to excuse horrific social events; that social groups or people who got in the way of history could expect no reprieve—though as a liberal he hoped that "the righteous" would not have to die. Whatever their crimes, however, the Bolsheviks would be absolved by history. Terror and excess, the police state and the gulag were its instruments at this stage of human development. Whatever might be the personal motives of men like Lenin and Stalin they were merely the instruments of the Zeitgeist.[60]

It was Steffens's good fortune to die in 1936, before the worst features of the Stalinist experiment in social engineering were widely known in the West. He was fortunate to die with his reputation intact. At one time his autobiography was compulsory reading in American schools. No other journalist of his time, wrote the *San Francisco Chronicle* in its obituary of the writer, had exerted so great an influence on the public mind.[61]

Steffens was essentially an intellectual fraud. He was not prepared to live by the principles he preached. As he admitted at the end of his life, the Stalinist terror was acceptable only to those who were ready to enter the future: "To those who are prepared it is heaven; to those who are not fit and ready it is hell". He himself, he conceded, was too old to cross the river Jordan into the future he had glimpsed in Moscow. He was too liberal. Despite seeing the path of salvation, he was beyond being saved.

Steffens is of interest as a writer because of his tendency to accept the vocabulary of the Zeitgeist on trust. He did not consider himself illiberal; far from it. But by temperament he was predisposed to write off entire social groups as expendable, to see history as a ruthless process of education that, though harsh, would eventually create a humanity more fitted to survive the travails that lay ahead.

Such views were threatening precisely because the ambition of their exponents was unlimited. It made conditional every act of mankind. The problem, wrote one of the earliest of the modern sociologists, Georg Simmel, was that life acts in total disregard of our rationally chosen ends. We are always disappointed with our achievements, for in attaining them we see how much further we have to travel or how little progress we have made: "Every goal or end of the will that actually is achieved can only be a point of transition and never a final destination".[62]

Because our will always wills more, we are constantly frustrated and disappointed by what we have achieved, an understanding, of course, which impels us to press on. This was one of the principal themes of the work of

Emile Durkheim, who argued that suicide was the endemic mark of the modern era. In a classic study he attempted to show that variations in suicide rates result from differences in the form of social life in different societies, and went on to classify suicide in accordance with the extent to which the individual was reconciled with or alienated from social life. Like Simmel he believed that progress gave rise to alienation precisely because an object of desire, once obtained or achieved, becomes less desirable. Yet another goal has to be set and then reached. Sadness, he wrote, does not inhere in things. "It does not reach us from the world and through mere contemplation of the world—it is a product of our own thought".[63]

The danger of this development, of course, was that if a better future cannot be realised, the present can at least be destroyed. The anarchist and social revolutionary, like the mystic, have in common a hatred for the existing order, a single craving to destroy or escape from reality. More frequently than not they hate the oppressor more than they pity the oppressed. In the end hatred of the tyrant rather than love of his victim may prove the stronger. Such urges can become suicidal if circumstances permit. That is why Durkheim called suicide "the ransom money" of civilisation, an arresting phrase that echoed Schopenhauer's claim that death is "the debt" that human beings pay to life.[64]

In the ruins of Europe after the Second World War, the intellectuals at last began to recognise the dangers of history. Albert Camus recognised in the aftermath of France's liberation that the West was in grave danger of dispossessing itself of its own future. In the last column he wrote for the Resistance newspaper *Combat* he warned his readers that history had not played false. It had not deceived them; they had deceived themselves. The world had been torn apart by their facile understanding of "the logic of history", which existed not in history but only in men's minds. It was a logic that would destroy them if they pursued it to its bitter end.

What history demanded of the human race was that it should never disinherit those who came after it. Every generation owed a duty to the next, and the duty it owed was to survive. It was true, Camus added, that humanity could not escape history altogether, "for we are in it up to our necks". But it could attempt to fight within history in order to keep a certain part of itself out of it at the same time.[65]

Roland Barthes was so depressed by Camus's lack of heroic determinism that he later called his novel *The Plague* "a refusal of history". Camus replied that he accepted that men would always have to fight for their principles, for the causes that make life worth living. But that was the point: life was to be lived, not sacrificed in the pursuit of a future that might never be attained. His answer to Barthes's challenge came when he was presented with the Nobel Prize for Literature in 1956. As he remarked in his acceptance speech, "by definition [the writer] cannot serve those who make history. He serves those who have to live it".

Chapter Four

War and Nationalism

"The brotherhood of nations", "happiness for humanity". And, thus preaching, the nations spit into each other's faces with relish.
—Maksim Gorky, *Fragments from My Diary*

Every society, wrote Octavio Paz, is about communication. Stated so boldly the proposition says very little. We have to ask, What do all societies say? All social discourse can be reduced to one simple phrase: *I am*. It is a phrase that admits of numerous variants: "We are the Chosen People" or "the master race" or the world's most important nation.[1] The discourse has been going on for centuries. In the premodern age humanity thought in terms of peoples—the tribes or ethnic groups with which they identified. In the modern era the principal conceptual unit has been (and perhaps still is) the nation-state. Nationalism is merely the most recent expression of the verb *to be*.

The verb itself, of course, is an empty one. It only really *is,* Aristotle reminds us, when it realises itself through an attribute: "I am stronger" or "I am a believer in a particular religion or creed". I am strong because the group to which I owe allegiance is strong; I am different from my neighbour because I worship a particular God. Everyone finds safety in the power of the particular group to which they belong. The modern age put a premium on security, for modernity (and especially industrialisation) made people feel particularly insecure.

In this respect nationalism is not rooted in atavistic dreams or nineteenth-century romanticism. It is an underlying condition of industrial life. The very nature of industrial production requires and engenders cultural homogeneity. Work entails communication with a series of previously anonymous interlocutors. It requires a shared literary culture. It also requires a sense of community to counter the alienation it produces. A collective national consciousness is one of the most effective ways of dealing with the modern condition.

If nationalism is a product of industrialisation, there is not much point in lamenting its growth or holding it responsible for everything that has gone wrong in the twentieth century. There is no point in judging stages of evolution that we all have to experience as good or bad, modern or atavistic. What the historical record does suggest is that liberal nations rarely go to war against each other. Indeed, they show a much greater reluctance than others to go to war at all.

For much of the nineteenth century the relationship between liberalism and nationalism was very close precisely because liberal societies were not considered to be particularly aggressive. Liberal writers, including John Stuart Mill, supported national self-determination in countries like Italy. Nationalists like Giuseppe Mazzini believed that once a nation had won its freedom it should have liberal democratic institutions. It is interesting that in the course of the century attitudes changed. Liberalism and nationalism were often seen to be in conflict with each other, a conflict that took the form of a perpetual tug-of-war between reason and passion.

It is a questionable conclusion to reach. Liberal nationalists were as passionate as their critics when it came to war. In 1940 Britain thought of the nation-state in highly romantic terms, wedded as its citizens were to a distinct historical consciousness, which Churchill was able to evoke in his speeches. In the early months of the war the British were profoundly attached to what a distinguished historian later dismissed as "the paste board pageantry" of national life.[2]

Indeed, it could be argued that illiberal nationalism was grounded in reason; that it was underpinned by intellectual argument, and packaged by philosophers and ideologues in equal measure. Liberal nationalism was much more impressionist, more intuitive than rational. If the illiberal version of nationalism tended to be more intellectual, this was not particularly surprising. Liberal societies were quite old. An illiberal country like Germany was not. Even the United States could boast the oldest written constitution as well as the oldest political parties. It could also claim to be one of the oldest political cultures in the world. Germany was a young country in 1871, and again in 1919, and once more in 1933. The Third Reich survived for a mere twelve years, for a far shorter period than the other two. With each change of political system Germany had to *redefine* itself as a nation. It had to justify the demand that the young die for their country in intellectual or ideological terms. It could not always appeal to history, or to nostalgia for the past.

In this chapter I have chosen three case studies to illustrate the high price that was paid for intellectualising the nation-state.

1. Cornelius Castoriadis reminds us that in every culture it is possible to distinguish the functional level of social relationships and another level that is imaginary. Waging war is functional: It increases the power or wealth of a society (or it is thought to do so, even if the historical record may often

lead us to question the rationality of those who think it). At the same time society imagines itself and the existence of other worlds. It speaks to itself and to others. It creates images of the future or what it would like the future to be. Social imagination in the twentieth century has been a particularly important agency of historical change.[3]

One of the defining themes of the nationalist debate in Germany and Central Europe was that a modern nation had to be equal to the metaphysics of its own being. It was not enough to have the trappings of nationhood, a language and an ethnic group to which they belonged. A people had also to act in character if it was ever to be at one with itself. It was an inherently subjective, even existential exercise; what it ultimately involved was the realisation of a collective destiny.

Such thinking was not confined to Germany. It was embraced too by much smaller nations that found themselves for much of the twentieth century in the antechamber of History. In the early 1930s the young philosopher E. M. Cioran dreamed of redeeming Romania from the position in which he claimed to find it. He hoped that one day it would escape its "subhistoric destiny", that it would transcend its condition as "a secondhand country", even if the price of its transformation would be war.

Writing in 1937 Cioran did not question that the risk of destruction had to be incurred. "Our entire political and spiritual mission", he insisted, "must concentrate on the determination to *will* a transfiguration in the desperate dramatic experience of transforming our whole way of life". The pursuit of greatness, the escape from a 'fallen' historical condition that had left the country "a little culture" might require martyrdom. In Cioran's vision the mystical 'will' was not objectless. It had a specific political content, and its stage was not the heart but the soul of history itself.[4]

The impossible was to be attempted whatever the cost. To that end all means were legitimate. Terror and crime, he contended, were only immoral when they were invoked by decadent nations. If they assisted in the "ascension of a people" they were virtuous. "All triumphs are moral", he insisted, a sentiment that echoed a passage from *Beyond Good and Evil,* Nietzsche's most radical work.[5]

A few years later Cioran chose to stand back from the abyss. He turned his back on the fascism of his early years, which had beguiled so many of his friends to fight in the Spanish Civil War—on the side of Franco. Recognising that Romania would never become a historically 'significant' nation, he took the logical step of renouncing his citizenship and leaving for Paris, where he lived for the next sixty years. If not suicide (which he had contemplated briefly), the next step was exile. When we next hear from him in 1949 it is in his first book written in French, *Précis de décomposition.* By then he had cast off his Romanian language and identity entirely and become a man from nowhere, an exile without a home.

2. In the 'catastrophism' of another Eastern European state, Poland, I shall look at another nationalist doctrine that required conflict as its medium. It was a distinctively East European phenomenon. At one time or another most East European peoples have suffered a loss of independence, even an emasculation of their cultural life. After a humiliation such as a historic defeat in war, a people can rebuild its self-esteem by cutting short its period of mourning and longing for the restoration of what was never really 'lost'.

Nations often nurse historical grievances in the hope of one day restaging a conflict and reversing history. It affords a peculiar form of revenge. Historical defeats are often in turn woven into a national mythology and transmitted to the next generation as a timeless hurt that, as long as it is remembered, confirms the integrity of the nation.

Trapped in a historical culture that was ruthlessly contemptuous of failure, the Poles chose to exalt their misfortune. Unlike the English and the French they were not a people who came into their own in the modern era. They could claim no civilising mission, no historically sanctioned dominance over others. Their greatest period of success lay behind them.

In these circumstances they found comfort of a kind in catastrophism, in the fact that they appeared fated to suffer more than others. What other countries had done for the world directly through victory in battle they could do indirectly through their own martyrdom.

It was an inverted Christian message that made a virtue of suffering. It was deeply held nonetheless. It was to be found even on the peripheries of the civilised world. "Our future is very dark", a young Boer officer wrote to his wife in 1901, at the height of the war with Britain. "Perhaps it is the fate of our little race to be sacrificed on the alter of the world's ideas. Perhaps we are destined to be the martyr race".[6]

3. Finally, in the writing of the Italian Marxist Antonio Gramsci, I will look at another peculiarly modern idea—that of war as an act of transcendence, a means by which a national consciousness could be forged.

As an idea it was especially attractive to many nationalist movements in the latter half of the twentieth century in their struggle against colonial rule. Many of their leaders were interested in winning political legitimacy, as well as political power, through success on the battlefield. Although their political manifestos often talked of transforming the armed struggle into a people's war, it became increasingly clear that the people's war would have to continue after independence if the liberation movements were ever to transform themselves into modern political parties and their countries into modern nation-states.[7]

If catastrophism was an inverted form of Christianity, the doctrine of national liberation was an inverted form of Marxism. Instead of class it posited the nation as the agent of history. Instead of class consciousness it looked to national consciousness to transcend the human condition.

Max Weber and the Destiny of the German People

In German the word sein stands both for the verb to be and for the possessive pronoun his.
—Franz Kafka, *Third Octavo Notebook* (1917)

"A mere ten days after the defeat of Austria in 1809, a young eighteen-year-old German named Stapps approached Napoleon and tried to assassinate him. The emperor interrogated the young man at length. He offered him his life in return for an apology. Stapps refused to provide one and in the end Napoleon had no alternative but to send him to his death. 'I never saw him so confounded', wrote Rapp in his memoirs. When the prisoner had gone, Napoleon remarked: 'This is the result of the secret societies which infest Germany. This is the effect of fine principles in the light of reason. They make young men assassins. But what can be done against illuminism? A sect cannot be destroyed by cannon balls'."[8]

Nationalism was not sectarian. It was the most important force of the modern world. It was also prepared to make use of cannon. As the critic Karl Kraus later complained in the early months of the First World War, he had no objection to the bombardment of Paris. What he did object to was the German propensity for inscribing their artillery shells with quotations from Kant.[9]

Napoleon's remark, however, illustrates a myth that is still prevalent in school textbooks, that of the German nationalist revolt of 1813, the so-called "war of liberation". Indeed, the myth was so deeply entrenched in popular feeling that by the end of the nineteenth century it had become almost axiomatic that a people could not achieve liberty except through armed conflict. "No nation in the true sense of the word", wrote Michael Howard, "no self-conscious community could establish itself as a new and independent actor on the world scene without an armed conflict or the threat of one".[10]

In fact historians now tell us that there was not much nationalist enthusiasm in Germany or anywhere else (England excepted). Nationalism played only a very small part in Napoleon's defeat. The nationalist aspirations of many of the German generals were as unconvincing as that of the Bavarian commander Wrangel, who first heard his German blood calling to him at the battle of Leipzig and made haste to change sides in time. In Prussia the peasants were unhappy at having to supply far more recruits than they had been asked to find by Napoleon. The landowners were worried about a peasant uprising. The bourgeoisie was horrified by the proposal that it should be conscripted for the first time. In the Waterloo campaign that brought Napoleon's career to an end, 10,000 Rhinelanders deserted the Prussian army long before the final battle.[11]

German nationalism was a product of a much later period, fuelled by the pace of industrialisation, the speed with which after 1870 a predominantly agricultural country became a predominantly urban one. What *is* true is that the intellectuals did glimpse the spirit of the age during the Napoleonic Wars and went forth to 'educate' a historically unresponsive people. It was they who set out quite deliberately to tell the German people what was demanded of them by history in the hope that they might make it on their own terms for the first time.

Germany was the only nation in which the national identity was propagated first in the universities. At the university of Jena in 1789 the poet and dramatist Schiller demanded the future now. "The commerce of history", he proclaimed, consisted of selling a people a future in exchange for a past. A few years later, in 1807, Fichte told his students, "if you go under, all humanity goes under with you without hope for any restoration".[12] Those who attended Hegel's lectures were told that of the four great ages of man, the Germanic would be the last. A century later Heidegger warned his own students that Germany offered the only hope of salvation for a world that was threatened on two fronts: the historical materialism of capitalism, and communism.

Perhaps of all the philosophers Fichte was the most influential, in part because he drew up the ground rules of the later debate. In the winter of 1807, a few months after the battle of Jena at which Hegel glimpsed the World Spirit for the first time, Fichte published his *Address to the German Nation*. He delivered his lectures at a time of great danger. Prussia had been effectively demilitarised by Napoleon and Berlin occupied by French troops. He dared not incite his students to rebel, so he dressed up his invocation to arms in the language of philosophy instead. That relatively few people heard his lectures or read them when they were published did not matter. The fact that he gave them at all was an act of defiance. That was how their author conceived his stance at the time, and that was how it was subsequently understood by the general public. Fichte, as a philosopher, had not simply made a political statement, he had performed a political act and had done so explicitly in the name of philosophy.[13]

Fichte's true importance in the formulation of a specific German consciousness stemmed from the fact that he was one of the first philosophers of note to suggest that there was something quintessentially 'Germanic' about the German people. Germanness, he argued, was a primordial characteristic. Indeed, they were the only people who had the right to call themselves one, because they alone had remained true to themselves. Even during the period of the Roman Empire they had escaped Roman rule. The French, by comparison, had Latinised their language and Romanised their culture, and had been transformed in the process into something other than their original 'self'.

The Germans alone had preserved their original language while others had adopted an alien tongue, transforming it into a bastardised vernacular. Only the Germans had a language rooted in nature and one that was therefore fully alive. The romance languages were largely rootless, and accordingly could only sustain a superficial life.

Secondly, since the Germans had a primordial culture, they were uniquely qualified to engage in primordial thinking. They were the only people to have great ideas and to produce great philosophers. That is what Fichte meant when he wrote that any enemy of Napoleon was by adoption a German, that German nationalism "encompassed the whole of mankind". That is why his contemporary, the much lesser known Ernst Moritz Arndt, declared the German to be "a universal man".[14]

Thirdly, philosophers like Fichte and, of course, Hegel after him, considered that they had a duty to educate the nation, to raise its political and national consciousness, to make it aware of its destiny, of tasks yet to be accomplished.

Taking all three arguments together we can see that many German writers saw nationalism in metaphysical terms. As one of the characters in Mann's novel *Doctor Faustus* remarks, nationalism had become "a tireless discursive argumentation and a cursed lot of dialectical tension". Although Mann's character was speaking about Russia, he might with equal force have been speaking of Germany, a nation that reinvented itself several times in the course of the twentieth century, mostly with catastrophic consequences for itself.

One of the reasons the Germans philosophised so much was the absence of great deeds in their history. The Russians too suffered from an inferiority complex, this time not in relation to Western Europe but to Germany itself. They did not even produce great thinkers. They were, wrote Hegel, a people without philosophy. Russia promptly proceeded to emulate Germany in every way possible, producing its own Slavophiles who were insistent that there was something definingly Slavonic about the Russian soul, just as German writers insisted that there was something specifically Germanic about the German *Geist*. Lenin merely took the logical step of restructuring Russia on a reading of two German writers, Marx and Engels.

The contribution that German philosophers made to Germany's identity can be seen in three areas.

1. What distinguished Germany from its neighbours was the belief in culture as the basis of nationalism. Many liberal democrats failed to grasp the full import of this distinction because of linguistic imprecision. They did not think in terms of culture at all; they thought in terms of civilisation. This difference is illustrated by the persistent mistranslation of one of Freud's major works, *Civilisation and Its Discontents*. Freud was not writing about civilisation at all but culture. The English and the Americans

make no distinction. The Germans do. *Das Unbehagen in der Kultur,* Freud called his book, and the correct translation of the title would be 'The Uneasiness Inherent in Culture'.

'Civilisation', of course, is a vague word. By the eighteenth century it had come to mean a society of different national cultures linked by a network of beliefs, concepts and institutions. Each culture might speak its own language but each shared a common one. By the eighteenth century Latin (the language of Christendom) had given way to French, the language of the Enlightenment.

The *Encyclopédie* redefined the world of knowledge and infused it with *philosophie* and the *"sociétés des gens de lettres"* named on its title page. Even though the focus of the Enlightenment shifted to the court of Frederick the Great and Catherine the Great, their ministers looked to the *philosophes* for guidance and legitimacy. All of them read French and nearly all of them consulted the *Encyclopédie.*

Different languages might give rise to different ways of thinking and feeling, but as a common language French imparted a set of ideas and even values that distinguished European civilisation from that of, for example, the Islamic world. French was not only the language of the Enlightenment but also the French Revolution. It generated an entirely new political vernacular with its reference to human rights and its division of society into left- and right-wing factions. In the course of the twentieth century English in turn became the common language of the West as well as the chief medium through which were communicated the ideas of liberal internationalism.

The French also invented the term 'civilisation' in the 1750s as an explanation of the superior accomplishments that were seen to have given Europe the right to colonise the world. The term did not refer to a distinctive mode of existence specific to Europe but to an ideal order of human society. For them the other people of the globe were merely living through stages of existence through which they themselves had passed, the apex of which was the European Enlightenment. For the French the nation-state was circumscribed by neither ethnicity nor culture. To be a Frenchman after 1789 was to be a man who espoused the Rights of Man. As the historian Jules Michelet claimed, the French mission was to help every nation to become free. In that sense, the history of France was the history of humanity.[15]

They were sustained in this belief even during the First World War. As Henri Barbusse wrote in 1917, it was wrong to imagine that in order to sacrifice one's life for one's country a patriot had to be stimulated by a narrow patriotism or "inebriated by hatred of a given race": "It is rather the lofty promise of final progress which leads the true men to give their blood. We who fight as Frenchmen and above all as men can say proudly that we are living proof of this".[16]

Barbusse's "lofty promise of final progress" was "the end of war". "We who fought as Frenchmen but above all as men" is a full expression of the predominant French ideology. Patriotism was sanctioned by reference to the human race. This internationalism was confirmed by the experience of the First World War. It served to remind the French that their humanity did not derive from nationality but vice versa. Many Germans, by contrast, considered that it was their 'Germanness' that made them human. In their own eyes, it gave them self-respect.

One cannot imagine Germany experiencing the Dreyfus affair, a scandal that divided the French into two factions, those who wanted to base their patriotism on the defence of the fatherland against Germany, whatever the cost to the rights of individual Frenchmen; and those who insisted, in the name of the revolutionary tradition, that justice was not above patriotism but consistent with "being French". As Jean Jaurès, the great socialist leader, declared during the crisis, "The human individual is the measure of all things: of fatherland, family, property, humanity and God. Here is the logic of the revolutionary idea".[17]

Most Germans, by contrast, considered that culture was much more important. It was the legacy of an ancestral tradition transmitted in a specific language and adapted to a specific way of life. German nationalism was *exclusive* rather than inclusive in nature. It was also intensely inward looking. Unfortunately, the Germans were so intent on making sure that others should give them due recognition that the horizons of their experience shrank significantly—to the point, in fact, where they lacked magnanimity in their dealings with the world. That is what made their nationalism dangerous for others as well for themselves.

It was also, in the end, deeply divisive. As Ernst Jünger complained, the German people knew that they were considered dangerous by others, that even their admirers did not trust them. The French would consider "every bushman as human before [they] will see us as human". As a result the German people were denied the self-esteem that stems from being respected by others. Ultimately they were even estranged from each other. "Our aversion to ourselves is a constant theme".[18]

As Spengler complained at the end of the First World War, what had defeated Germany was its lack of national cohesion, which was due in no small measure to the alienation of what he termed an *'innere England'*—an inner core of Germans who were drawn far more to Anglo-American liberal ideas than to those of their own culture.[19] Thomas Mann alluded to the same dilemma in his apologia for Wilhelmine Germany, *Reflections of a Nonpolitical Man* (1918), an early work in his cultural development that was not translated into English until 1982 and hence that barely penetrated the Anglo-American consciousness. "Germany has enemies within its own walls," he wrote at the end of the Great War, "the allies and proponents of world-democracy." What rendered his own reflections so pertinent was that he recognised that, as a writer, he was partially aligned by the act of writing itself with the force of democracy, whatever his misgivings: "Am I to harbour within me . . . elements which further the 'progress' of Germany? Could it be that I am destined . . . to further Germany's progress towards that condition which in these pages is named with the quite inauthentic name of 'Democracy'? And what sort of part of myself then could that be? Perhaps the *literary* . . . for literature is at its most basic democratic".[20] It was a question that was to haunt him throughout the 1920s and that was, at the end of that disastrous decade, to align him firmly with the Anglo-American camp. As a result he spent a large part of his life in exile in two of the most democratic societies in the world, Switzerland and the United States.

There was no 'inner Prussia', of course, in England or the United States, no body of opinion that identified with the Prussian idea of the state, or found the force of Prussian militarism particularly compelling. It is interesting, however, that when the Americans were at last confronted by communism—the only major illiberal challenge that *was* internationalist in its appeal—they too went on the defensive. In the early 1950s a despairing attempt was made to define what was authentically 'American' thinking. The American people were asked by their leaders to see themselves for the first time not as a country so much as a contract with history that the Founding Fathers had entered into in 1776. The United States, they were told, was an idea, or a *proposition* contained in the Declaration of Independence. They were encouraged to believe that America was defined by its thoughts as well as its actions, that there was a definingly un-American way of thinking as well as behaving.

Error, in short, had to be engaged at home first, before America could venture forth into the wider world to redeem humanity. It was one of the few examples of a phenomenon that we tend to identify with the illiberal world, the 'intellectualising' of the nation-state.

2. Ultimately the emphasis the Germans put on protecting their cultural heritage might not have been problematic but for its military bias. What made liberals so critical of Germany was its indifference to what they themselves considered to be one of the most significant values of Western civilisation—peace. "The Germans", wrote Nietzsche in 1888, were "an *irresponsible* race which . . . at all the decisive moments in history were thinking of something else".[21] What he meant by 'irresponsible' was that they did not consider that what was true for them had to be construed as universally valid for everyone else. They broke with a post-Enlightenment tradition that considered values such as peace to be principles discovered by reason. For Germany the very word 'civilisation' took second place to 'culture' or *Kultur*, which the allies in both world wars did so much to mock for being 'uncivil', that is, warlike.

Even before the Great War a number of German writers had been critical of the pretensions of Prussian militarism. Nietzsche was among the first to take his own countrymen to task for thinking that their culture (rather than the army) had triumphed in 1870 in the war against France. Germany's victory, he insisted, had been due not to the superiority of its culture but to the iron discipline of its army and the army's superior generalship. The Germans had not lacked clearsightedness and courage. They had not prevailed because they had been culturally superior to the French, however. They merely happened to be better organised.[22]

Later the Germans tried to reduce the plurality of voices in Western civilisation to one. Liberalism was stifled early in the history of the Second Reich, and banished from the Third. The state, fearful of social divisions inside the country, and even more fearful of threats from the outside world, became an expression of naked power. It used war to impose its own discourse on others. War is born of non-communication. It aims at one end: to replace it with mono-communication, the word of the victor.

It was not surprising, therefore, that during the Second World War the Allies should have determined to transform Germany by force. In the Great War they had sought unsuccessfully to eradicate Prussian militarism, an exercise that H. G. Wells had referred to as the most important example in history of "sanitary engineering".[23] Later still, in demanding the unconditional surrender of the Third Reich, they insisted on bringing Germany into their world by force of arms. In order to make it a more historically responsible nation they had to make it more *responsive* to the terms on which the West believed history should be lived.

3. Apart from militarism, what made German thinking particularly un-Western was its racial view of nationalism. What made it particularly distinctive was that it combined two concepts not to be found in the nationalism of the liberal world: revolution and race. It combined them in a way that liberal societies still find puzzling.

The liberal world thinks of revolution as a 'progressive', liberal or left-wing phenomenon. Race tends to be regarded as conservative or reactionary, a phenomenon that is necessarily devoid of revolutionary content. That has been its own experience, and with its commitment to universalism it expects this to be true of the rest of the world.

German revolutionary thinking, however, as found in the works of such nineteenth-century writers as Bruno Bauer and Wilhelm Marr, was predicated on the belief that the German race was the most revolutionary of all, for it was in Germany that revolutionary humanity would find its ultimate fulfilment. German revolutionary thinking transcended the categories of left and right that had been introduced into European thinking with the French Revolution. The Germans believed that a genuine revolution could only be embodied in a movement, not a political party, in a nation not a faction. Revolution was not the birthright of a class but of an entire people.

It followed logically that the model of the false revolution, the French, should be destroyed. In August 1870 Wagner actually wrote to Bismarck to urge him to raze Paris (as he had demanded in his famous Revolutionary Manifesto of 1850). The true revolution, he insisted, would have to begin with the burning of Paris, the city of Robespierre, Saint-Just and Danton.[24] Hitler, in turn, though impressed by French culture, was clear that in his New Order there could be no place for France as a nation. Its revolutionary tradition would have to be expunged from the memory of man.

Race was also a central element in the concept of 'Germanness', which is why anti-Semitism was not only endemic in German life but crucial to the politics of identity. Long before Hitler the Jews were identified as an alien strain in German society, in large part because they were associated with a liberal commercial spirit that was considered to be a product of English or French, not German thinking. The revolutionary philosopher Jakob Fries called for the "extermination of the Jewish commercial caste" as early as 1816. Even Marx, in his notorious essay *On the Jewish Question* (1844), was among the first to see the Jews as 'parasites'. This racial element of German thinking was reinforced after 1871 by a peculiar reading of Darwin that can be found in the works of Ernst Haeckel and his imitators who laid the intellectual foundations of German national socialism.[25]

It would be easy enough to take one of the many illiberal German writers of the early twentieth century to illustrate each of these themes. It is important to recognise, however, that they also influenced the liberal imagination. They can be found in the early work of Max Weber, a writer with an excellent reputation in the English-speaking world.

Weber himself stood halfway between an authoritarian and a liberal tradition but squarely within the nationalist camp. Even after Germany's defeat in 1918, he wrote to his friend Ferdinand Tönnies, he "had never felt it so much a gift of destiny to have been born a German".[26] The German influence was never more pronounced in his writings than in the 1890s, when he wrote about the position of German smallholders east of the Elbe.

In the course of his inquiries he claimed to have discovered an economic struggle between Germans and Slavs in which the 'inferior' race had gained the upper hand. The advance of German culture in the east during the Middle Ages had been predicated on the superiority of an older and 'higher' culture. Now, he warned, the process was being reversed by market forces, by employers whose only interest was cheap labour. If the influx of untutored immigrants went unchecked a rural population might soon arise that could not be assimilated by "the historically transmitted culture of the country".

Polish immigrants had driven out the much stouter and stronger German workers because of their willingness to live at a subsistence level, because, as a people, they were lesser men, because they represented, in the jargon of the hour, "a less developed *cultural* type". The Poles had been able to secure jobs because their own standard of living was lower than that of the Germans, and because their cultural demands were lower still. What had happened in East Prussia was the triumph of the unfittest race. It was a triumph that threatened German culture in the east and the national security of its eastern frontier. Weber was quite unforgiving. If necessary, he insisted, Germany would have to be prepared to reverse the process, "to trample a whole generation into the ground" in order to safeguard its future. The "Slavic flood" could only be stemmed, he added, by a policy of recolonisation by German farmers, or what our more cynical generation has come to call 'ethnic cleansing'.

What is significant about Weber's views is that they were not at all unusual. They were quite consistent with mainstream German thinking. They can be found in many tracts of the time. They were even more forcefully expressed by Weber's friend, the historian Friedrich Meinecke.

A nation, Weber contended, was usually anchored in the superiority, at least irreplaceability, of its cultural values. Language was an essential element by which values were communicated. The capacity of a community to develop self-consciously and to sustain values that were distinctively different from those of other countries was linked to its success in developing a *literary* culture. A community without a literature (and the ideas that literature embodies) was uncultured, or in his own phrase, *kulturlos*.

Weber had accused the Poles of lacking a culture, in terms of both education and literacy. He had not on that understanding suggested that they should be suppressed. He wanted them instead to be given their own state. This would be more desirable than allowing them to live within the Reich as cheap labourers, threatening the jobs and therefore the economic culture of the German nation.[27]

In short, Weber drew a distinct contrast between the Polish and the German people that cast the former in a particularly unfavourable light. The Poles were an inferior people because of their inability to develop a sense of individuality compared with the Prussian community among whom they lived. "At least the majority of them had no self-consciousness nor any strong need to distinguish and separate their lives from their German-speaking fellow citizens". In that sense, they were parasites living off a stronger culture. "If anybody says that we have degraded the Poles to second-class citizenship," he added in the 1890s, "let the truth be spoken: we have turned them from animals into human beings."[28]

Hitler too, of course, considered the Polish people to be *kulturlos,* fair game for enslavement and colonisation. But he made the same claim, far more forcefully, about the Jews. Where he differed from Weber was in the importance he attached to national myths. As a rationalist Weber saw the problems of assimilation purely in political and social terms. For Hitler the importance of the cultural construction of identity was that a nation was the lived-out realisation of a myth. We cannot understand this point unless we see in mythology more than just a story (or series of stories) with a moral locked into the occasion of their first telling. Mythology involves a process, a complex set of culturally specific ways of thinking about the world and its history.

As Alfred Rosenberg wrote in his fevered study, *The Myth of the Aryan Race,* "Today we Germans are beginning to dream again our original dreams". Dreams revealed the inner psyche of a nation in its discourse of national formation. The community was imagined. "The imagined community . . . thinks of the representative body not the personal life". Such essentialism meant that anyone who did not conform to a representative type was necessarily an 'outsider'.[29] It followed that the Jews could never constitute a people because they had been forbidden by God to dream of the future. In terms of Nazi ideology they were a profoundly unaesthetic people because of their attachment to an ethical order, a Mosaic Law that forbade the construction of secular idols.

Let me return to the argument with which I began this chapter. Society is about communication. So is nationalism. Herder and Fichte had preached the gospel that the German people were only as strong as the language they spoke. In this respect, one of the most haunting images of Germany's role in the Holocaust is Georges Perec's *The Disappearance.* It is an experimental novel that contains not a single 'e' throughout the text, an omission that has the effect, of course, of rendering the reader even more conscious of the missing letter than if it had been sprinkled over its 300 pages. Perec was inspired by the fact that the French pronunciation of the letter 'e' is more or less indistinguishable from that of the word *'eux'* meaning 'they'.

Perec lost his mother in Auschwitz and was haunted by her death until the end of his life. What has disappeared from his book is 'they,' the Jews of the Holocaust. In his eyes, the Final Solution had been an attempt to eradicate a letter from the human alphabet, an act that could only end in impoverishing the language of human discourse.

The importance of that discourse is that it preserves diversity. It refuses to render one voice more marginal than another. It recognises that the suppression of a voice is a denial of the future, because with it, a human possibility disappears too.[30]

Catastrophism and the Agony of Poland

> *Love no country; countries soon disappear.*
> *Love no cities; cities are soon rubble.*
> —Czeslaw Milosz, 'Child of Europe'

The Jews or 'the Chosen People', wrote D. H. Lawrence in the last book he wrote, had always had an idea of themselves as an imperial people. They had tried to create an empire and failed disastrously in the attempt. They then gave it up. After the destruction of Jerusalem they ceased to imagine a great national Jewish empire. "The prophets became silent forever". "The Jews became a people of *postponed destiny* and then the seers began to write apocalypses".[31]

The early Christians were even more apocalyptic than the prophets of the Old Testament. The prophets of the New, Lawrence tells us, anticipated the apocalyptic thoughts to be found in the writings of men as diverse as Péguy, Proudhon, Sorel, Bakunin and Herzen, all of whom, at one point or another, had looked forward to the end of the world just as thoroughly "as any primitive Christian awaiting with pious satisfaction that much canvassed event".[32]

One of the last and most poignant expressions of modern Christian 'catastrophism' was formulated in the ruins of Nagasaki by an unusual Christian, a Japanese doctor named Nagai Takashi. Takashi later became a symbol of his city's suffering, just as a schoolgirl named Saki Sadako became a symbol of Hiroshima. Sadako was two years old when the bomb exploded a mile from her home. She died of leukaemia ten years later, but not before trying to fold a thousand paper cranes as a symbol of longevity.

Takashi was a professor of radiology at the University of Nagasaki when the city was bombed. He had contracted leukaemia before the war, perhaps as a result of his laboratory experiments. He was a devout Catholic but also a Japanese patriot who was devastated by Japan's defeat. But then, as he wrote in his best-selling book *The Bells of Nagasaki,* he had a flash of religious inspiration. The bomb, he concluded, had been "a great act of Divine Providence" for which the people of Nagasaki should thank God. The city, "the only holy place in Japan", had been chosen as a sacrificial lamb "to be burned on the altar of sacrifice to expiate the sins committed by humanity in the Second World War".

In this vision Takashi added the Catholic victims of the bomb to the long list of Nagasaki's Christian martyrs. They were the spiritual heirs of the Christian believers who had been crucified in the seventeenth century for their faith: "How noble, how splendid was that holocaust of August 9, when flames soared up from the cathedral, dispelling the darkness of war and bringing the light of peace. From the very depths of our grief we reverently saw here something beautiful, something pure, something sublime. Eight thousand people, together with their priests, burning with pure smoke entered into eternal life. All without exception were good people whom we deeply mourn".[33]

Nagai was unusual only for his religious sensibility, for his belief in God. If most other twentieth-century visionaries were distinguished by their secularism, of course, their apocalyptic visions were frequently expressed in religious terms. Hegel himself had referred to God when describing the character and development of the absolute spirit. He even went so far as to call his own philosophy a 'theodicy'. His most important twentieth-century interpreter, Alexandre Kojève, was much impressed by his remark in *The*

Science of Logic that logic was "the thought of God before the creation of the world", which could be interpreted to mean (as it often was) that his logic was "the logic, thought, or discourse of God".

On such a view philosophy took over from religion as the source of ultimate coherence in people's lives. And being based on reason rather than revelation, it was considered far superior because it was both conclusive and universal. Hegel can be read either as a philosopher or a prophet, and it was largely as a prophet that he inspired men such as Feuerbach and Marx and others like them, who were intent on transforming the story of mankind into a coded blueprint for a new Jerusalem.

Let me add parenthetically that the Anglo-American imagination was not entirely inaccessible to what has been called catastrophism, to the idea of the nation-state as the medium of the apocalypse. D. H. Lawrence, a fundamental critic of the liberal conscience, was obsessed with the crisis through which Europe was passing, which he hoped would result not in the revaluation but in the renovation of man. In the early days of the Great War, he hoped that the English would play a major role in that change. "Our death must be accomplished first, then we will rise up", he told Bertrand Russell in May 1915. "Wait only a little while", he wrote to Russell's mistress, Ottoline Morell; these were "the last days" of mankind, "the last wave of time".[34]

Lawrence was so obsessed with the apocalypse, wrote Frank Kermode, that he can well be described as a 'moral terrorist' (Kant's term for the historians of his day who thought that the evident corruption of the world presaged an immediate appearance of the Antichrist). Kermode traces the origins of his eschatological thinking to the doctrine of Joachitism (so named after St. John, the author of the book of *Revelation*, a faith that postulated three historical epochs, one for each person of the trinity, with a transitional age between each).

The apocalypse was given particular force in Lawrence's wartime writing. In another letter to Ottoline Morell he wrote of the arrival of the first zeppelins over the skies of London as presaging "a new cosmic order". As always, the new age could not be realised without "smashing". *Women in Love,* one of his most important works, may avoid all explicit mention of history—"I should wish the time to remain unfixed so that the bitterness of the war may be taken for granted in the characters", he wrote—but it is a deeply historical book all the same, for "it was in 1915 that the old world ended" and the Great Transition began.[35]

Lawrence's apocalyptic poetics eventually ran into a dead end. By the time he died he had lost faith in war as a medium of redemption. He had no faith either that a country as materialistic as England could ever spearhead the advent of a new age.

Unfortunately, in Eastern Europe catastrophism remained a potent political force. Its origins dated back a long way. One of the holiest occasions, for example, of the Serbian Orthodox calendar coincides with the day in

1389 when Prince Alazar Hrebeljinovic and his forces were crushed by the Ottoman Turks in the battle of Kosovo, which ushered in 500 years of Muslim rule. According to Serbian legend, the angel Elijah appeared to Alazar on the eve of the battle and offered him a choice over the outcome of the next day's fighting. He could have a victory and win an earthly kingdom or choose martyrdom and a place for his people in Heaven. He chose the latter, ensuring in the process that a military failure was turned into a spiritual triumph and that the battlefield became the birthplace of the Serbian mission to recover the national homeland.

"Wipe away Kosovo from the Serb mind and soul," wrote Milovan Djilas, "and *we* are no more. . . . If there had been no battle at Kosovo the Serbs would have invented it for its suffering and its heroism".[36] In 1982 the Serbian Orthodox Church published an appeal for the protection of the historical site of the battle, arguing that the question of Kosovo involved nothing less than the "spiritual, cultural and historical identity of our people". Exactly how spiritual, the Serbs and everyone else were soon to find out, at the end of the Cold War, when it gave rise to the most wasteful conflict Europe had witnessed in fifty years, in the course of which 250,000 people lost their lives.

Catastrophism recommended itself especially to the peoples of the East, perhaps because their quotidian of misery and suffering at the hands of non-Europeans was greater than any other—the Serbs under the Turks, the Russians under the Tartars, the Poles under the Russians. When Poland was invaded by the Russians for a second time in 1944, its people were treated far more cruelly by the Red Army—with which this time they were 'allied'—than they had been in 1939, perhaps because on the second occasion some of the Russian units included a large number of Uzbeks and Chechens, once nomadic warriors who had roamed the steppes. Did they not in 1944, asks one historian, revenge themselves on the white race that they had once subjugated?[37]

Perhaps the main reason, however, that catastrophism became popular in Eastern Europe was the historical contingency of existence with which many of its people had to live. All small nations experience an uncomfortable sense of always being answerable to history. All of them, at some point or another in their past, have passed through "the antechamber of death". Their very existence has been brought into question, a fate never experienced by England or France even in the darkest periods of their history. Even today observers are still amazed by the often astonishing intensity of their self-affirmation, especially their cultural life.[38]

In Poland's case that identity took on a particularly intense meaning. In the mid–nineteenth century the country's most celebrated poet, Adam Mickiewicz, found a bizarre form of consolation for the fate of his nation after the failure of the November rising in Warsaw in 1831. His response was to formulate a messianic view of nationalism that made the Polish people God's chosen nation. A measure of God's grace was evidenced by its repeated crucifixion under Russian rule.

Mickiewicz went so far as to identify the nation as a collective reincarnation of Christ and its revolt against Russia as a form of messianism. The fall of Warsaw twice (in 1794 and 1831) would be followed by the rise of Warsaw on the third day. With the resurrection of the Polish nation, war between Christian nations would cease altogether.[39]

The roots of Polish catastrophism ran deep. It stemmed from a mixture of Jewish and Russian messianism. In the seventeenth century the country had played host to the largest Jewish concentration in the world among whom messianic sects flourished. We can find it in the writings of the rabbi Sabbatai Zevi (a native of Smyrna), who declared himself to be the messiah and attracted thousands of Polish Jews who sold their property to join him. It included the self-professed eighteenth-century messiah Jacob Frank, who spent his youth in Thessalonica until a vision instructed him to travel to Poland, the promised land. For several generations the Frankists (who were finally expelled from the synagogue in 1759) married exclusively amongst themselves. It is perhaps no coincidence that Mickiewicz's wife was a member of the community. For him it was quite natural that Polish Jews should take part in the country's unique mission, that even a regiment of Jewish light cavalry should have fought to defend Warsaw against the Russians and Prussians during the 1794 rising.

Only later did the Poles reveal that they had little sympathy for Mickiewicz's Zionism. During his life, however, Catholic anti-Semitism, although widespread, did not yet pretend to represent the patriotic interest. It was only in the second half of the nineteenth century that nationalists began to preach that a true Pole was a Polish-speaking Catholic Slav and that all other communities that existed in Poland, especially the Jews, were obstacles to the construction of an authentic nation.

The other source of Polish catastrophism came from Russia, where it can be found even in the writings of philosophers such as Pytor Chaadayev. "We are one of the nations," he wrote in the 1820s, who do not appear "to be an integral part of the human race but exist in order to teach some great lesson to the world . . . who knows when we will rejoin the human race and how much misery we must suffer before accomplishing our destiny".

Rather disturbingly, this passage appears in connection with the United States on the concluding page of the memoirs of the Polish-American writer Zbigniew Brzezinski, President Carter's national security advisor in the late 1970s.[40] The United States too has often seen itself as a country outside history, an agent rather than an actor, a nation in which the extraordinary is commonplace. The difference is that a nation that has tried so hard not only to redeem mankind but also to dehistoricise tragedy, has never accepted that its own martyrdom is the inevitable price to be paid for the redemption of the world from eighteenth-century kings, Nazi gauleiters or communist commissars.

It might have been expected that when Poland became a nation in 1919, its intellectual elite would abandon catastrophism. Far from it: Writers such as Jozef Czechowicz and Marian Zdziechowski believed that the world was passing through a great crisis, one that had been heralded by the revolution in neighbouring Russia. Zdziechowski was a cultural historian who voiced his catastrophism in such essayistic works as *The Spectre of the Future* (1936) and *The End Envisaged* (1938). Both writers came from the east. Though born in Lublin, Zdziechowski spent long periods of his life in Belorussia. He was nurtured on Russian literature in the early 1920s. No wonder, writes the poet Czeslaw Milosz, that catastrophism remained a potent cultural force, one that was instinctively pessimistic about Poland's future.[41]

Milosz himself was the witness to the force of the idea when the people of Warsaw did indeed rise again in 1944, this time against not the Russians but the Germans. Warsaw in fact witnessed two revolts against the German army: the first was that of the Jewish ghetto or "the forbidden city", as Malaparte called it. It was fitting that it should have fallen to an Italian to give it its most haunting name, for the Italians have been associated with urban life more than any other people, and have speculated more imaginatively than any other about the cities of the future. It is an imagination that encompasses Augustine's City of God; Dante's Infernal Metropolis; Campanella's City of Walls, in which the inhabitants were walled in by the city fathers; Piranesi's Ruined Cities; Giacometti's haunted spaces; and more recently the "invisible cities" of Marco Polo's imagination, dreamed up by the author Italo Calvino.

None of these writers, however, could have anticipated what the Germans made of city life halfway through the twentieth century. In 1944 Warsaw offered a nightmarish vision in which its citizens were randomly arrested and deported to the countryside. Even their children had to be educated in secret. The dangers were enormous: if caught their teachers were killed and their parents sent to concentration camps. The children themselves were often sentenced to hard labour.[42]

According to one participant, the uprising was the result of four years of "nervous exhaustion". Milosz was at hand to record it. It was a futile act that resulted in the death of 200,000 people in two months of fighting. It was a young persons' uprising. It was also a poets' war as the Spanish Civil War had been for the English. Milosz mentions some of his fellow writers who lost their lives—the twenty-year-old poet Christopher, who died at his post sniping at SS tanks, his wife later dying in hospital, grasping an unfinished manuscript of her husband's verses; and the poet Karol who, together with Marek, were blown up on the barricades. Both men died defying history, uncomprehending to the end of the real historical forces that were being played out at their country's expense.

One of the stories Milosz tells is of a friend, called Alpha, the pseudonym of a well-known writer who had spent much of his life describing the tragic moral conflicts that were such a distinctive feature of his country's history. During the years of the German occupation he had contributed to the underground literature produced by the resistance movement, writing works that were mimeographed on the run.

When the two men finally returned to the city after the war, they found themselves walking through a wasteland of ruined buildings and gutted houses. One day they stumbled upon a little plank fastened on a metal bar. The inscription read "Lt. Zbyzek's road of suffering". It was a cry of justice, a cry of the dead. Why had the lieutenant died, what had he died for, and what had he imagined was the reason for sacrificing his life in those last hours of his existence?

Alpha had railed against the people responsible for such a futile sacrifice of life. But, as Milosz asks, was he not one of those most to blame?

> Actually, Alpha was one of those who were responsible for what had happened. Could he not see the eyes of the young people gazing at him as he read his stories in clandestine authors' evenings? These were the young people who died in the uprising: Lt. Zbyzek, Christopher, Barbara, Karol, Marek, and thousands like them. They had known there was no hope of victory and that their death was no more than a gesture in the face of an indifferent world. They had died without even asking whether there was some scale in which their deeds would be weighed.
>
> The young philosopher Milbrand, a disciple of Heidegger, assigned to press work by his superiors, demanded to be sent to the line of battle because he believed that the greatest gift a man can have is the moment of free choice: three hours later he was dead. There were no limits to these frenzies of voluntary self-sacrifice.[43]

In the end, the uprising was betrayed by the Polish people's supposed allies, not their enemies, for the Red Army was ordered to dig in before Warsaw and allow the resistance movement to be crushed. It did not come to their aid. It even went so far as to shoot down Allied planes flying in aid from England.

But then, Milosz remarks, why should they have helped? What was the use of blaming the Russians, who had their own messianic understanding of history? They were "the force of history", they were intent on liberating Poland not only from the Nazis but from its past. They had no wish to be met by a functioning government when they entered the city. They represented a historical force, Communism, whose triumph they expected would be complete. History, Milosz added, is brutal when it pronounces its sentence. There is no place for pity or regret.

The Warsaw uprising, as it happened, was "the swansong of the [Polish] intelligentsia". Those who had survived the uprising were arrested by the new regime when it came to power and disappeared from history altogether. They were betrayed by their own apocalyptic thinking, for imagining that they could make history on terms of their own choosing.

Wars can create nations, but they can also destroy them. It may have been Christ's destiny to die on the cross, but it was not Poland's, any more than the suffering preceding that 'final' act of despair the Warsaw uprising, was fated for the victims or the anguish following it for the survivors. The Poles were betrayed by the peculiar language of nineteenth-century history, that vocabulary moulded by a tradition of thought that dates back to Hegel. The rhetoric of suffering displayed a fatal capacity to reconcile the victims to their supposedly ordained fate.

Milosz's conclusion in *The Captive Mind* displays a moment of stunning clarity, which is why it was received so critically by many of his countrymen, communist and nationalist alike, who still considered it a privilege to be members of a martyr race. Their subsequent experience of forty years of communism, another messianic creed that used a nineteenth-century vernacular, enabled the intellectuals to see their country's history in a more rational, clearheaded light, to recognise belatedly that there is no nobility in martyrdom not freely chosen.

Gramsci and National Liberation Wars

In the opening pages of Michael Howard's book *War and the Liberal Conscience*, the Trevelyan lectures that he delivered at Cambridge in 1978, the author describes the association of the man after whom the lectures are named, and his study of the Italian war of independence. George Trevelyan had no doubt that the *Risorgimento* had been "a good war" and that war was the stuff of history, heroism and the progress of the race. As a liberal he admired John Bright, the peaceful Quaker MP, but he also admired Garibaldi and he saw no conflict between the two men. Bright's journals report Garibaldi greeting him when he visited England with the words "I am of your principles, for if I am a soldier, I am a soldier of peace". He was, adds Howard, not the last "freedom fighter" to make such a claim.[44]

It is easy to see why the cause of Italian nationalism was so popular with liberal England, the first European country to gain a national identity, if not always a great understanding of itself. Yet the story of Italian nationalism in the nineteenth century is being rewritten at an alarming rate. Garibaldi himself has lost much of his reputation, for he is seen increasingly to have been neither a true fighter nor a true nationalist but an opportunist who made the best of the modest hand history had dealt him.

"You are the bastards of humanity", declared Mazzini, addressing not his foreign adversaries but his compatriots.[45] The *Risorgimento*, in which

Mazzini took such a prominent part, historians now tell us, was not about the creation of a greater Italian state. Charles Albert's fight for Piedmont, Cattaneo's for Milan, Manin's for Venice, and the Romans for their republic in 1848 were not part of a much greater struggle. Cavour had no wish to bring southern Italy into the union with the north until Garibaldi forced his hand. Both men died disappointed, realising that the new Italy was not liberal at heart.[46] Instead it was waiting for Mussolini, whose own rise to power ensured that the south would be treated even more ruthlessly as a 'colonial' appendage of the north. As Massimo Taparelli, Marquese d'Azeglio, concluded in a famous phrase, "The founding fathers had made Italy but failed to make Italians".

One of the few Italian intellectuals who addressed this dilemma, the Marxist writer Antonio Gramsci, recognised from the first that Italy's 'nationalisation' had been incomplete, for the *Risorgimento* had not involved the people. Mazzini might have preached armed revolt, but he had wanted only a local insurrection, not a genuine armed rebellion. The result had been a war of liberation fought not by the Italian people but by Piedmont, engaged in a tactical alliance that united the industrialists of the north with the reactionary landowners of the south. It had succeeded without creating a proper nation.

In the south Gramsci found an impoverished Third World society anchored to the First World. He found a colonial people despised by the northerners as an inferior race. For several decades after unification, the south, like a colony, was in a chronic condition of peasant revolt, which the government denounced as 'brigandage' and which it put down with extreme force.[47] Gramsci knew this revolt and repression at first hand from the rising in 1906 on his own home island, Sardinia. In his youth he had been an enthusiastic secessionist.

One of Gramsci's contemporaries who discussed his country's lack of national consciousness was the writer Carlo Levi. In the mid-1930s he was banished by Mussolini to a primitive village in Lucania, a remote province of the south, where he discovered a way of life that he had never previously suspected to exist. The peasants, he found, did not even think of themselves as Christians. Christ, he was told, had stopped at Eboli and his message had never been taken farther. A Christian in their mind meant a human being. They did not, alas, think of themselves as men but as beasts of burden, forced to scratch for whatever subsistence living they could.

Nor did they consider themselves to be Italians. For them Rome meant very little. It was the capital of a foreign, hostile world that taxed them and conscripted their sons to fight in its name. Naples had more right to be their capital, and in some ways it was—the capital of poverty. But at Naples there had been no king for a long time, and the peasants went there only to embark for other shores. The world to which they went, the other world, the future, was not the north but America: "New York rather than Rome or Naples would be the real capital of the peasants of Lucania if these men without a country could have a capital at all. And it *is* their capital in the only way it can be for them, that is as a myth, a place where they could become men, where they could have a future".[48]

Levi's emigrant race was the despair not only of politicians on the left but also of Mussolini and his supporters. "We are an emigrant nation", lamented Enrico Carradini, an early Fascist writer who was a typical member of a struggling intellectual circle that took refuge in cultural pessimism in the early years of the century. The complaint that he put into the mouth of one of his characters—"The time does not allow for magnanimous feelings"—accurately sums up his own state of mind.

Emigration and war were the twin themes of his books. The first had made the Italians slaves, the latter would liberate them. To obtain work or merely to live, people had to do so outside Italy. War was the only alternative. It was a 'moral' imperative, "a means of national redemption", a reaction, in short, to "the cowardice of the present hour".

Taking up the same theme, Curzio Malaparte attributed the absence of a true national consciousness to the fact that the people had never been asked to fight for their freedom, save for a brief moment in the *Risorgimento*. As a result they had developed an aversion to suffering. A people who had no wish to suffer, and no enthusiasm for martyrdom, could never expect to forge a nation. Unlike Gramsci, who hoped for a revolution, Malaparte looked forward to a civil war that would once and for all condition the Italian people to suffering. "Our people must suffer . . . only deep and atrocious suffering experienced by all . . . can transform us into a magnificent imperial people". Mussolini, he added, would "need to be merciless to us at home . . . and must not fear to make war on those of his own blood before showing no mercy to those outside". "His war against us", he concluded, would be an element of his "inevitable function in Europe".[49]

It was all to end in tears, of course, and for that there is no better witness than Malaparte himself, who acted as an interpreter for the U.S. Fifth Army when it entered Naples in 1944. The last months of the war saw a fratricidal struggle of Italian against Italian, between those who remained loyal to Mussolini's Salo Republic in the north and those who had gone over to the Allies. "It was the usual sordid war between Italians begun on the usual pretext of liberating Italy from the foreigner".

When Malaparte entered his own home city, Florence, he surrendered his automatic rifle to an American soldier so that he would not be tempted to kill any of his compatriots.

> "Why don't you fire? Are you a conscientious objector?" I was asked.
> "No, he isn't", answered Jack, "he is an Italian—a Florentine. He doesn't want to kill Italians, Florentines". And he looked at me with a sad smile.
> "You'll regret it", Mr. Bradley shouted to me. "You'll never have another chance like this as long as you live".[50]

Fascism, of course, could unify Italy no more than communism could. Its own brand of nationalism suffered from a major contradiction. On the one hand, the nationalists insisted on the need for unity; on the other, their contempt for human life violated the minimum conditions or principles on which a community must be based. The Fascist principle could not promote a national consciousness that could effectively unify the Italian people.[51] Nor for that matter, could socialism.

Unfortunately, after 1950 the language of national liberation wars was imbued with a socialist gloss that gave the writings of Gramsci's successors, in particular Sartre and Frantz Fanon, a spurious credibility. Nation building was very much the theme of the decolonisation era. By the end of the century, however, it had become patently clear that a nation cannot be forged in blood without paying a high price in social alienation.

George Orwell and the Myth of England

In the same year that Chesterton wrote *The Napoleon of Notting Hill,* he penned a short book, an intellectual and spiritual autobiography. In putting forward the philosophy in which he had come to believe he chose to present his readers with a set of mental pictures rather than a set of deductions. It was a telling decision, for he identified in himself what he later came to believe was most impressive about English patriotism in the critical years of the Great War. He recognised that *liberal* nationalism traded in images of the past—in images, not ideas.

What he deplored most about English nationalism was its jingoist element; and what he disliked most about jingoism was (contrary to received opinion) its tendency to trade in ideas:

> The worst jingoes do not love England, but a theory of England. If we love England for being an empire, we may overrate the success with which we rule the Hindoos. But if we love it for only being a nation, we can face all events: for it would be a nation even if the Hindoos ruled us. . . . A man who loves England for being England will not mind how she arose. But a man who loves England for being Anglo-Saxon may go against all facts for his fancy. He may end (like Carlyle and Freeman) by maintaining that the Norman Conquest was a Saxon Conquest. He may end in utter unreason—because he has a reason.[52]

In a passage of which Nietzsche would have approved, he added that *rational* optimism tended to lead to stagnation; irrational optimism, to reform. The man who rationalised his patriotism was an essentialist determined to preserve what he regarded as the timeless character of his own country. The irrational patriot who was prepared to love his country whatever changes it underwent was the one who was the more modern of the two. Because he was more modern his country was likely to fare better in its wars.

Chesterton would have been surprised (if not aggrieved) to learn that Nietzsche too spent a large part of his life condemning such essentialism. He remained profoundly unhappy at the way his generation interpreted the rise and decline of states. The purpose of history, after all, was not to discover the essential roots of a nation but to transcend them. Its significance as a subject lay not only in celebrating the elements of continuity in a nation's history but also in underlining the importance of discontinuity as well.

In one of the essays that form his *Unfashionable Meditations* Nietzsche was particularly critical of his own country's obsession with authenticity, its perpetual search for an authentic self. He was scathing of its historians for continually grubbing around in the soil for roots, forever attempting "to conserve for posterity the conditions under which we were born". A true historian, Nietzsche asserted, should take every period at face value. He should not judge one more morally uplifting than another. He should not place conclusions at the beginning and make last things first. The role of a historian should be to celebrate the aspects of a national story that make one age inherently different from the next.[53]

Nietzsche also attacked the essentialists on a second count. They wanted the history of a nation to 'ring true'. They were inclined to judge its success or failure by whether it had acted 'in character' or not. As a result they tended to write off entire ages or epochs as low or high moments in a country's past, the highest of all, of course, being the most authentic, when the nation was most 'true' to itself. German historians, he complained, tended to accomplish this fact by getting as near as possible to the past, placing themselves at the foot of mountains looking up, adopting "the perspective of frogs".

Ultimately, what he considered most self-defeating was the fact that decline is a value-laden term. In its static sense it requires a disjunctive logic of 'higher' and 'lower', or 'earlier' and 'later'. The earlier point, of course, set the standard for every other. To decline, a state had to fall away 'from' a previous standard. Consequently, distance in time tended to become difference in value. Speaking of historical decline becomes not only a matter of early or late, but also of better or worse. It is a value judgement that historians are invariably not competent to make.

Nietzsche finally attacked the concept of essentialism as one of the abiding vices of nineteenth-century historiography. It was the historian's task to be a physician, not a philosopher, interested in the health not the destiny of his patient. His task should be to keep the patient alive rather than to hurry him off to his death. "The conviction reigns that it is only through the sacrifices and accomplishments of our ancestors that the tribe exists", he wrote. "One has to pay them back with sacrifices and accomplishments. One thus recognises a debt that constantly grows greater".[54]

Writing in the same vein an English historian once criticised Churchill for being "the price the British people paid for reading history".[55] In this case, however, the past served Churchill particularly well in his dialogue with the nation, and the nation in its discourse with itself. Of all leaders Churchill more than most could instil in those who listened to his radio broadcasts in 1940 a sense of national destiny, which he constantly evoked to fortify the present.

Nietzsche is an important philosopher because the overriding concern of his later years was to offer an effective critique of the culture of his day in the hope of contributing to its improvement. If much of his work is pervaded by medical terms, these are more than conventional metaphors. He was well aware of the dangers of analogising, but he also recognised that philosophers are inveterate analogisers and that he could not avoid the habit himself. The metaphors that he encourages us to use do not rest merely on analogies between the body's working and the activities of the mind. They are also based on structural and functional analogies between the human body and such larger units as political cultures. When he wrote of a culture in decline he compared it to a patient going into decline, consumed by sickness, by anxiety, by a loss of confidence in the future—in a word, by depression.

In later life he came to couch his general theory of man's cultural development even more exclusively in medical terms, arguing that unless societies were dynamic they would die. Their life could be best prolonged by "inoculating them with something new", by embracing transience and change, not retreating from them.

What was so important about liberal societies in the twentieth century was their willingness to live with historical change, with the transience of the past in the present. In his essay 'On Transience,' Freud, who was to die in exile in England in 1939, described taking "a summer walk through a smiling countryside" in the company of "a taciturn friend and of a young but already famous poet". The identity of the two men cannot be established. Perhaps Freud made the story up.

> The poet admired the beauty of the scene around us but held no joy in it. He was disturbed by the thought that all this beauty was fated to extinction, that it would vanish when winter came, like all human beauty and all the beauty and splendour that men had created or may create. All that he would otherwise have loved and admired seems to him to be shorn of its worth by the transience which was its doom.[56]

"The demand for immortality", Freud concluded, "is a product of our wishes too unmistakable to lay claim to reality: what is painful may nonetheless be true".

No one can contemplate his own mortality with indifference, but we might, with Freud, dispute the pessimistic poet's view that the transience of what is beautiful involves any loss in its worth. The intellectual idea of nationalism suggests an unchanging being or an authentic self. The liberal view is one that allows us to come to terms with transience, with the fact that a national character changes over time and that a nation changes with it. A nation is only as true as what the living, not the dead, demand of it.

Chesterton was right therefore to stress the importance of the visual image in celebrating what made a country distinctive in its own imagination. What distinguished the German and the English responses to history most was that the German bourgeoisie defined itself intellectually. What distinguished it from its English counterpart was its obsession with its own identity. The German bourgeoisie was the principal bearer of German national thought and nationalist doctrines. It looked continually to other cultures to better understand its own.[57]

The poetics of German nationalism first found a voice in the verse of Novalis and Hölderlin. Later it found a voice in the philosophical texts of the nineteenth century. German historians may have furnished the conscious recovery of a national myth, but it was its philosophers who delineated the cognitive map of the German nation. By contrast, the essential characteristic of the English mind was predominantly its *visual* nature, a vision in which a nation with a modest history of pictorial representation was captured mostly in its poetry and prose. Visual pictures usually are related to an atrophy of the intellect. Ideas are conjured away, only images remain. The English did not rationalise or intellectualise their sense of nation; they couched it in visual terms instead.

Above all, the English imagination was a poetic one. The poets of World War One invented a pastoral tradition for which the English had fought, and yet which at the same time they were conscious was being destroyed in the Flanders mud. That poetic image survived into the 1930s. Early in the Second World War Tom Harrison, the founder of Mass Observation, carried out a poll that asked soldiers what they were fighting for. Few replied in terms of king and country, church and state, freedom or democracy. Quite overwhelmingly they replied in terms of an idealised picture of a timeless rural England, one that George Orwell glimpsed through the window of a train when he returned from Spain in 1938:

> Here it was still the England I had known in my childhood . . . the railway cuttings smothered in wild flowers, the deep meadows where the great shining horses browse and meditate, the slow moving streams bordered by willows, the green bosoms of the elms, the larkspurs in the cottage gardens, and then the huge peaceful wilderness of Outer London: the barges on the mirey river, the familiar streets, the posters telling of cricket matches and royal weddings, the men in bowler hats, the pigeons in Trafalgar Square, the red buses, the blue policemen—all sleeping the deep sleep of England from which I sometimes fear we shall never wake till we are jerked out of it by the roar of the bombs.[58]

This was *not* the England he had seen two years earlier, which he recorded in the first part of *The Road to Wigan Pier*. The latter offered an unforgettable depiction of the very texture of northern working-class life that had nothing pastoral about it. There was nothing redeeming about the scene Orwell glimpsed from another train as he returned to the south, that of an exhausted young woman trying to unblock a pipe: "She knew well enough what was happening to her—understood as well as I did how dreadful a destiny it was to be kneeling down in the bitter cold, on the slimy stones of a slum back yard, poking a stick up a foul drainpipe". The full extent of the horror he found in the north was conveyed by his use of adjectives. His account is punctuated with words such as 'dreadful' (top of the list), followed by 'frightful', 'appalling', 'disgusting', 'hideous', then 'unspeakably', 'horribly', 'obscenely'.[59]

Nor had Orwell drawn a very flattering picture of England the year before when he was present at the funeral of George V. What had struck him most was the "physical degeneracy of modern England". The English had become a people of puny limbs and sickly faces. As the coffin passed by, men took off their hats and "a friend who was with me in the crowd . . . said to me afterwards, 'The only touch of colour anywhere was the bald heads'". Even the guardsmen marching beside the coffin seemed inferior to the soldiers he remembered before the war. But then, he concluded, the Great War had selected the best men, nearly a million of them.[60]

The England that the researchers of Mass Observation recorded before the war also differed significantly from that observed by others in 1940. Tom Harrison, who was the father of Mass Observation, was an old Harrovian, a Cambridge dropout, a self-taught anthropologist, the eventual curator of the Sarawak Museum in Kuching. He 'went native' in Bolton and began to study the Lancastrian way of life. Victor Gollancz, who had commissioned Orwell's *Road to Wigan Pier,* also provided financial support for Harrison's studies and published his findings. In a sense, he helped to anthropologise the British people.

The English did not have to travel to Spain to find a different world. Between the wars, noted Frances Donaldson, the upper and middle classes regarded the working class as quasi-foreign. When they moved among them they did so with a view to improving their lot "as anthropologists . . . or missionaries visiting a tribe more primitive than themselves".[61]

In short, the England for which the English people fought was not bounded by the reality they had experienced during the Great Depression. Briefly in 1940 it was defined by a myth, a powerful one, of course, which helped to sustain a people fighting for its life. But it was not one that could be sustained for long. The pastoral picture painted in such vivid colours by Orwell may still obtain in the imagination, but as a political force it soon lost its hold over the English people. It really did disappear with the welfare state proprieties of the 1940s and the decline of the country as a political power.

That this might be problematic for the liberal world—that it might herald a postmodern age—began to become clear in the postwar years. Writing in 1964 Rebecca West broke off her story of the three traitors, Burgess, Philby and MacLean, who had shocked their countrymen's faith in the future by defecting to Russia, to relate another story, that of a young British hero of the Korean War, a Lt. Walters, who had died for his country. Dying for one's country, West noted, had become almost embarrassing—dying for a country that was no longer 'great', whose people had begun to find patriotism itself rather ridiculous:

> For the comprehension of our age and the part treason had played in it, it is necessary to realise that there are many English people who would have felt acutely embarrassed if they had to read aloud the story of this young man's death. . . . They would have felt more at ease with many of the traitors in this book. . . . They would also have felt that Walters' heroism had something dowdy about it, while treason has a certain style, a sort of elegance . . . or sophistication.[62]

West expressed a view that was shared by a good many of her compatriots. It was echoed by the two most widely read novelists of the time, Graham Greene and Evelyn Waugh. Greene, who served under Philby during the war, wrote an introduction to Philby's autobiography, *My Silent War*, which was published in Moscow in 1968. "Who has not committed treason", he asked, "to something or someone more important than a country"?[63] Waugh's greatest achievement, his war trilogy, which was completed two years earlier, has as its hero the naive if admirable Guy Crouchback, a man who concludes the war knowing that the patriots have had their day, that the modern age ("the real enemy", he calls it) has no time for patriotism and very little interest in war.

"Never forget", the Greek poet Constantine Cavafy wrote to E. M. Forster, "that we are bankrupt. Pray that you—you English with your capacity for adventure—never lose your capital, otherwise you will resemble us restless, shiftless liars".[64] In concluding this chapter I have quoted Cavafy for two reasons. The first is that by then patriotism had lost much of its appeal. It was Forster himself who famously proclaimed after Philby's defection that he hoped that he would have the courage to betray his country, not his friends.

Secondly, in the early 1960s the fate of the Greeks looked likely to be the English fate as well. During a trip to the National Portrait Gallery in London Cioran was shocked by the contrast between the virile faces of earlier generations and the bland and unheroic features to be found in contemporary life. The English of the 1950s, he wrote, were as remote from their forebears as the Greeks of the Roman Empire must have been from those of Aeschylus. Gone was the arrogance and passion in the eyes of Elizabethan statesmen or Victorian men of commerce. Britain's empire had been built by adventurers. It had been lost by a new generation of Englishmen who were less interested in power than they were in correct behaviour, "an idea they had come dangerously close to realising".

The contemporary Englishman was determined to be happy. His happiness exempt from risk had become "an enveloping mediocrity". The English were no longer a nightmare for anyone. They had been domesticated. They had become a *'postmodern'* people. Struck by the change, Cioran concluded his account by formulating a new principle of history: "Only at the price of great abdications does a nation become normal".[65]

Chapter Five

The Will to Power

The glory of the great—of what account is genius if it does not communicate to him who contemplates and reveres it such freedom and elevation of feeling that he no longer has need of genius. Rendering themselves superfluous—that is the glory of all great men.
—Nietzsche, *Human, All Too Human* (1878)

The Napoleonic Wars made clear to everyone that the world was now subject to rapid change and that war was the chief instrument not only of the revolution (at home as well as abroad) but also of self-determining humanity. If we consult an early eighteenth-century work by the Enlightenment philosopher Diderot we may better appreciate the significance of the change. The hero of the tale, Jacques the fatalist, joins a regiment and is seriously wounded in battle. Marked for life, he will limp for the rest of his days. But what war has he fought in and what battle ? Diderot does not tell us. War was not that important, and one war was very much like another.

It was only really from the start of the Napoleonic Wars that novelists like Balzac and Scott began to make clear which wars they are describing in their fiction. Characters like Stendhal's Fabricio, who fights at Waterloo, live in precisely dated times. Most of them are also acutely aware of the significance of the age in which they live. Even when they are unsure of their own historical importance, or of what later generations might find worthy of note in their lives, they are conscious of being agents of history.

Long before Nietzsche pronounced God dead divine law had given way to history. Although God had remained at the centre of Western consciousness until the Enlightenment, it is notable that he had ceased to speak to man for some time. If we believe the Bible, Job was the last prophet with whom he conversed directly. His silence thereafter was one of the significant factors of the Judeo-Christian experience. He no longer took a direct part in human affairs.

The upshot was that by the mid–nineteenth century man was more conversant with history than he was with the scriptures. History had replaced divine sanction. Those in tune with it, the great men of the age, were, in de Maistre's celebrated quip, merely "functionaries of the Absolute". Hegel set the trend in arguing that in any given historical period all individual human beings were merely moments of the Spirit. Even those who were unconscious agents of History carried out its most important tasks.

No one was more conscious of that responsibility than Napoleon. From the first he spoke in terms of history as personal destiny. As Spengler wrote almost a century later in *The Decline of the West*, Napoleon had a strong feeling for the deep logic of 'world-becoming' and in such moments could divine the extent to which he *was* and to what extent he had a destiny. At the beginning of the Russian campaign in 1812 he noted: "I feel myself driven towards an end that I do not know. As soon as I shall have reached it, as soon as I shall become unnecessary an atom will suffice to shatter me. Till then not all the forces of mankind can do anything against me".[1]

The problem, of course, was that as a force of history he could never stop. He had to permanently test the limits of his own destiny. As William Hazlitt noted in his life of the Emperor, for Napoleon "there could be no line of retreat", for history can never be put into reverse.[2]

The modern age demanded its heroes, whether or not they were in fact functionaries of the Absolute. Napoleon set the trend. Long after his death the Napoleonic myth continued to live on in the Western imagination. As early as the spring of 1814, René de Chateaubriand predicted that a long time would elapse before posterity would be "disinterested" enough to sit in judgement on him as a person. "When will the time come when Europe will have put off mourning his crimes?"[3]

1. In the first section of this chapter I will look at the great man theory of history that Napoleon made popular for a time. For Julien Sorel in Stendhal's *The Red and the Black,* Napoleon represented colour, action and nobility. For Balzac the universe was full of Napoleonic models. Vautrin was the Napoleon of crime, Nucingen the Napoleon of finance, and the novelist himself, in the scope of his creative energy, resembled a Napoleon of the pen.

Even after the defeat of Hitler—a man who like Napoleon believed in his own indomitable will—the Dutch historian Pieter Geyl was surprised to find that Napoleon still cast a spell. He was particularly struck by a translation of General Bertrand's memoirs. Bertrand was with the emperor when he died on St. Helena in 1821, a prisoner who like Prometheus had been bound to a rock, not in the Caucasus but the south Atlantic. Geyl confessed that he had been taken aback by the unashamed hero worship he found in the editor's introduction, the florid pages of purple prose that evoked the greatness of a man who had brought his country to the verge of ruin. "How startling to find that [Napoleon worship] has survived not only the horrors the First World War but also the catastrophe the Second World War brought to France". Geyl was surprised that even in a Europe that had suffered the humiliation of being divided between two non-European powers, hero worship was still not "extinct".[4]

2. When the modern age was not disputing the role of its military heroes, it worshipped at the shrine of its national heroes, personifying the nation in arms as a heroic type. There was nothing very heroic, of course, in the industrialised slaughter that war had gradually become. But there was something heroic in the national will to continue fighting, particularly in the willingness of soldiers to fight against the technology that threatened to overwhelm them.

War became in the eyes of many writers the supreme test of the nation's will to win. In the face of modern technology, even the generals were able to find a spurious consolation in the power of the will, or what Henri Bergson, the most influential French philosopher of the twentieth century, termed a nation's *élan vital*. What was this response to the logic of modern war but a vain attempt to maximise human agency, to insist that countries could will victory whatever the odds against them. Hitler never doubted that his own willpower would see the war through to a successful conclusion. So did the Japanese leadership in 1941, who foolishly contrasted their own will to win with the material soullessness of America's reliance on industrial production.

For the French, the upshot of this thinking was realised on the killing ground of the western front. It was a conflict that was so massive in scale that it was later held responsible for having drained away their own vitality as a nation. The bloodletting at Verdun was thought to have claimed the best blood. In a sense they never really recovered. Defeatism was implanted long before the events of 1940. France's eventual defeat had been anticipated long before it happened. As Heidegger put it with his usual sententiousness, what it lacked as a nation was the will to exist, or "the metaphysics equal to its own being".

3. In the philosopher Ludwig Wittgenstein I shall be looking at another strategy for coping with the alienation of modernity: an attempt by man to master himself. In his highly personal response to the First World War, Wittgenstein tried to discover the heroic in himself, in a conscious attempt to become "a better man".

The problem with this strategy of survival was that it devalued politics and political action. It was largely solipsistic. The hero was engaged not in making history or advancing a cause but in an existential experiment, the sole end of which was intensely self-regarding—to experience himself. What makes Wittgenstein's own response so interesting is that he placed himself outside history at the very time that many societies were trying to turn their citizens into a historically responsive people.

4. I shall conclude the discussion with reference to a very modern manifestation of the will to power: the general will, and the willingness of those

who invoked it to commit evil in the name of a greater good. "The great epochs of our life", Nietzsche wrote in his most compelling work, *Beyond Good and Evil*, "come when we gain the courage to rechristen our evil as what is best in it". Like many of Nietzsche's titles it is brilliant, unforgettable and usually misunderstood. It was especially misunderstood by Max Horkheimer and Theodor Adorno, who presented Nietzsche and Kant as the producers of a negative dialectic of the Enlightenment.[5] The idea of the hero as criminal, however, is to be found in its most characteristic form not in the work of either philosopher but in the fevered imagination of the Marquis de Sade.

It was Sade who took issue with the Enlightenment's conception of freedom. For all their devotion to liberty the *philosophes* had still insisted on the people's need to be constrained. Voltaire, though himself an atheist, believed in the power of belief in damnation to keep man in check. Diderot thought that although the wise man does not need laws to make him behave well, most men, who are not wise, do. Even Rousseau, who believed in the perfectibility of human nature, was insistent that men enter into a binding social contract that exchanged natural license for socially approved freedoms.

Like all the authors of liberation ideologies the *philosophes* merely set out to replace one set of rules by another. It was Sade's unique contribution to argue that there should be no rules constraining the human will. In his cosmology natural forces make God redundant; physics replaces Providence; nature's iron law replaces divine love. It was Sade who put d'Alembert's "experimental physics of the soul" into practice in the darkest corners of cruelty. It was Sade who insisted that, like nature, consuming, destroying and creating, man is pure egoism. In such a vision of the world, in which evil becomes a virtue, only the criminal is a true hero.

On Napoleon and Napoleonism

Napoleon has taught our children to play the game of hocus-pocus with popes, priests, kings and other straw stuffed scarecrows. They (for we, their fathers, still cling to the rocking horse and the rattle), despising the toys of our own times, will cast them aside and play a manlier game.

—De Ruyter, circa 1811, in
Edward J. Trelawny's *Adventures of a Younger Son* (1831)

Napoleon dominated the imagination of the nineteenth century long after his death. He dominated it, of course, even more during his lifetime. The German poet Heinrich Heine saw him once riding into Düsseldorf. In later life he saw the Emperor as a titan who had used his intellect to make history. Small wonder then that he went on to compare Philippe Paul Ségur's *Histoire de Napoléon et de la guerre armée pendant 1812* with the other great epics of world literature like the Edda, Nieblunglied and Mahabharata.[6] What they all had in common is that they celebrated the decline and fall of a heroic epoch.

If Napoleon was dead by 1821 and the heroic era had come to a tragic close, Heine still believed that history was capable of moving on. From his reading of Hegel he was acquainted with the idea that the purpose of man was revealed in history. When he wrote of Napoleon as a *noumenal* historical figure and a prototype of human spiritual achievement, he was steeped in Hegelian thought. He died believing that the Emperor's *example* (rather than his deeds) could charge men with the enthusiasm to pursue their own revolutionary aims and themselves make history as he had done. The age, at least, had still been given great tasks to undertake, if it had the will to realise them.[7]

Described so memorably by the great men of his own day such as Goethe and Hegel, it is not really surprising that Napoleon should have continued to cast a shadow well into the nineteenth century. It would have been more surprising if he had not. Even towards the end of the century Charles Fourier was accused of a "Napoleonic style" when formulating his utopian system of government. When not applying the Napoleonic mobilisation of the nation to the arts of war, he applied it to those of peace. Sorel later accused both Fourier and Saint Simon of "a Napoleonic disposition", but in his own *Reflections on Violence* Sorel was guilty of Napoleonism as well. What had he done, after all, asked Wyndham Lewis, but to encourage the workers to conceive of their class struggle epically, requiring them to become perfect heroes who could be led into battle even in a futile cause"?[8]

The Napoleonic principle became part of the fabric of modern life even in spheres other than politics, particularly music. A character in one of Wagner's early Parisian short stories discourages his friend from hearing Beethoven's *Eroica Symphony* as a musical portrait of the emperor, despite its original dedication to him. Instead he urges him to recognise it as an act of heroism in itself, an emulation of Napoleon's deeds. Beethoven too "must have felt his powers aroused to an extraordinary pitch, his valiant courage spurred on to a grand and unheard of deed". Ten years later two of the foremost musicologists of the age interpreted the first forty-five bars of the symphony as the representation of a "singularly obsessed hero fighting against a recalcitrant external world".[9]

Arguably, Beethoven himself impressed his heroic principle of music making on the Western canon. For the past 200 years composers have developed their own recognisable style, one so strong that it no longer acts as an overt part of our musical consciousness. In his *Life of Beethoven*, Romain Rolland wrote that Europe was urgently in need of the heroic principle in life. "Open the windows again. Let in the fresh air. Let us breathe the breath of heroes".[10]

In the remainder of this section I will discuss three very different interpretations of Napoleon's career by three quintessentially illiberal writers: Carlyle, Nietzsche and Franz Grillparzer, an Austrian playwright little known in the English-speaking world. Although their interpretations of the Napoleonic myth differed significantly, each offered a unique insight into different aspects of the illiberal imagination.

Carlyle and Napoleon as the Hero Who Turned Inside Out

It is not all that surprising that Napoleon should have made an impression even on his most implacable enemies, the British, or that he should have captivated the young Carlyle. Napoleon was for him the model of the great man. He had broken into pieces the hollow certainties of eighteenth-century Europe. He had been the modern world's window on history. He had been the first man to believe in the power of the will. It was Carlyle's particular distinction to have turned an affection for Napoleon into a system, a belief in the heroic principle of history.

On History, Hero Worship and the Heroic in History—such is the full title of the lectures Carlyle wrote in 1840. They state a number of propositions. The world could not be understood by the old philosophies, but rather by history and intuition. History was evolutionary or organic. Organisms occasionally fail. Periodically they are visited by catastrophes and have to be reborn. "There is nothing else but revolution or mutation", we learn in his *History of the French Revolution*. In this cruel process courage was more valuable than compassion. The hero or man of courage was the only hope of the hour. He was a man who acted intuitively without constraint of philosophy or morality. He was in tune with history's march and was himself an instrument of history. Through him history moved forwards, not backwards. It followed that history was the biography of great men.

Carlyle had no doubt that Napoleon was the most heroic figure of all. He was deemed to embody in his own person something that was definingly modern about the modern age—the constant need for conflict in life. "Man is created to fight; he is perhaps best definable of all as a born soldier; his life a battle and a march under the right general". In an earlier work, he had written of Napoleon: "He himself . . . was among the completest, ideologists at least, ideopraxis: in the Idea *(in der Idee)*, he lived, moved and fought. The man was a Divine Missionary though unconscious of it; and preached through the cannon's throat."[11] What Carlyle ultimately found most redeeming about Napoleon, while recognising his "outer manoeuvrings and quackeries", was his faith in the spirit of the age. In the early years of his career he had set out to tame the French Revolution, the better to contain its anarchical spirit and thus fully realise its political potential. Only when he had departed from this agenda, when he had set out to crown himself Emperor of the French and to construct an empire rather

than a new order, had history deserted him. Once he parted company with
the spirit of the age he was lost. History had chosen to invest no longer in
him but in a national spirit that took the form of the wars of liberation in
Spain and Germany, to which Carlyle attributed his eventual eclipse.[12]

After it, however, the world had turned inside out. The heroic principle
of history had given way to the unheroic role of the market. The spirit of
the age had changed for the worse. What had followed his defeat was a
great ennui, those fifty years of peace in which Europe seemed to offer
nothing but the same sterility of ideas and actions. What Carlyle most disliked about the period in which he lived was that it made a nonsense of
Napoleon's very existence.

A reflection of this mood can be found in Alfred de Musset's *Confessions
of a Child of the Age* (1836), a book that caught the mood of a generation
obsessed with memories of events in which they had taken no personal
part. Another is the complaint of Ernest Renan that those born at the end
of 1830 between Waterloo and the uprising against Charles X were subject
to an optical illusion. "We have seen great things so we refer back to the
revolution for everything. . . . That is our horizon, the hero of our childhood, our end of the world".[13]

What resulted was a profound sense of alienation. This became one of
the principal themes of nineteenth-century literature, whose authors regretted the fact that progress had been taken out of human hands and invested
instead in the industrial process. History was now forged in the money
markets, or on the assembly line, by the bankers or the new industrial
workforce penned up in the tenements of the cities. Not for nothing were
the martial names of the mid–nineteenth century evoked in economic
terms—the 'captains of industry', or the 'Napoleons of finance'.[14]

The bourgeois world accomplished much in this period, but it found a
discontent within itself that was bound sooner or later to bring it up
against modernity's limits. What remained heroic had grown dull. What
ideas were expressed had their roots in hard, ungiving ground. It seemed as
though Europe was condemned to live off its intellectual annuities, including the memory of the Napoleonic epic.

One of the main reasons why men looked back, of course, was that they
were unsure of where history was heading. Even the dogmatic Carlyle
wrote in 1830, "The whole frame of sincerity is rotten and must go for fuel
wood—and where is the new frame to come from? I know not and no man
knows".[15] Of course, the eighteenth century had known; although Carlyle
called it the "age of doubt", the Enlightenment had a faith in humanity that
the nineteenth century lost.

Carlyle himself, after all, was a disillusioned Scottish radical who had
imbibed radicalism along with Presbyterianism from his parents and lost
faith in both. Brought up as a Calvinist he naturally believed that the world

was not a beautiful place but one of struggle and suffering, "not a May game . . . but a battle and a march, a warfare with principalities and powers". Words could never alter anything. Deeds could. The problem was that he lived in an age without heroes.

One of the other reasons that Carlyle's work proved so popular even in liberal England was that it was at one with a new mood abroad, the revolt against materialism. Matthew Arnold's preface to his 1853 collection of poems is a plea for modern poetry in the grand style. Ruskin gave "the sight and history of noble persons" a central place in education so that nineteenth-century man could develop the faculty of hope. He was perhaps not the best placed to provide it, but he professed to being both "a violent illiberal" and "a communist of the red school—reddest also of the red". Even Mill, good liberal though he was, deplored the fact that individuals were "lost in a crowd".[16]

Hero worship, in other words, was to be expected of an age in which social life was becoming notably marked by bourgeois values. Bourgeois self-hatred was an important element of the illiberal conscience. 'Bourgeoisphobia'—the word is Flaubert's—inspired a wealth of complaints, more or less rational or irrational as the mood took its authors. By the end of the century, attacks on the bourgeoisie had become so commonplace that a disgusted Jules Renard adjudged the phenomenon to be 'bourgeois' itself.[17] The important point about it was that it was not delimited by class. Being bourgeois was a question of attitudes and beliefs rather than social position.

By the time the heroic principle of history was reaffirmed, the Napoleonic myth had begun to tarnish. The hero worshippers had begun to look elsewhere. Marx and Engels were the first writers, in fact, to portray political life as a play of class interests, a petty game of petty politics. Whatever their own misconceptions of history, and they were many, they appreciated at least that Carlyle's hero had become an anachronism. Writing about the events of 1848–1852, Engels observed: "It really seems as though old Hegel, in the guise of the World Spirit, were directing history from the grave and, with the greatest conscientiousness, causing everything to be re-enacted twice over; once as grand tragedy, the second time as rotten farce, Caussidière for Danton, Louis Blanc for Robespierre." That was the point about heroes. There were only so many roles they could play, and most had been played before. The problem was that they had to reenact history when circumstances had changed. Marx developed this point at greater length. History never repeats itself completely; it proceeds by analogies:

> Hegel says somewhere that upon the stage of universal history all great events and personalities reappear in one fashion or another. He forgot to add that on the first occasion they appear as tragedy, on the second as farce. Caussidière replaces Danton; Louis Blanc, Robespierre . . . the nephew Louis Bonaparte re-

places his uncle. . . . Men make their own history but not of their own free will; not under circumstances they themselves have chosen. . . . The tradition of the dead generations weighs like a nightmare on the minds of the living. And just when they appear to be engaged in the revolutionary transformation of themselves . . . in the creation of something which does not yet exist, precisely in such epochs of revolutionary crisis they timidly conjure up the spirits of the past to help them; they borrow their names, slogans and costumes so as to stage the new world-historical scene in this venerable disguise. [18]

What had happened to the Napoleonic myth? Eight years after Marx penned the passage above the much despised and dismissed young man, Louis Napoleon, made himself President of the Second Republic and then Emperor of France. His reign was not without its highlights, but it was inglorious and decidedly unheroic. Even when it ended in military defeat, as Tocqueville predicted it would, Sedan was not Waterloo. His exile in the bourgeois comfort of Chislehurst was also a far cry from his uncle's lonely sojourn on St. Helena.

The real heroes of the second Napoleonic epic were the Communards, the radical working men who seized the government of Paris after the city had been besieged by the Prussian army in the last phase of the Franco-Prussian war. They held out for seventy-two days before being crushed by forces loyal to the new Third Republic. Marx himself had little time for the Commune, but he recognised it as the forerunner of a new period in history: that of the working man.

The idea of the working man as hero had been affirmed twenty-five years earlier in *The German Ideology* (1845–1846), the first recognisable 'Marxist' work. In direct contrast to German philosophy, which descended from heaven to earth, the authors of *The German Ideology* affirmed that their own ascended from earth to heaven. "We set out from real active men".[19] In their belief that real men not abstractions made history, Marx and Engels had as little time for the liberal idea of the social contract as they had for Carlyle's worship of great men.

They had a point. In the modern age political discourse was principally focused on the task of making man the agent of his fate. It presupposed that man had the capacity to evaluate the world and his own place in it, and in accordance with that knowledge to act upon it, to forge his own future for the first time. The problem with liberal political thought was that it often seemed to be lacking in compassion for its citizens in leaving them at the play of market forces or in marrying agency to such metaphysical assumptions as the existence of natural destinies (Locke, Bentham), or natural rights (Locke), or social contracts that were based on myth rather than a strict reading of history. In the liberal world the agent was often an abstraction divorced from the social and cultural milieu that, we are told, makes agents what they are.

In Marx's reading of history the narrative ordering was reversed. The hero was now the slave, not the master. A new set of events claimed the reader's attention. The relations between labour and production took precedence over relations between kings and people. Unfortunately, just as the king and emperor as heroes gave way to the working man, the working man in turn rapidly became an abstraction: History. The proletariat became the object, not the subject, of its own story. History was deemed to unfold of its own accord, independently of the creative powers of its supposed subject—Man. The proletariat ceased to be a living human community and became instead an abstract concept in a new system of scientific determinism.

Perhaps the best way to appreciate the change that Heine witnessed from the era of the great man to that of humanity in general, at the level of symbolic truth, is to look at the fate of Napoleon himself. His extraordinary career gave rise to one of the most unusual books ever written, an attempt to find out the true significance of his place in history by invoking the methods of Jewish mysticism in general and the Kabbalah in particular. In 1912 the French writer Léon Bloy wrote a spirited book called *The Soul of Napoleon* in which he set out to decipher the symbol 'Napoleon', considered as the precursor of another hero, another man and a symbol hidden in the future.[20] On the purely symbolic level, however, he had no need to look to the future: The past told a very different story, that of a hero who had become a victim of history, a man who had turned inside out.

In his later years this was precisely Napoleon's fate. The Emperor steadily grew fatter to the point of obesity. He also suffered increasingly from attacks of somnolence. He even lost his legendary decisiveness on the battlefield. The man who appeared at Waterloo was a shadow of his former self. Some historians attribute his illness to a neuroendocrinological syndrome. Others suggest that he suffered from Zollinger-Ellison syndrome, in which multiple small tumours in the pancreas secrete the hormone gastrin, which in turn gives rise to malignant tumours in the pituitary glands. It may also result in secondary kidney disorder, reducing the thyroid function and producing obesity, fatigue, whiteness of skin and the loss of skin hair, all of which Napoleon suffered in the last years of his life.

Of his fifty-two-year career Napoleon probably spent a good half attempting to overcome his multiple afflictions, over which even his willpower could not prevail. His political retreat was, by a tragic irony of fate, in step with the disintegration of his personality. Long before his death the Emperor had lost himself. When he was finally anatomised he was found to have developed beautiful white skin and breasts, and his genitals had atrophied almost completely.[21]

A kabbalist like Bloy should have found the change profoundly important as a symbol. There was also another, pregnant with significance for the future. On Napoleon's death he was still wearing his old dark-green coat. He had by then long outgrown it. But since green cloth was not available on St. Helena his old uniform had to be unpicked at the seams, underlaid and turned inside out. Was that not also the fate, asks Miroslav Holub, of one of the most powerful men in history, the archetype of the modern hero? Was that not also what eventually happened: the great man as hero turned into the leader or voice of the nation, into the representative of great *men?*

Grillparzer and the End of the Napoléonade

> *Just when the difficulties of the winter campaign in the East had reached their height some imbecile pointed out that Napoleon like ourselves had started his Russian campaign on 22 June. Thank God I was able to counter that drivel with the authoritative statement of historians of repute that Napoleon's campaign did not, in fact, begin until 23 June.*
> —*Hitler's Table Talk* (19 July 1942)

Of the three writers I have chosen to discuss Franz Grillparzer is the only one who actually saw Napoleon: when he entered Vienna in 1809 after defeating the Austrian army at Wagram, one of his last significant victories. Grillparzer is little known in the English-speaking world. J. B. Priestley, in his book *Literature and Western Man,* devotes only five lines to him, and even then only as a point of comparison with Goethe. As a playwright, however, he was much respected in the German-speaking world and was avidly read by many earlier twentieth-century authors, including Kafka. What makes his general body of work interesting is that he detected in himself a kinship with Schopenhauer and his theory of the will long before the latter's influence on men of letters became clearly discernible.

His most famous play, *King Ottokar's Rise and Fall,* was inspired by Napoleon's death a few years earlier. Ottokar's last speech, the longest in the play, expresses the guilt of the would-be 'hero', a man with an indomitable will to win, in sacrificing men by the thousands for his own aggrandisement. In Grillparzer's view Napoleon was just such a man, an egomaniac obsessed with assertion for its own sake. In pursuit of his own personal ambition he had brought the curtain down on eighteenth-century rationalism and ensured that romantic nationalism would take its place. Even at the time Grillparzer was writing, the seething tide of nationalism was threatening to break over the old European order. In his eyes Napoleon represented "the fever of a sick era", one that could only be cured by catharsis, or in this case perhaps nemesis—his own destruction. In Napoleon he saw a man whose humanity was only in evidence in defeat, whose greatness was to be found only in the humiliation of exile.[22]

It was a version of history that was far from the truth, of course. Napoleon was perhaps even more vain in defeat than in victory. On St. Helena he set out to remake the image of himself as a man of peace who had been forced to spend his life on the battlefield by the British, his most implacable foe, a people who had succeeded in chaining him like Prometheus to a rock in the south Atlantic.

Grillparzer was correct, nonetheless, to see that the seeds of the emperor's destruction lay in his impatience to get to the end. In what Nietzsche called "the Napoleonic tempo" or demonic drive, the emperor ignored everything that was secondary or ephemeral in pursuit of a single goal: his own aggrandisement. Every citizen became expendable. So too did every state. Even France was almost lost to his personal ambition. In short, Napoleon was the most dangerous man of the nineteenth century. It is precisely this feature of Napoleon's character, of course, that attracted his later admirers, as so nicely illustrated in Dostoyevsky's character Raskolnikov in *Crime and Punishment,* a man who identifies specifically with Napoleon's criminality. He was "a real *ruler of men,* a man to whom everything is permitted", Raskolnikov proclaims applaudingly. He "takes Toulon by storm, carries out a massacre in Paris, *forgets* an army in Egypt, *wastes* half a million men in his Moscow campaign". "Such men," he adds approvingly, "are not made of flesh and blood, but of bronze".[23]

Raskolnikov captures one of the key ideas behind the "will to power", namely that mankind is divided by nature into two categories: an inferior one whose only purpose is to reproduce its own kind, and a superior one that possesses the gift to make history anew. "The great mass of people—the masses—exists merely for the sake of bringing into the world by some supreme effort, by some mysterious process we know nothing about . . . one man out of a thousand." Such a man is "absolutely entitled, in accordance with the dictates of his conscience, to permit himself to wade through blood, all depending of course on the nature and scale of his idea."[24] The greater the idea, the greater the sacrifice.

Grillparzer was among the first contemporary observers to identify the central dilemma of Napoleon's career. He had been interested only in the political, or what he called the *Hauptsache,* the main point. Everything else was peripheral. In pursuit of this aim he was prepared to turn everything into the political: the private into the public, life into war, the individual into the collective will. He was even prepared to 'requisition' the nation for the duration, to militarise it, to turn it into a supremely effective instrument of war.[25]

Grillparzer grasped what his contemporary, the Prussian general Clausewitz, also recognised, that there was a unique dialectic at work in modern life: not so much the transformation of the private into the public as the political into the military. One of the reasons that Clausewitz is still read is that

he perceived the tendency of limited war to become absolute. In his own lifetime Napoleon never grasped this fact. All his wars tended to escalate out of
control until they finally engulfed him. In a twenty-five-year career he won
campaign after campaign, only to find that final victory eluded him. Ultimately he failed in his attempt to transform the political into the military—to
turn Europe into an armed camp. Clausewitz recognised that a successful
general was one who never allowed himself to lose sight of political goals,
who grasped the principle that war was a continuation of politics by other
means, not politics a continuation of war. He held to this position all his life
because of the unideological nature of his thinking. By nature Clausewitz was
a dialectical thinker, but he was not a Hegelian. Like most early-nineteenth-
century writers he engaged in dialectical thinking, observing the traditional
distinction between subject and object, theory and reality, war and politics,
attack and defence, intent and execution. It is precisely these dualities that
Hegel tried to transcend, as did Marx, in the hope of finding a synthesis of
the two. To do that they both needed to adopt a philosophy of history, one
that Clausewitz could not or would not provide. Although his work shows
an affinity with Hegel in his vigorous use of dialectical tools, it shows little
affinity with Hegel's metaphysics, idealism or conception of history.[26]

In recognising that in war the unpredictable is always to be expected,
that the best-conceived plans are always frustrated by chance, that all wars
are uncertain in their outcome, Clausewitz insisted that politics must never
be lost sight of. A nation that was on a permanent war footing would not
survive for long.

At no point in Napoleon's career was this element clearer than in the
tragic and futile 'hundred days' that marked the last phase of his career.
Within three months of his return from Elba hostility to Napoleon had in-
creased so dramatically that the cities in the south and the west had to be
put under martial law. When he went on campaign he had to leave behind
thousands of troops to control, combat or crush them. The only way for
him to survive politically was, as usual, to go to war, even if it meant fighting all the major powers of Europe. War had once again become a condition of peace at home, a theme I have discussed at greater length in a previous chapter.

Grillparzer himself, of course, was a conservative, a traditionalist, a sup-
porter of the Hapsburg monarchy, which was bested by Napoleon time and
again in the course of the Napoleonic Wars. It triumphed in the end and
survived long after Napoleon's fall. In Grillparzer's work the Hapsburg dy-
nasty stands for life, the contingent and transient, life in the minor key, the
life that is worth living. Napoleon's career, by contrast, he saw in terms of
death, the eternal, the transcendent, life in the major key—a life worth sacrificing. The latter was melodramatic, the former truly heroic, for life is to
be lived, not sacrificed in the name of a higher being, however heroic.

Nietzsche and Napoleon as Zarathustra

*I no longer have the slightest idea which of my views do good, which
harm . . . this is the torment of every great teacher of mankind: he
knows that he has as much chance of becoming its curse as its blessing.*
—**Nietzsche, letter (April 1884)**

While teaching at Harvard in 1942, Crane Brinton wrote that without
Nietzsche's most notorious book, *Zarathustra,* the First World War would
never have broken out or the Second followed so closely upon it.[27] Even in
the early months of 1914, one of the few English magazines to defend
Nietzsche's reputation reported a disturbing incident in a bookshop in the
Charing Cross Road when two soldiers asked to see a copy of *Zarathustra,*
only to return it to the bookseller, baffled to find no mention of the Kaiser
in its index.[28]

Nietzsche was the first to recognise that he would be misunderstood, that
his ideas would be used unscrupulously by people who had never read him
or who would read him without understanding his work. He was particularly concerned about the "plundering soldiers" who would take his philosophy apart bit by bit and use and preserve whatever pieces they found useful for their own purposes.

It must be conceded, of course, that he did not help his own cause. As he
grew older his rhetoric became more violent as he attempted in vain to
shock his readers into action. He was nothing if not candid, but his readers
were carried away by his candour as candour, not by its content. They
tended to accentuate the nihilistic and destructive side of his teaching until,
in the end, the destructive side took precedence over the creative in the general understanding of his work.

What his readers still misunderstand most is his concept of the will to
power. What they still misconstrue is his interpretation of the man of destiny, the hero who heroises history. For Nietzsche, as for Carlyle, there was
no greater example of the phenomenon than Napoleon himself. "The history of Napoleon's reception", he wrote in *Beyond Good and Evil,* was almost the history of "the higher happiness attained in the century in its most
valuable human beings".

His own age, by comparison, was a wretched time in which to live. Europe in his own day appeared to be at the mercy of little minds and petty
politics. He railed against the "moral hypocrisy" of those who commanded. Governments protected themselves against their own "bad conscience" by posing as executors of higher commands, such as God or the
law, or more ancient authorities such as constitutions. Politicians had
tamed the public by appealing to them to do nothing for themselves, in the
name of the public spirit, moderation or modesty. What Nietzsche deplored

most was not only the fact that the citizens had ceased to be soldiers; the rulers had even ceased to be commanders. All parliamentary constitutions, he claimed, had their origin in this unwillingness to fight for one's future.[29] Nietzsche's dislike of both constitutionalism and parliamentary democracy is a persistent feature of his work. As Zarathustra declares, "war accomplishes greater things than love of a neighbour".[30] Nietzsche's argument was that war makes one intellectually stronger—as long as it does not destroy intellect itself, of course. His statement in *Twilight of the Idols* that "war educates for freedom" is consistent with this reasoning.[31] True freedom must include the freedom to commit oneself to goals and to hold oneself accountable for the consequences of one's own actions. This was the true expression of the will to power, as well as the only reality of true freedom. It provided the experience of being an effective agent in the world, one who is able to transform what 'is' into what 'will be'.

"The nations which were worth something, which became worth something, never became so under liberal institutions; it was great danger that made of the nations deserving reverence; [it is] danger which firsts teaches us to know our resources, our virtues, our weapons for war, our spirit which forces us to be strong".[32] What Nietzsche is asserting here should not be misconstrued. All that he was saying was that power alone sustains the values that liberals extol such as rationality, moral responsibility, autonomy and freedom. Human agency in history is concrete, real and contingent and constantly must be fought for.

He believed that rights, particularly those so beloved by liberal philosophers, could only be secure when they had been won, not when they had been conferred by the state. The 'will to power' was grounded in human action. Nietzsche knew nothing of rights grounded in legal maxims or claims to natural justice. If societies wanted rights they would need to defend them. His was the aristocratic Athenian view of self-esteem in which the self-reflective individual values himself so much that he is prepared to respect his own laws. "Is the social state unimaginable in which the wrongdoer will bring a denunciation upon himself and publicly dictate his own punishment in the proud feeling that he is thus honouring the law he has made himself and that in punishing himself he is exercising power over himself"?[33]

Governments that obey their own laws do so not because they are powerless but because they respect the laws they have passed. In other words, they respect their fellow citizens. That is why, for Nietzsche, Periclean Athens was one of the few examples of a noble state in history. The crucial point was not that in Athens equal rights were sustained by law, but that the Athenians were the first people in history to respect each other. This was the historic and cultural condition in which equality was born. In turn, it was the basis of the definition of power in Greek society. And this, in turn, presupposed an equal ability to will.

Now, we should be very clear on what conclusions Nietzsche drew from this argument. He was fully aware that the Greek city-state model (the noble model of politics) could not obtain in the modern age. But he was also profoundly distressed by the absence of spirit in the 'slave' societies of modern Europe, the industrialised, democratic liberal democracies that he so despised for their mediocrity. In his most profound moments of gloom he doubted whether his age could produce heroes. Even when its composers, such as Wagner, wrote music about larger-than-life figures—the Brunnhildes, Siegfrieds and Wotans of the *Ring* cycle—he came to believe that there was something counterfeit about them. They failed to ring true. He never gave up hope, however. Even if he despised his own age for always counting the cost of its heroes and the price of following them, he believed it could throw up another Napoleonic figure. When that man appeared, Nietzsche believed, he would remake Europe and thus redeem it from the soullessness that he foresaw could prove nihilistic, that could breed the two poisons he feared most, anarchism and anti-Semitism.

It is also important if we wish to do Nietzsche justice to recognise that unlike Carlyle he had no illusions about the criminality of history's heroes. He was not oblivious to the price societies paid for reading history too often, or for failing to read between the lines. He once described Napoleon as having the "innocent conscience of a beast of prey". He called him and others like him "triumphant monsters". "Great men, like great ages, are explosives in which tremendous force is stored up".[34] "I do not spare you, I love you", declares Zarathustra. He loves his supporters so much that he wishes to redeem them, even at the cost of destroying them in the attempt. His love is indeed a dangerous gift. Earlier Zarathustra had claimed to love mankind. When challenged by the Holy Man he denies it and says that he was bringing man a gift. The trouble is that Zarathustra's love destroys. His love is one that poisons in order to produce health. He is the loving force of destruction.[35]

Nor was Nietzsche under any illusion about the nature of history itself. What was it, he asked, but "a disgusting procession of murder, arson, rape and torture"?[36] These are not the words of a man who believed that history should be made on these terms. In Nietzsche's philosophy Napoleon incarnates in his person the *problem* of the noble idea, not its solution. In the *Genealogy of Morals* he contended that in Napoleon "the problem of the noble idea was such as was made flesh . . . Napoleon a synthesis of the inhuman and superhuman".[37] Slave cultures had found in humanity too high a price to pay for the superhuman and had agreed to settle for all-too-human mediocrity instead. Noble societies had judged it better to have inhumanity rather than not to produce the superman at all. Nietzsche's question was this: Was the connection between the two one that could be severed?

He was, of course, to be disappointed. The key to that disappointment seems to me to lie in nationalism. Nietzsche praised Napoleon for being the enemy of the nation-state. He abhorred Germany for producing the wars of liberation in 1813 that had finally unseated the emperor and ushered in a nationalistic age. He looked forward to the coming of a new Napoleon who would finally unite Europe and thus help to engender a new European, "a supernational and nomadic type of man", a citizen who would not need to find his roots in a country or his salvation in following a political cause.

Nietzsche had no truck with the heroes of his own day. He railed against Bismarck's Germany for taking the "petty politics" of nationalism to its logical extreme. In his last book he accused his countrymen of having on their conscience all "the perpetuation of European particularism, petty politics". He saw nationalism as a neurotic condition, a mortal sickness, a threat to the existence of Europe itself. In contrast to Hegel, he also had little regard for the state, not least because of its tendency to go to war for no purpose other than to increase its own power. He called the nation-state "the slow suicide of life" and predicted the impending suicide of Europe in an age of total war.

Most of all, he feared his own country, Germany. In one of the notes that form part of his projected work *The Will to Power* he observed that it would be "anachronistic" for him to write the book in German. He would prefer to write it in French instead, so that it would not be used to support German nationalist aspirations. "The Germans today have ceased to be thinkers." They would only understand the title of the book, he complained, not its argument, and then only the last word of the title, 'power', which they would misconstrue.[38]

Unfortunately, the would-be Napoleons of the twentieth century, the Stalins and the Hitlers, worked through the nation-state. Was nationalism rather than the will to power as such therefore at fault? Nietzsche would probably have reached this conclusion. In accepting that Napoleon had been corrupted by power, he saw corruption as a contingent force, not a factor inherent in the power structure or in the will to power itself. Napoleon's corruption, he insisted, was the result of circumstance: "He himself was corrupted by the means he had to employ and lost *noblesse* of character. If he had to prevail among a different kind of man he could have employed other means. There would thus not seem to be a *necessity* for a Caesar to become bad".[39] Today, of course, we are more inclined to see that corruption lies in power itself. But then so too did one of the few men Nietzsche admired to the end of his life, his former colleague at the University of Basle, Jacob Burckhardt.

Burckhardt was one of those rare historians of the nineteenth century who were prepared to call evil by its name. "From the fact that good may come from evil and from disaster comes happiness", he wrote in *Reflec-*

tions on World History, "it does not follow that evil and disaster are not what they are". All power, he regarded, was predominately evil. Napoleon he called a "personified absurdity" for not realising it in time.[40]

In the end Nietzsche asked too much of humanity. In the subtitle of *Zarathustra* we are told that here is "a book for all and none". The book is for all because it is directed at humanity. It is for none because Nietzsche recognised that no one was yet ready to accept his teaching. On the one hand, he wanted to accelerate the destruction of European culture, to clear the ground of rubble in order to make possible an act of radical reconstruction. On the other hand his task was to produce disciples, the instruments of that destruction. Of course he could prophesy the coming of the superman confident that his appearance would be welcome, but the danger was that the prophecy might itself result in the appearance of disciples who were unworthy of him—men like Hitler and Stalin, who were so unworthy, in fact, that they made impossible his coming.

But then Nietzsche would probably not have challenged this conclusion. In the last years of his working life, when self-criticism was not especially conspicuous in his work, he added that it was not necessarily desirable to accept his ideas in an uncritical spirit. On the contrary, a dose of curiosity might be an "incomparably more intelligent position to take".[41] He may not have been a liberal, but he was a man who loved humanity enough to want to offer it what it merited most—self-respect. He was clear that it would forfeit its own self-esteem if it unquestionably followed its own prophets to perdition. Even *Zarathustra* ends with a caution: "You say you believe in Zarathustra? but what does Zarathustra matter? You are my believers, but what do my beliefs matter? You had not looked for yourselves. Then you found me. This is what all believers do. That is why belief is worth so little—Now I bid you to lose me, then find yourselves".[42]

Renan also imagined a radical rewriting of the scriptures in which Christ would say to his followers, "You must leave me if you would be my disciples"—a Christ who would lay upon his followers the goal of truth, insisting that they should follow the truth of their own experience even if the truth led away from the Cross. This was, of course, the great challenge of the twentieth century to which the Europeans failed to rise: Instead of honouring each other, they turned on each other at the behest of their tribal gods.

Of no nation did Nietzsche have greater concern than his own, for he identified as its worst characteristic the sin that Kafka too called the most heinous, namely, impatience. This, he wrote in *Twilight of the Idols,* in a section devoted entirely to the problem the German people might pose for Europe in the future, was "the first preliminary schooling of spirituality": "*Not* to reach immediately to a stimulus but to have the restraining stock-taking instincts in one's control. Learning to see, as I understand it, is what is called in unphilosophical language "strong will-power"—the essence of it is precisely *not* to will: the ability to *defer* decision".[43]

Bergson and the '*Élan Vital*'

The will to power was of more than just academic interest, a hobbyhorse of philosophers and lesser thinkers, a cliché of the hour. It was an idea that was in the air, especially in military circles, where it was interpreted in national terms. In the face of the continuing mechanisation of warfare and the development of greater firepower that threatened to spell the end of the period of heroic warfare, thoughts turned to how the human will might circumvent the material conditions of life. Nowhere were these thoughts more developed than in France.

One of the country's most important military 'thinkers' in the run-up to the First World War was the head of the Third Bureau (Ops) of the General Staff. He served under three commanders in chief and was one of Marshal Ferdinand Foch's star pupils. He closed the second of two General Staff conferences with the assertion that it is always necessary in battle to do something that would be impossible for men in cold blood. It was quite possible for soldiers to march under fire if they were in a high pitch of excitement. Even in the face of the most intense firepower they could prevail over men in a low state of morale. "Our conclusion must be that we must prepare ourselves and others by encouraging with enthusiasm, with exaggeration and in all the infinite details of training everything that bears, however little, the mark of the offensive spirit. Let us go far as excess".[44]

Élan and *cran* (guts) would do it all in a succession of charges of body-to-body blows. This widespread attitude in the French armed forces on the eve of the Great War was perhaps captured best by a remark at the end of a General Staff conference in 1913: 'impudence' in an offensive is the best form of security.[45]

It was widely believed that battles would be won in the future by demoralising the enemy. For that to happen, of course, an army had to take the offensive. Defensive battles seldom brought victory. Victory went to the army that was sustained by moving forwards, whatever the strength of the enemy fire. The president of the French Republic, addressing the Conseil Supérieur de la Guerre in 1912, insisted that the "offensive alone is suitable to the temperament of our soldiers". One military manual of the time, introduced just on the eve of the First World War, insisted that "battles are above all else moral struggles", determined not by the defensive but the offensive, the will to assert oneself, all obstacles notwithstanding.[46] Belief in *élan* was one of the few examples of the direct influence of philosophical thinking on the military mind—in this case that of the most important philosopher of the hour, Henri Bergson. It was Bergson who led the counterattack against positivism in the sciences. As a professor of philosophy at the Collège de France as well as the author of a seminal work, *Creative Evolution,* he was much quoted and read in his lifetime. His influence in his own day was as great as that of Descartes or Pascal in theirs.

It counted for much that the Collège de France was the country's highest institute of learning. It had no students and no examinations. Its lectures were public. Bergson's brilliance as a lecturer ensured that his lectures would be attended by politicians and writers such as Valéry and Péguy. Even the generals attended. Indeed, one of the ironies of the First World War was that, contrary to some of the gross caricatures that gained popular currency in the interwar years, most of the generals were well-educated and sophisticated men. Perhaps they were too intelligent for war. Perhaps they took ideas too seriously.

Bergson's ideas shaped the military mind because they were put forward at a time when the harsh reality of war, in particular the growth of increasing firepower and the intensity of artillery barrages, were beginning to rob war of its glamour and romantic appeal. His philosophy was as much a belated rearguard stand against materialism as were the views of the offensive put forward with such passion by General Foch, the refusal, that is, to countenance what many already knew, that war was becoming butchery, little better, in fact, than mass murder. The coincidence in ideas between Bergson's principles and those propounded by the offensive school of war were marked. Bergson believed that all intelligence in matter was shaped by a force called the *élan vital.* It consisted, he claimed, of a compulsion to create. But the will could not create absolutely "because it meets in front of itself matter, that is to say a movement opposed to its own". The way to resolve that dilemma was to ensure that the will to create was at one with creation. "Consciousness ... is the origin of life ... but this consciousness which is an urge to create only manifests itself when creation is possible". If men intuitively grasped reality they could act in accordance with it: "When we replace our being in our will and our will in the impulsion of which it is part, we realise that reality is continuous growth, a creation that continues without end. Our will already creates this miracle".[47]

In other words, provided that an army remained at one with the spirit of the times, it could march to the sound of the guns with as good a conscience as a man marching to the sound of history. The generals who attended Bergson's lectures were heartened and enthused by these claims, for it was clear how much in common they had with their own views of the offensive spirit. It is important nonetheless, wrote Theodore Zeldin, to recognise that Bergson was not an antirationalist. What he chose to deny was that reason necessarily produced clear results or that emotion was necessarily a source of confusion. He gave new status to the 'inner life' that science appeared to have explained away as an amalgam of mere physical stimuli.

Science, he argued, could not penetrate beyond time and space to the permanent core of the individual. Inner life was the source of human liberty. The best reason for action was not to have a reason but to act because "it is me". In that way the *élan vital,* which was a development of the eighteenth-century doctrine of vitalism, was transformed into a symbol of a new, early-twentieth-century reality: the will to power.[48]

Bergson's ideas struck a particular chord because they were readily consistent with the need for collective action, the belief that a society that was mobilised completely would have a distinct advantage in any conflict with others. Such thinking was widespread. It was part of the public consciousness. It is an excellent example of how ideas ring true with a wider public.

Towards the end of his life, for example, Renan had anticipated him by taking the theme of *élan* further than anyone before him. In a lecture he delivered at the Sorbonne in 1882 he concluded, in a passage that subsequently became famous, that "a nation is a soul, a spiritual principle . . . [it is based on] the will to continue living". A nation was "the result of a long history of effort, sacrifice and devotion". It existed only because of the will of its people that it should. It had to be reiterated in a silent, daily plebiscite. It was a community "created by sacrifices borne together and the wish to bear further ones in the future".[49] It was the nature of the sacrifice that would determine the extent to which a nation's *élan* was adequate to the demands of the hour.

Long before the First World War, in fact, the demands of modern warfare were such that victory and defeat were no longer technical matters to be decided by opposing armies, but final conclusions about the viability of a people and its way of life. Well before the First Word War, historians had begun to suspect that they would be writing not about armies on the battlefield but about entire societies at war.

Unfortunately, the culmination of Bergson's philosophical stand reached its inevitable apotheosis in Verdun, the bloodiest battle of the First World War. In 1916 the German High Command took the decision to bleed the enemy white by attacking the city and forcing the French to defend it to the bitter end. At the end of two months it was clear that the strategy had failed, that Verdun was a fortress that could neither be taken nor successfully invested. Nevertheless, for reasons of national prestige the battle went on. In the battle of attrition the Germans were bled white almost as much as the French. In time the engagement became entirely a matter of whose resolve would be broken when supplies rather than men ran out. Only the British attack on the Somme in July provided an excuse for the High Command to call off the battle.

Verdun was crippling for the German army, but it was much worse for the French. What gave it its particularly atrocious character was the size of the battlefield. 800,000 casualties in all were sustained in an area measuring little larger than the combined acreage of the London parks. Years after the victory the battle continued to haunt the French nation. At one time or another more than three-quarters of the entire army had fought there.

No one knew that better than the most successful of the field commanders, Philippe Pétain, who years after the war remarked, "The constant vision of death penetrated [the French soldier] with a resignation which bordered on fatalism". For a symbol of what Verdun did to France one need hardly look beyond the tragic figure of Pétain himself, the hero of 1916, the resigned defeatist of 1940.

After the war the French increasingly came to accept that they had lost their vitality as a nation in world affairs. In a sense they lived in a different time zone from the rest of the world, firmly anchored to the past, to the period in which they imagined they had had a future. They had won the war, but they found themselves looking back nostalgically to an age they understood much better. As their problems mounted, as international life became more complex and frustrating, their disappointment was transformed into a form of fatalism, all the more pernicious because it was so deeply entrenched in the thinking even of successful generals like Pétain.

We can take as an example of this malaise the work of the writer Roger Martin du Gard. When he began writing *Les Thibault* the war was not the central event of the series. Shortly after the armistice he had drawn up a plan for a family chronicle in which the war itself would play only a minor role. Although Jacques was to be killed, the lives of the other characters were to go on in a world that was fundamentally unchanged. As late as 1927 he called the volume covering the war only a 'prologue' to what was to come.

By 1932, however, he had come to see the war as a catastrophe that had brought the stable bourgeois world of the Thibaults to an abrupt end. "The Thibaults disappear, wiped out in the war", he wrote, "and it is an entire society, a whole form of the bourgeoisie that the war wipes out with them".[50] Paul Nizan praised the book at the time for this reason—for making it clear that since 1914 "all life had become public", not private. In such a world all private manifestations of heroism or *élan* had little appeal.[51]

One of the most memorable episodes in the final pages of Martin du Gard's chronicle is Jacques Thibault's reckless, forlorn mission to scatter propaganda from the air behind German lines. When his plane crashes not far behind the French side of the front the gendarmes who remove his body from the charred wreckage have no way of understanding the heroism of his intended gesture. One writer described this ending as "the ultimate confrontation of the privileged hero with the realities of twentieth century history, as the last nineteenth century act in a major work of French literature".[52] It also marked something more profound: the discrediting of a nineteenth-century idea, the will to power.

Wittgenstein and the Sanction of Battle

I demand the right to settle matters with myself. To be face to face with myself. Perhaps from my confrontation with myself something else may emerge.
—Eugène Ionesco, *Fragments of a Journal* (1967)

At the end of 1916 Ludwig Wittgenstein was posted to a fighting unit on the Russian front, an artillery regiment attached to the Seventh Army. For some time he had been pressing to see active service, and so it was all the more annoying that when it came time to join the new unit he fell ill. His illness passed quickly and he was not left behind as he had feared. When he was told that he still had time to join the battle, he prayed: "If only I may be allowed to risk my life in some difficult assignment". Once at the front, he asked to be assigned to the most dangerous position of all, that of an observation post for the artillery, one that made him automatically the object of enemy fire. "Was shot at", he recorded laconically in his journal on 29 April, "thought of God".[53] On 4 May he was detailed to go on nighttime duty, one of the most dangerous assignments of all. "Only then will the war really begin for me", he wrote, "and maybe even life".

One of the reasons he welcomed the job he had been given was that it was a solitary occupation. He did not have to endure the company of his comrades, in whom, he complained, it was impossible to find "a trace of humanity".[54] Unlike many of his friends, Wittgenstein did not derive any value from seeing himself as a member of a community. His feeling towards the men to the end was one of contempt, not understanding. Not for him that camaraderie between men of all classes that was invoked so often after the war in the memoirs and reminiscences of the soldiers who survived. For much of the time Wittgenstein regarded his fellow soldiers as barely human: "When we hear a Chinese talk we take his speech for inarticulate gurgling. Someone who understands Chinese will recognise language in what he hears. Similarly, I often cannot discern the humanity in a man".[55] "The people around me", he added, "are not so much mean as appallingly limited". Within their own circle they were clever enough, but unimaginative. "They lacked character and therefore breadth". They were not ready to make anything of themselves. Despite their experience of war they had not grown as persons. Instead, he found among the rank and file a general indifference to patriotism, a stolid, dumb commitment to life, a determination to survive, whatever the cost.

Wittgenstein's attitude was in part a testament to his social background. He came from a very wealthy Jewish family that, though excluded by race and class from the upper reaches of Viennese social life, answered the call to arms readily enough. The men whom he commanded did not need the war in the way that he did. They did not find it morally redeeming. Indeed, if asked, they would probably have preferred to have remained at home. The Czechs and Poles serving under the Austrian flag had been pressed into service. Unlike Wittgenstein, they did not volunteer.

Wittgenstein continued to throw himself into the fray until the end of the war. His service on the eastern front only came to an end in the year that witnessed the last Russian offensive, a desperate attempt by the new and ill-fated Kerensky government to win public support for the continuation of the struggle, an attempt that, like every other, fizzled out in failure.

Later he volunteered for service in Italy and in May 1918 was posted to a mountain artillery regiment. He took part in the Eleventh Army's last offensive, in the course of which he was decorated for bravery. After Austria's surrender he found himself a prisoner of war, first at Como and finally at Monte Cassino, where he concluded much of his first work, the *Tractatus Logico-Philosophicus,* the only one of his books to be published in his lifetime.

The will to power could be as much an individual as a collective act, which Wittgenstein's experience of war illustrates quite clearly. Standing eye-to-eye with death enabled him to appreciate the value of life, to know rather than imagine what gave it meaning. He had gone to war to escape a sense of self-estrangement that had become more pronounced as the years advanced. He had gone to war determined, in his own words, to become a different kind of man, "a decent human being".

In retrospect, there can be no doubt that the war was central to his development, not only as a philosopher but also as a man. As his mentor and friend Bertrand Russell later wrote, war was a telling way of testing the logic of a man's life against the dogmatism of shells and bullets. Before the war he had written to Russell: "I keep on hoping that things will come to an eruption once and for all so that I can turn into a different person. . . . How can I be a logician before I am a human being? The most important thing is to settle accounts with myself".[56]

Many of his fellow Austrians who served in the war shared a similar point of view. One of them, the artist Oskar Kokoschka, wrote that the story of Christ's Passion was the eternal story of man. The miracle of the Resurrection could only be understood in human terms if it was grasped as the truth of the inner life. "One does not become human once and for all just by being born. One must be resurrected as a human being every day".[57]

Even Wittgenstein's philosophical enquiries were given a boost. As he submitted many years later, a "knockout" blow in military thinking could be paralleled by the "big push" in life. One more intellectual offensive was all that was needed to come to terms with the remaining problems of philosophy. Throughout his years at the front he continued to record his thoughts on the problems of logic and philosophy in the notebooks he carried in his rucksack. The *Tractatus* had begun life as a treatise on the nature of logic. During his service in the army he was encouraged to extend its scope to an understanding of life itself.

His experience in the war confirmed him in the fundamental tenet of the work: the fulfilment of will as self and the fulfilment of self as will. Life, he contended, is entirely what we will. At the moment of our death, of course, the world does not change for us. It ends. In that sense death is not an event, for we do not live through it. Life is willed by the individual. Death is simply a suspension of that will. As such, for us, it is a nonevent.

In short, man is not imprisoned by history because history is only what we will. It follows that the only proper conduct for man is to live for the moment: Live in the present, he wrote. Life's significance is not what the soldier but the historian thinks it to be. War cannot legitimise a cause, and no one can seriously die for one because causes are what historians make of them. In that sense, he argued, it is purposeless to fight for a future one will never experience. What the *Tractatus* affirms more powerfully than any other of his works is his belief that the purpose of existence is to live, not to die. What he said of God he could also claim for man. "How things are in the world is a matter of complete indifference to what is higher. God does not reveal himself in the world".[58] Two propositions were drawn from this:

> 6.44. It is not how things are in the world that is mystical, but that it exists.
> 6.45. To view the world *sub specie aeterni* is to view it as a whole—a limited whole.
> Feeling the world as a limited whole—it is this that is mystical.[59]

Like Nietzsche, Wittgenstein had no truck with the idea that the purpose of life is its moral or political improvement. It is a condition of his being that man should struggle to escape the present to arrive at the future sooner. Both men believed that life could be devalued by spurious political action. Both were highly personal, even autobiographical in their philosophy. Both were lyrical and aphoristic in their writing. Both were also violently antisystemic in their avowed distaste for philosophy itself. Wittgenstein thought that it was a disease and that the job of the philosopher was to study it as a physician studies malaria, not to pass it on to his patients but to cure them of it.

In the end Wittgenstein remained true to this central belief. Though much of his philosophical thought changed, in this respect he was consistent. As a philosopher, he insisted that he could not discover empirically how men ought to behave, in part because empirical science is concerned with facts, not values. All that philosophy can provide is knowledge about the goals that we seek to achieve. Philosophers are not qualified to judge the worth of these goals, or even to suggest why we should pursue them. If we are ruthlessly philosophical, we must admit that there is no more ratio-

nal justification for peace than there is for war. A society that believes in the
virtue of peace is merely a peaceful society. A distaste for war does not necessarily mean that it is morally wrong.

Freud had a similar perspective on life. Neither man formulated policies
on how to promote peace. Like those who would have welcomed shorter
working hours but feared what the workers might do with their leisure,
Freud like Wittgenstein would have welcomed a more peaceful world. Both
men were interested in private ethics, however. They had no grand designs
for a better life. "You can't build clouds", Wittgenstein once wrote, "and
that is why the future you dream of never comes true".[60]

Wittgenstein did not deny, however, that war had a purpose for those
who fought in it. Men joined up in the twentieth century to fight their own
demons. They did so for their own salvation. The causes for which they
fought defined them as people—what they stood for, what they wanted to
be remembered for, what they wanted to see themselves as in their own
imagination.

In a few brief and unsystematic remarks in the last four pages of the
Tractatus he indicated why he thought it was worth acting in the world,
even dying for a cause. Good or bad acts of will may make no difference to
the world, in the sense that they do not always change history. But they do
alter our horizons. They affect our sense of moral agency. Accordingly, to
the good-willed agent the world appears altogether different from the
world of the bad-willed agent. "The world of a happy man is a different
one from that of the unhappy one". Good-willing—or fighting for the values in which we believe—may make us happier than not fighting for them.

Ultimately, however, Wittgenstein's position was a deeply ambiguous
one. Unlike many of the Cambridge philosophers, of course, he fought in
the war. He did not spend part of it in prison as a conscientious objector
like Russell, or observe it as an armchair critic like G. E. Moore. In
Wittgenstein's later life, when someone remarked that Moore's childlike innocence was to his credit, Wittgenstein begged to disagree: "I can't understand that", he said, "unless it is also to a child's credit. For you aren't talking of the innocence of a man who has fought, but of an innocence which
comes from a natural absence of temptation, from pursuing a sheltered
life".[61]

Later still, in the 1950s, Russell was involved in the movement for nuclear disarmament. He assumed that a liberal society could command peace
as a moral right. His support for unilateralism was informed by a vision of
a second Eden to which man could be readmitted by rejecting the fruit of
the tree of the knowledge of good and evil and attaining a second innocence. It was another example that Wittgenstein would probably have considered (given his positive attitude towards nuclear weapons) of a childlike
response to history.[62]

What is most disconcerting about Wittgenstein's stand, however, is his apparent lack of political commitment. We find the same failing even in the work of Julien Benda, who did so much to expose the conspiracy of intellectuals, the writers who had allowed their scholarship to be used in a way that conflicted with the intent and spirit of philosophical enquiry. Unfortunately, the twentieth century was one that demanded political commitment on the part of its thinkers. Even Benda himself could be found in 1937 delivering impassioned speeches on behalf of the embattled republicans in Madrid.[63]

Wittgenstein's position ultimately illustrates another example of the *trahison des clercs,* one that Benda did not address in his study. If the first was the willingness of philosophers to put themselves at the service of politicians, the second was to deny that political action and philosophy were inextricably linked. Unfortunately, as Paul Ricoeur notes, philosophy reflected the violence inherent in twentieth-century life.[64]

First, there was the violence of its point of departure. Husserl described his philosophical mission as goal-oriented, predestined and demonic. It was his task, he believed, to provide an exact knowledge, a task the natural sciences had surrendered at the end of the nineteenth century. Here was an attempt to replace the natural sciences, to prescribe (as well as proscribe) what should and should not be life's calling.

Then there was the violence of the trajectory that the philosophers chose to argue their case. They were always locating their own ideas in a tradition, one that vied for primacy with others. The result was to insist on the truth of their own presuppositions to the exclusion of every opposing one. In this respect, Wittgenstein differed not a jot from Heidegger, despite the very great differences in their thinking.

Finally, there was the violence of the premature conclusion inherent in the belief that they were on the brink of solving all the remaining puzzles of life, the belief that it was possible for humanity to live without questions about its own condition. Wittgenstein too claimed that one final push or knock-out blow would solve all the remaining problems at the centre of philosophical discourse. What was this if not an often unconscious desire— shared with Marxists and many others—to bring history to an end, to a grand conclusion.

When Wittgenstein later rejected this position he adopted another that was no less dogmatic: that the philosopher could say very little, and that the rest was silence. His major work, *Philosophical Investigations,* tells us that it is not the philosopher's task to propound theories but only to describe facts about language that are perfectly obvious, or should be, designed in such a fashion as to break the hold on the mind of philosophical paradoxes and confutations. What was this if not a retreat from the heroic, if this time not from 'the will to power' but 'the will to truth'?

Sade and the Brotherhood of Man

In the early days of the French Revolution the notorious Marquis de Sade was still incarcerated in the Bastille. By then he had been in prison for ten years and in the Bastille since 1784. We know that he harangued the crowd the day before the prison was stormed. He appears to have employed as a loudspeaker a pipe used for emptying his dirty water. One of his many provocative acts was to yell out that the prisoners were being slaughtered on the orders of the king.

When the crowd finally broke in they found only three prisoners, none of them at risk. Sade paid dearly for his mischief. In the confusion some of the manuscripts on which he had been labouring, including *The 120 Days of Sodom,* were lost. "Instead of liberating its author", wrote Georges Bataille, the mob lost the manuscripts on which he had laboured for so many years, an incident that "was the first expression of his full horror of liberty".[65]

It would be more true, perhaps, to say that it marked his first intimation of the cost of what Rousseau in particular had written of so eloquently, the general will. In addition to the idea of the individual will there was another, that of the collective will, that of an entire people mobilised for action. It was an idea that fitted in naturally enough with another—the brotherhood of man.

One of the first philosophers of note to grasp the danger inherent in both concepts was Hegel. Hegel set out to restrain the longing for total freedom that had manifested itself in the nihilistic phase of the French Revolution. He also tried to counter the hero worship of Napoleon. He did not believe that there would be any more world individuals like Napoleon, for he believed that humanity had finally become conscious of its true end, the struggle for freedom, and that history no longer needed to depend on the unconscious actions of individuals.

Hegel also believed that the attempt to attain absolute freedom would inevitably lead to disaster, and he tried to redirect this longing towards a more limited and rational end. In the Terror he saw a classic illustration of what happens when individuality goes mad and insists on absolutising itself by force in order to forge a single, indomitable will. The Terror was the logical result of the pernicious demand for absolute freedom, for a will that was unhampered, unrestrained, arbitrary and capricious. The drive to absolute freedom could only destroy, not rebuild anew. And when the old order had been laid to waste it would turn its destructive energies elsewhere, on itself. It would end devouring its own children. The beheading of those lacking in civic virtue or human content would become of no more importance than "cutting through cabbages". In this respect it was entirely fitting that the guillotine should have become the chief instrument of the Terror.[66]

Hegel recognised, from the beginning, that a viable society could not be constructed on the foundations of an undifferentiated will because every society requires differentiation of function, a fact that has to be embodied in such political structures as an executive, legislature and bureaucracy, each in creative conflict with the other. The Robespierrean state of course could not tolerate any differentiated structures. Liberty, the great voice of revolutionary virtue, Louis Saint-Just declared, "must prevail at any price. You must not merely punish traitors but the indifferent as well. . . . We must rule by iron those who cannot be ruled by justice".[67] If indifference were permitted it would constitute a constraint on the supposedly unconditional freedom of the rational will to remake the world as it wished.

If much of Hegel's influence in the twentieth century derives from the interpretation given his works by Alexandre Kojève, a Russian émigré living in Paris in the 1930s, much of Sade's impact on the modern mind derives from a seminal study of his writing by another émigré, Pierre Klossowski. Twenty years later he was one of the first philosophers in postwar France to set out to penetrate the meaning of Sade's work for the modern era.

Klossowski was one of the first intellectuals to show how the passions of the revolution that the eighteenth-century *philosophes* had seen as a grand experiment aimed at liberating man could also give rise to men such as Sade. It was Sade, not Robespierre or Saint-Just, who was the greatest exponent of the general will in pursuit of the ultimate goal: the brotherhood of man.

For the general will to be forged, the revolution would have to accomplish three ends. First, it would have to throw up a leader, a great unifying figure. Sade saw the revolution as the first chance in history for the man of destiny to rise to power, a figure of whom the masses should indeed have been wary since such men are quite capable of accomplishing, or at least willing if they fail, "the end of the whole human condition": "The mass . . . is composed only of individuals and the individual represents the species intrinsically; and there is no reason why the species should escape the risks involved for it in the success of an individual".[68]

The more the man of destiny was successful, the more he would concentrate the diffuse energies of the age in his own person. And, of course, the more dangerous he would become. Hegel had seen Napoleon as the first man of destiny, but not necessarily as a destroyer. Napoleon, however, had gone on to wage a series of wars in pursuit of an impossible imperial dream in the course of which a million or more Frenchmen lost their lives.

Napoleon, wrote Klossowski, had known how to discharge in his person all that the age had accumulated in him. From the point of view of the masses he was perfectly sane, at least in terms of how the masses themselves judged sanity. "The best index of the health of the man to whom the masses submit is his resolve to sacrifice them".[69] The masses had to be prepared to be sacrificed by a leader of unlimited vision if they were to have any hope of transcending their own condition or of revising the natural and divine order on their own terms. To be sure, the great man would be a criminal, but one whose crimes would be a means to a much greater end.

Secondly, Sade wanted the revolution to make man in his own image, not God's. He wanted a revolution that would engage in criminal action, that would legislate against nothing, that would impose no laws except one, the right to do anything one chose, including the pursuit of the impossible—for if the revolution was only about the 'possible', it would only be half complete. A revolution that allowed the impossible, of course, would have the virtue of being unending.

Sade hoped that the revolution would bring into existence a republic that would treat 'insurrection' as a condition of its being. The only order a true republic would know would be a permanent state of emergency. That, alas, wrote Walter Benjamin in the 1930s, is what political life had become in the modern era. It was a nihilistic doctrine, for the essence of modern nihilism lies not so much in the longing for a substantial goal but in the repeated rejection of all attained goals as limitations on human freedom. The upshot had to be permanent revolution. The author with whom this principle is still most widely associated is Leon Trotsky, who argued that permanent revolution would raise man to a new plane and create "a higher social biological type . . . or if you please a superman".[70]

Trotsky's superman was not Nietzsche's. We must also ask whether Nietzsche himself really believed that the day of the superman would ever arrive. The last part of the book ends with Zarathustra's failure to storm the heavens and his return to the human world, where he finds the higher men he has taught living in a more degraded state than he left them. These higher beings are wounded souls unable to overcome or renounce a world they despise. It is a mark of Nietzsche's achievement to have exposed Zarathustra's pedagogical failure to teach the higher men wisdom as well as to expose the unworkability of his own ethics of self-deification.[71]

Sade's third premise, which he put forward in an admirably clear and consistent fashion, stemmed from the other two. If the impossible were to be attempted God would have to be taken out of the picture altogether. "Let us not be content with breaking sceptres. We will pulverise the idols forever".[72] Only by demystifying God could the revolution be rendered permanent. "Since you labour to destroy all prejudices, do not let any of them subsist because it only takes one to bring them all back". What Sade proposed was that the revolution should go beyond killing the king to killing God.

All our Christian virtues, he believed, had triumphed because they had reinterpreted human suffering by lending it a vicarious meaning. Christianity had restored the dignity of man, but only by valuing those attributes of human nature that enabled man to gain entry into the next world, which were not necessarily the values necessary to live a full life in this one. Sade wanted redemption now rather than later.

Unfortunately, he could not escape using Christocentric ideals altogether. Nor could those who followed him. Dostoyevsky later painted a picture of an 'incomplete nihilist', Stavrogin. Or was he an incomplete Christian? Sade was responsible for reformulating a secular language that included all the old Christian themes: redemption, martyrdom and the search for a state of grace. If God disappears from the text, evil does not. The loss of a metaphysical reference point does not extinguish sin. The absence of God merely means that there is no remission from it. Sin ceases to be an accident and becomes a permanent condition of man.[73]

What was frightening about the late nineteenth and the twentieth centuries was that many revolutionaries were prepared to redeem man from sin by suffering themselves in eternity. As Georg Lukács wrote of the Russian Revolution, the death of freedom was one of the tragic historical situations, its tragedy lying in the fact that it was "impossible to act in such a way as not to commit sin". The ultimate measure of a man's greatness was not his choice of causes, but the extent of his own sacrifice.[74]

The individual, when forced to choose between two evils, "chooses correctly when he sacrifices the lower to his higher self." Still, Lukács left his readers in no doubt that this tragic choice between evils showed man at his best, not his worst. His willingness to sacrifice himself for the permanent good of others was to be considered the defining mark of his humanity.

Such sacrifices could be made not only by Marxist revolutionaries but also by anarchists like Boris Savinkov, who in the run-up to the Russian Revolution of 1905 claimed that the ethical validation of his own terrorist acts lay "in the fact that he sacrificed for his fellow human beings not only his life, but his purity, his morality, his soul". The supreme sacrifice, Savinkov declared, "is to become evil in the service of the greater good and commit the evil deed that is truly and tragically moral".[75] In short, murderous acts could be described as ethical when those who committed them were prepared to imperil even their immortal soul.

The point is made compellingly by Borges in a short story set at the turn of the century. It tells of a theologian, a scholar, Nils Runeberg, who stumbles upon the real identity of the Messiah. God, the Bible tells us, lowered himself to become a man in order to redeem humanity. His sacrifice, however, was perfect, and not attenuated by any omission. To limit what he underwent to the agony of one afternoon on the cross would be blasphemous; to maintain that he was a man incapable of sin would be more blasphemous still. If the redeemer could feel cold, fatigue, hunger and thirst, and in the end even despair, surely he could also commit a sinful act.

The vision of his coming in Isaiah 53:3, "He is despised and rejected of men; a man of sorrows, and acquainted with grief", is for many a future version of Christ at the moment of his death. For Runeberg it is a prophecy of eternity. God makes himself a man but a man more despised and rejected than any other in history, a man held in universal contempt. To save the human race he could have chosen any of the destinies that make up history's complex web: "He could have been Alexander or Pythagoras or Rurik or Jesus. He chose the finest destiny of all: He was Judas". Condemned to the lowest circle in Dante's vision of Hell, it is his fate to suffer agony until the Day of Judgement. Borges encapsulates the reality of that myth with a quotation at the head of the page from *The Seven Pillars of Wisdom*, T. E. Lawrence's overromanticised account of the desert campaign against the Turks. "There seemed a certainty in degradation".[76]

Criminal acts on the scale that the twentieth century occasionally 'demanded' were so monstrous, in fact, that once they had been enacted all record of them would have to be expunged. The epigraph in Borges's story attached to the prologue of Runeberg's work *Den Hemliqe Fralsaren* (1909) is from the gospel by John: "He was in the world and the world . . . knew him not". In his own will Sade took this logic to its ultimate conclusion, leaving instructions that once he had been buried his grave was to be sown with acorns so that in future all trace of his tomb would disappear completely. So too, he hoped, would the world's memory of him. He wanted his very name to vanish from the memory of men. It was a response that, he was the first to admit, was required because of the enormity of what he preached.

A hundred and fifty years later, addressing a group of SS officers who had assembled in Poznan on 4 October 1943 to discuss the progress of the Final Solution, Himmler announced that once the campaign was completed all memory of it would have to be covered up. The Final Solution, he insisted, would be "a glorious page of our history", but it would have to remain unchronicled by historians of the future.[77] After dismantling the camp at Treblinka as the Russian army advanced, the Germans sowed the fields with grain, planted pine trees and used the bricks from the crematorium to build a farmhouse. In this respect, Borges grasped the point of a secularised Christianity or inverted Christian creed. The true redeemer would be unknown in the future precisely because no one would know his deeds.

The chief problem with this philosophy was not that it rendered the professional criminal a moral outcast, but that it transformed him into a moral man. One of the few criminals to have understood this was that permanent recidivist Jean Genet, who many years later was transformed into an international figure by his patron, Jean-Paul Sartre. In *The Journal of a Thief* Genet charted his progress through Europe in the 1930s, dressed in rags, suffering contempt and oppressed by fatigue. Everywhere he charted his experience of the same pattern of bars, flophouses, robbery, prison and expulsion. For him it was a voyage of discovery beyond all moral laws. It was the expression of a philosophy of vice, the working out of an aesthetic of degradation. Even he, however, professional criminal though he was, found disturbing a society that made vice a civic virtue:

> I walked from Breslau to Berlin. I would have liked to steal. A strange force held me back. Germany terrified all of Europe. It had become, particularly for me, the symbol of cruelty. It was already outside the law. Even on the Unter den Linden I had the feeling that I was strolling about in a camp organised by bandits.
>
> I thought that the brain of the most scrupulous bourgeois concealed treasures of duplicity, hatred, meanness, cruelty and lust. I was excited at being free amidst an entire people that had been placed on the Index. Probably, I stole there as elsewhere, but I felt a certain constraint for what governed this activity and what resulted from it—this particular moral attitude set up as a civic virtue was being experienced by a whole nation which directed it against others.
>
> "It's a race of thieves", I thought to myself. "If I steal here I perform no singular deed that might fulfil me. I obey the customary order. I do not destroy it. I am not committing evil, I am not upsetting anything. The outrageous is impossible. I am stealing in a void".[78]

Totalitarian states were precisely that, moral and political voids. No one could have expressed it as forcefully as Genet, a criminal who was affronted by the criminality of the new order, a man who, devoid of any political consciousness, had a natural aversion for crime as a political act.

Conclusion

Sade himself was fortunate to have escaped the guillotine. He spent the last years of his life incarcerated in the mad ward at Charenton, acting out plays on an improvised stage with other inmates as the players. After his death he was burned in effigy. The next century would take its writers more seriously.

It would be wrong, of course, to conclude that liberals balked at the idea of committing sin in pursuit of their aims. Reinhold Niebuhr was insistent that an individual is always forced to choose some evil to do good. That was what he saw as the "irony of American history", an irony that constituted the tragedy of a society that had set out to dehistoricise tragedy from political life, one that, in Hegel's words, was determined to be happy. What made the world a tragic place was that good could only be attained by transgressing the God-given order or what Niebuhr called "the harmonies of nature".[79]

We cannot eliminate sin because we are never entirely in the right. But the clue to limiting evil is to recognise that our ambition must have limits, for an unlimited aim is a hubristic one that must inevitably end in failure.

The English historian Herbert Butterfield, speaking as another committed Christian, also believed that evil and good were inextricably linked, that "one can hardly fail to recognise the element of tragedy in many conflicts which take place between a half right that is perhaps too wilful and another half right that is too proud".[80] But an unlimited aim is more dangerous still because it requires one side to be entirely in the right. Arguing in this vein in the wake of the Second World War, he contrasted the Christian modesty of the victors with the pagan self-confidence of the Nazis: "The hardest strokes of heaven fall in history upon those who imagine that they can control things in a sovereign manner as though they were kings of the earth playing Providence not only for themselves but for the far future with the wrong kind of farsightedness".[81]

Butterfield's view of Providence was a liberal one. No generation can control the direction of history because it can never aspire to transform itself out of its own limits. As Leopold von Ranke once wrote, every generation is "equidistant from eternity".

If the West learned this after 1945 it took the non-Western world much longer as it emerged from the chrysalis of the colonial era. Many revolutionary leaders who had sat at the feet of Sartre and Althusser in Paris, or read Marx and Engels in their youth, believed that by will alone they could transform their dormant, listless societies into modern, socialist states. Conceiving of their development programmes and five-year plans as military campaigns, they tended to treat society as if it were a military headquarters. History, one Algerian author wrote of his own country in the 1960s, "was made in the imperative mood, in a Schopenhauerian world in which people lived as if all that mattered was the will to power".[82]

The upshot was a fundamentalist revolt that in the first five years of the 1990s claimed 60,000 victims. Whatever are the inadequacies of religion— and there are many, including sectarian strife, the stupidity of dogma and intolerance towards other faiths—it is, at least, the institutionalised expression of an idea that in the face of life a sense of awe is not irrelevant. In the absence of God life can become unbearable. It can produce what Milan Kundera calls "a certain lightness of being". No forced march into history can compensate for that.

Sade's work is a good note on which to conclude this chapter, for it illustrates the central flaw in the concept of the will to power. Its exponents set out not to circumscribe but to expand human agency, to make man the master of his own fate, to imbue him with what liberal societies denied their citizens, the freedom to attempt the impossible, the restructuring of human nature through political action.

The chief problem of the will to power was that people willed too much. Modern political theory is littered with words that presupposed that human beings were subjects of social action—words such as rationality, responsibility, legitimacy and rights. Liberal writers sought to secure greater agency without doing harm to those values; illiberal thinkers tried to achieve a much more unconditional freedom, which in the end served merely to circumscribe man's freedom of action more than ever.

A free man is one who is conscious of himself as a thinking, active, willing agent responsible for his choices. He is free, however, only insofar as he also accepts that there are limits to human agency, that he obeys the laws he has imposed on himself or found in his uncoerced self.

What ultimately makes Nietzsche a philosopher on the side of freedom (his later reputation notwithstanding—in a world that took his language rather than his ideas as the measure of the man) was his understanding of freedom: not in terms of obedience to God's law or nature's, still less to that of a Hegelian World Spirit, but to man's *self-given* laws. He may well have devoted most of his active life to challenging the numerous constraints on man's will, but he was among the first to recognise the danger that if it were possible to remove all constraints, if it were possible to master necessity, then there would be no reason not to do so. If Europe were ever stalked by the fear that what it did not master would master it, then it would have no reason not to aim for total freedom—at the price, of course, of permanent war or unending revolution.

Most illiberal writers, by contrast, agreed with Napoleon that a belief in the impossible was "the spectre of the timid and the refuge of the coward".[83] Nietzsche, like most of the liberal writers he despised, insisted that limits had to be placed on freedom as a necessary price to pay for human action. Reason requires us to reason out the limits of our actions, to accept that they have to exist.

Let me conclude this discussion by invoking a more liberal version of the Napoleonic myth (if this is not a contradiction in terms). In Shaw's inimitable portrayal of the young general, *The Man of Destiny*, Napoleon succeeds because he is devoid of ideals and idealism. He finds it possible to be irresistible without working heroic miracles. Even when he adopts an oracular tone no one believes him. It is the incredulity of his supporters that makes him so irresistible. It is the greed of his army that makes it serve his cause. His army in Italy succeeds not because each soldier carries a marshal's baton in his knapsack (as Napoleon himself claimed) but because he hopes to carry half a dozen silver spoons there the next day.[84]

Shaw's Napoleon is even without courage. He insists that fear is not to be surmounted but outflanked. If Nietzsche's hero is beyond good and evil, Shaw's is beyond courage and cowardice. He is a fraud but also a thoroughly modern man. In his cynicism and self-deprecation he is almost a Wittgensteinian hero, a postmodern man. Whatever he is, however, he is not a liberal. No Shavian hero could ever claim to be that.

Chapter Six

War and the Illiberal Unconscious

Man is the animal whose nature has not yet been fixed.
—Nietzsche, *Beyond Good and Evil* (1886)

All intercourse among men is based on this: that each is able to read the interior soul of the other and the common language is the sonorous expression of a common soul.
—Nietzsche, 'Notes on Reading and Writing' (1873–1875)

The illiberal temper was not restricted to the writers and intellectuals I have cited so far in this study. Many of their ideas 'rang true' in the popular mind (even if they were recycled in more simplistic formulas that were more immediate in their appeal). They confirmed people's experience or reinforced it. In short, the ideas that I have discussed would not have had such an impact but for the fact that they resonated in the unconscious mind.

One need not to subscribe to the ideas of Carl Jung on the 'Unconscious' (a word first coined by Coleridge) to find persuasive the idea that people were predisposed to entertain illiberal thoughts subconsciously, that some of the most extreme ideas found them out. The alienation of modernity was intense in the early years of the twentieth century, as Nietzsche recognised with his usual insight. Europe, he concluded, was suffering from "an over-stimulation of nervous and thinking capacity . . . so much so that the cultivated classes in the European countries are completely neurotic and all of their great families have a relative on the brink of madness".[1]

The late nineteenth century does appear to have been particularly stressful. If Peter Gay is correct to see in the early Enlightenment years a "recovery of nerve" after the religious wars of the seventeenth century, perhaps we can say that the late modern age demonstrated a loss of it.[2]

John Keane prefers to call it 'social fatigue'. Civil society in modern Europe created a 'space' in which peace broke down within society long before war broke out between states. Did one mirror the other, or produce it? Did the high tension within civil society that Nietzsche identified—the enforced intimacy and stresses of modern family life in particular—presage what some historians call 'the European civil war' that broke out in 1914 and extended to 1945 and beyond?

In Jaroslav Hasek's great work of twentieth-century fiction, *The Good Soldier Svejk,* the hero finds himself at a loss to know what the war is about. His only concern is personal survival:

> Vaneck asked with interest: "How long do you think the war will go on, Svejk?"
> "Fifteen years", answered Svejk. "That's obvious because once there was a Thirty Years War and now we're twice as clever as they were before, so it follows that thirty divided by two is fifteen".[3]

Though the Great War lasted only four years, Svejk was nonetheless right. In the minds of many of the veterans returning home, particularly to the defeated countries, the war continued in the street fighting that brought fascist regimes to power, in the traumatised minds of an entire nation that never really recovered from the experience of the front. The war did indeed go on, not for fifteen but for thirty years, and may be said to have come to an end only with the collapse of the Third Reich.

Nietzsche, in this respect at least may well have been right to talk of modernity not as a pathological condition but as one that could give rise to antisocial behaviour. Civil society, its greatest achievement, did not eliminate fear or uncertainty. It merely contained it, or tried to. It regulated the constant competition by social groups each struggling to advance themselves or simply survive. The changing fortunes of social groups amplified life's essential contingency. Nothing could be taken for granted; nothing was permanent. There were no "transcendental guarantees of absolute certainty".[4] To quote Nietzsche once again: "We are more free than ever before to look around in all directions; nowhere do we perceive any limits. We have the advantage of feeling an immense space around us—but also an immense void".[5] Modernity constantly tested the reality of the world to the point where many people craved a restoration of the 'real' in its most absolute, uncontingent form.

Let me look at three forms of civil violence that, it seems to me, anticipated the violence of international social life after 1914: blood sports, sexual murder and child abuse. None of them were new, of course, but all of them were discussed in the modern world as they had never been before. In time they became a central part of the modern world's understanding of itself.

1. In Chapter 1, in the section on Arthur Conan Doyle's novel *The Lost World,* I discussed the depiction of the bloodlust of otherwise normal men when confronted with a danger or challenge. Even when the ape-men have

been hunted down to extinction Malone returns to the plateau of his own free will to continue slaughtering some of the other species that Prof. Challenger's party had also encountered.

What Doyle depicts is the late Victorian obsession with blood sports, especially in the form of big game hunting in Africa, the dark continent that had also been 'sealed off' by history until the Europeans trekked inland from the coast in the latter half of the nineteenth century. The scramble for Africa, of course, was followed by the Great War, which saw the greatest bloodletting in history.

What we have here is perhaps a fairly good example of the civilising process itself not being strong enough to discipline individual behaviour. Blood sports may have been a reaction to the rise of civility itself. On the eve of the next world war the German sociologist Norbert Elias, suspecting that the study of the unconscious in relation to violence was in need of urgent attention, called for a new science, 'historical psychology', which as yet did not exist. He was particularly critical of contemporary historians for believing that changes in thought, including the rise of liberalism, were caused by changes in the psychological disposition of individuals. In this respect, he reproached psychoanalysis as well for conceiving "the unconscious" as "an id without a history".[6]

Much of Elias's later work (written in England after he had fled from Nazi persecution in Germany) was about the weakness of civil society in internalising the prohibitions on violence that had previously been imposed from the outside—by the state. He wrote eloquent pages on the apparent internalised need for violent action, of which he found a particularly strong manifestation in sport.[7]

Freud, in his own study *Civilisation and Its Discontents,* had written at length about the same phenomenon, in psychological rather than sociological terms. Again, *Das Unbehagen in der Kultur,* the actual title of the book, roughly translates as "what makes us feel uncomfortable about culture". The civilising process, he contended, makes people unhappy by repressing their aggressive instincts. It impresses upon the citizen commandments that in the premodern world it would have been absurd to observe because they were at odds with human nature. To love one's neighbour as oneself is absurd; to love one's enemies impossible; to turn the other cheek, positively dangerous:

> The element of truth behind all this, which people are so ready to disavow, is that men are not gentle creatures who want to be loved, and who at most can defend themselves if they are attacked; they are, on the contrary, creatures among whose instinctual endowments is to be reckoned a powerful share of aggressiveness. As a result, their neighbour is for them . . . someone who tempts them to satisfy their aggressiveness on him, to exploit his capacity for work without compensation, to use him sexually without his consent, to seize his possessions, to humiliate him, to cause him pain, to torture and to kill him. *Homo homini lupus.*[8]

Those instincts are only contained, argued Freud, not because the state polices the citizen and punishes any attempt to challenge its own monopoly of violence, but because the social institutions that make up a civilisation make the citizen feel guilty about his innermost instincts. In a word, the citizen is *shamed* into behaving well. He is not restrained, he restrains himself by developing a guilty conscience. The civilising process disarms individual aggression and sets up within man a self-regulating agency "like a garrison in a conquered city".[9]

It is culture that produces guilt, though its instrumentality is not often acknowledged but expressed instead as an unconscious malaise or discontent for which people usually seek other explanations. In short, the disenchantment that the civilising process produces is inherent in the process itself. The price we pay for civilisation is a feeling of unhappiness, or permanent discontentment.

2. In the work of H. G. Wells I identified a quite widely held obsession with eliminating those who were different, who did not fit in, those who like the Eloi in *The Time Traveller* were too weak or too unthinking to save themselves from the Morlocks emerging from their subterranean kingdom at night. At the end of his life Wells despaired of a society whose deeply divided members seemed able to coexist only by threatening their own atomic destruction, a society that seemed intent on murdering itself.

By the turn of the century many other writers began to be aware of the pathological condition of their own age. What Jacques Le Rider says of the pre-1914 world also applies to life in the interwar years:

> The individual had been challenged to overcome with nothing but his own subjective resources problems which were far beyond his capacity. ... [He was] faced with the consequences and sometimes even the failure, of the great strategies of emancipation and with the slackening of the old bonds of cultural integration ... the crisis of the psychological whose "libidinal economy" ... was attempting to control conflicts which remained insoluble within social reality. The attempt could end in pathological upset.[10]

Economic stress in Weimar Germany produced a particularly vivid response to the threat to sexual identity, which in turn contributed to the rise of serial murder. The experience of war also seems to have lowered the threshold of what was deemed possible, altering the rules on both the domestic and fighting fronts in ways that few historians have begun to investigate systematically.

Among the evidence of a traumatised society that was troubled not only by defeat in war but also by the hyperinflation of the 1920s was society's response to the phenomenon: the projection of all negative, *a*social moral qualities such as lust and cowardice onto the murderers themselves. Their crimes were explained almost entirely in terms of the inner psychic life of the nation. From there it was not far to criminalising entire social groups or racial minorities. One reinforced the other, at least in the case of psychic stereotyping.[11]

3. In Shaw's play *The Simpleton of the Unexpected Isles* I also discussed a morality play that ends with the appearance of the Exterminating Angel, the Angel of Death, who heralds not the end of the world but the end of its childhood. The Angel promptly snuffs out the childish elements in life who will not grow up, the selfish, the mischievous, the bankers and the politicians. Was there not in the late bourgeois attitude to children something quite new in the history of infancy, a totalitarian insistence on transparency? Children were not only punished for failing to conform to adult standards of behaviour; they were also often made to forfeit any feeling of self-respect.

This was true even for the victims of totalitarianism like Anne Frank who spent two years with her family hiding from the Gestapo in a secret annex of a house in Amsterdam. Anne wanted to become a journalist and knew she would make a good one. She looked forward to the day of liberation when she could once again emerge into the outside world.

The very last words she wrote in her diary, her only expression of freedom in the closed world of the annex, the world of her own consciousness, show that she was hiding not only from the Germans but also, to some extent, from her own family as she experienced the pangs of adolescence: "I can't keep this up. If I am watched to that extent I start by getting snappy, then unhappy and finally I twist my heart round again so that the bad is on the outside and the good is on the inside and keep on trying to find a way of becoming what I would like to be".[12]

The phenomenology of self-address is still a subject in need of further study. In the twentieth century its main form was the journal and the autobiography. The latter, wrote the anarchist Herbert Read in the preface to his own account of his life, was the only way of establishing a man's individuality in the face of what he saw as the permeating power of a collective death wish.[13] Anne's world in the annex can serve as a metaphor for the childhood of many children in the modern age, who were punished for what they were 'on the outside' by parents who wished to remould them from 'the inside' in their own image.

The Archduke Franz Ferdinand and the Pathology of Hunting

An annual murder festival in Sarajevo. The population is dressed in the animal hides of Franz Ferdinand's victims. . . . On the corner the man playing Princip leaps out and shoots the mass murderer in the heart.
—Elias Canetti, *The Human Province* (1973)

In 1875 Marie Thurn-Hoffer, the daughter of Prince Eugen Hohenlog-Waldenburg, married Prince Alexander von Thurn und Taxis. It was a brilliant match. The prince was a gentleman of the old school, a competent violinist and a brilliant fencer. He was also a big game hunter and went on several hunting trips with the Archduke Franz Ferdinand, the heir of the Austrian-Hungarian emperor.

Thirty-four years later, in the summer of 1914, the archduke stayed as a guest at the prince's residence at Duino, on the Adriatic coast. Shortly afterwards he was assassinated by a Serbian nationalist, an event that precipitated the First World War.

One of the guests at Duino that summer recorded the visit of Lord Kitchener, who landed at Trieste on his way from Egypt, where he had been High Commissioner, bound for his next job—of which he had no inkling at the time—to become secretary of state for war. The two men met on a hunting trip:

> Two men of power who came to violent ends, not without a certain resemblance in their facial features and expressions. Kitchener's eyes had something of wounds in the flesh about them while the Archduke's gaze penetrated as though through the barrel of a rifle. He was a great killer of animals. It was said that he hoped to bring the number of those he'd shot up to a million. . . . Standing on the terrace, the two men no doubt looked across to the nearby Italian border with different if not contrasting emotions.[14]

In June 1916, while Marie Taxis watched through a telescope from her hotel balcony the destruction by Italian artillery of her Duino estate, Kitchener went down in the cruiser HMS *Hampshire* off the Orkneys, in the North Sea, en route to Russia.

No host could have been more cultured than the prince. He was used to the company of men like the poet Rilke. Yet he was also a ferocious huntsman. So too was Franz Ferdinand, who had come to Duino in 1914 hoping to bring his tally of 'kills' to a million. In retrospect, there was surely something deeply pathological about the European enthusiasm for hunting in the late nineteenth century, not so much its practice as its scale. It afforded an intimation of what on the killing ground of the western front was to become not the first but the most vivid example of serial death, or mechanised warfare. Whether the archduke killed his millionth animal or not, more than a million men lost their lives in the first year of a war that was fought ostensibly to avenge his assassination.

Virginia Woolf tells us that in the years before the war the average 'bag' of the Duke of Portland was 1,212 head of game for a day's shooting at Chatsworth. On the royal estate at Sandringham thirty years earlier there was a record slaughter.[15] On one November day (14 November 1896) 3,144 pheasants were shot. "I love shooting more than anything else", wrote the future heir to the British throne to his father George V. The following year on the Beaconsfield estate of Lord Burnham all previous royal records were shattered. "My left arm ached from lifting my gun, my shoulder from the recoil, and I was deaf and stunned from the banging", the young Edward VIII later recalled. They shot 4,000 pheasants that day. He recorded that his father was proud of the way he had shot that day, "but I think the scale of the bag troubled even his conscience".[16]

If blood sports were extensive in Europe, they were much more so in Africa, where the British congratulated themselves on their superior sportsmanship, compared, for example, with the Germans, whom they accused of hunting in a thoroughly unprofessional but 'methodical' manner, getting the Askaris or native bearers to fire volleys at herds of elephant or buffalo.[17]

Frequently in the descriptions of African life almost no reference is made to people. They are invisible, taken for granted, or dismissed as bearers or porters who have no other function but to assist in the organised hunts of their new masters. If in the Victorian imagination Africa may have been empty of people, it was never empty of game.

Take Charles John Anderson, who served his apprenticeship as an African explorer under Francis Galton, a scientist-explorer who was a cousin of Charles Darwin. In the late 1840s both men explored the unknown region of southwest Africa. When Galton returned home Anderson continued to hunt big game. In 1851 he organised an expedition to Lake Ngami, which had been discovered two years earlier by Livingstone. Reaching the lake, he pressed on north. His journey was remarkable, writes Frank McLynn, for his fanatical crusade against lions. There are lion hunting incidents on almost every page.[18]

Some of explorers, such as Henry Stanley and John Speke, had no interest other than game hunting. For his great expedition to Lake Victoria and beyond in the late 1860s Speke chose as his companion an unassuming Scotsman, James Grant, who besides being an amateur artist and expert botanist liked game hunting as much as Speke did. What such expeditions actually meant can be found in the experiences of the French explorer Paul Du Chaillu, who made three long journeys in the interior in the late 1850s and summed up his experiences as follows: "I travel always on foot and unaccompanied by other white men about 8,000 miles. I shot, stuffed and brought home over 3,000 birds, of which more than 60 are new species and I killed upward of a thousand quadrupeds, of which 200 were stuffed and brought home with more than 80 skeletons".[19] Du Chaillu's main claim to fame was that he was the first white man to observe—and shoot, of course—a gorilla, which he saw as the missing link in the story of human evolution, a claim that led to an outbreak of fighting in the halls of the Ethnological Society in London when he lectured there in 1861.

Possibly, an elephant named Pollux, a great favourite of the Parisians when it was displayed at the zoo, may well have been one of those Du Chaillu brought back from Africa. Its popularity did not prevent its being eaten during the siege of Paris in 1871. The de Goncourt brothers found his carcass on display at Ross's, the English butcher's shop on the Boulevard Haussmann, where it fetched 40 francs a pound.[20]

The instances of butchery are quite extraordinary in the writings of the period. Particularly horrific was a scene in the Sudan when hunters set the grass aflame and drove herds of elephant into the inferno.

> No resource for escape is left to the poor brutes. Driven by the flames into masses, they huddle together young and old, and they cover their bodies with grass, on which they pump water from their trunks as long as they can, but all in vain. They are ultimately either suffocated by the clouds of smoke or over-powered by the heat, or so miserably burnt that at long last they succumb to the fate that has been designed for them.[21]

A "war of annihilation", the author called it, in which neither young nor old, neither male nor female, were spared—and for what? "No other reply seems possible but what is given by the handle of our walking sticks, our billiard balls, our pianoforte keys, our combs and our fans, and other unimportant articles of the kind".

As McLynn observes, it would be anachronistic, of course, to expect late-twentieth-century attitudes to animal conservation to have been common among nineteenth-century African explorers or big game hunters. But a study of African exploration reveals a very clear dichotomy between the sportsmen like Samuel Baker and Speke and those with a genuine feeling for animals like Livingstone, Burton and Stanley. Burton despised Speke for his lust to kill, and Stanley severely reprimanded a fellow explorer for his hunting mania on the grounds that it was not an occupation to satisfy serious or intelligent minds.[22]

What are we to make of these blood sports? Nietzsche was among the first writers to suspect that the huge energy of the late Victorians was a sublimation for war, or a form of what Elias termed 'internalised violence'. The English, he wrote, had not renounced war. They had merely seized on a different means of "engendering their fading energies", those perilous journeys of discovery, navigation and mountain climbing which, though undertaken purportedly for scientific ends, were in effect a surrogate for other more martial pursuits.[23]

Nietzsche did not refer to blood sports by name, but he might as well have. Joseph Conrad (who was also not English) called them 'imbecile rapacity', the 'pitiless folly' of firing at every animal they saw. Conrad also identified the phenomenon as a need to expend surplus energy that would otherwise be repressed at home. In *Heart of Darkness,* he wrote, "There was an old hippo that had the bad habit of getting out on the bank and roaming at night over the station grounds. The pilgrims used to turn out in a body and empty every rifle they could lay hands on at him. . . . All this *energy* was wasted".[24]

Two German refugees had some interesting speculations on the phenomenon. The first, Erich Fromm, drew a distinction between what he termed 'elite' and 'traditional' hunting. Elite hunting, or killing for sport, included a certain amount of sadism characteristic of power elites. It tells us more about the psychology of the hunter than it does about the psychology of hunting. Fromm maintained that power over people (or in this case animals) was a compensation for the inability to be a complete person.[25] Certainly Africa attracted its fair share of Europeans who, having failed to impress themselves on their fellow countrymen at home, found in the Dark Continent a theatre to impress themselves on others—on animals and Africans alike.

In the course of his life Conrad was able to observe a certain type of individual who would engage in the wilful slaughter of animals or men (in their eyes not far removed from them). Possibly the model for Kurtz in *Heart of Darkness* was the German colonist Carl Peters, who openly admitted that he was fed up with being counted among the pariahs at home and "wanted to belong to a master race". Even Conrad's gentlemen like Axel Heyst are irresistibly attracted by a world in which they could do anything "in that great wild jungle without the law".

Perhaps that is what Stanley meant when he observed that the slaughter of wild animals was not an occupation for an intelligent person. Was this need for 'control' amplified in the late modern era? Did the inauthentic man suffer even greater alienation than in previous ages? As men appeared to lose control over life, as the industrial world transformed centuries-old traditions, did the need for self-assertion as self-affirmation increase correspondingly?

In Conrad's *Victory* the white interlopers appear to Heyst himself to be remarkably similar "to those myths current in Polynesia of amazing strangers who arrive at an island, gods or demons, bringing good or evil to the innocence of the inhabitants—gifts of unknown things, words never before heard". That too was the experience for many in Europe of the industrial age, that "fantastic invasion" of technology and social forces that promised both good and evil, light and darkness, salvation and damnation. Africa gave such men a chance to remake the world anew in their own image, to take possession of it—or if they could not, then to "exterminate all the brutes", Kurtz's last injunction. So too, perhaps, the more indiscriminate hunters could slaughter the game even if they could not impress themselves on the jungle.

Elias also has some interesting observations on blood sports in another discussion of the civilising process and the way in which societies had internalised violent passions. If despite society's rules against the use of physical violence, violence in sport was still real, it was increasingly hedged in by rules and conventions. Tight rules in boxing were introduced, for example, and competitors matched according to weight. Gentlemen promoted contests between working-class professional fighters at the same time as they took up the sport themselves in place of duels.

Elias was not surprised that sport had been taken up most avidly of all in a country that by the nineteenth century was a parliamentary democracy. Indeed, the very word was English. He linked the process of 'sportisation' with that of 'politicisation', with the manner in which political conflicts, like sporting contests, were now played out according to agreed rules, the 'rules of the game'.[26]

Even the sport of fox hunting was transformed in the public imagination. The idea of shooting a fox, which had been quite common in the eighteenth century, was made impermissible. The point was not killing so much as the pleasure of the chase. The sport, in other words, was taken out of the hands of the huntsmen and given by proxy to the hounds. Later the hunter absented himself even from that. In the novels of R. S. Surtees and Anthony Trollope the kill is never mentioned. The purpose of the hunt was to make it less easy to kill the fox; it now became a professional sport for hunters, with some risk to horsemen and horses alike.

What changed in the nineteenth century was the expressive or instrumental violence of sport. The emphasis was less on the kill than on competition and achievement. Big game hunting, by contrast, was entirely about the kill. It had no instrumental value and observed no rules. It was also ultimately nihilistic, for it depleted the stock of victims and threatened the continuation of the sport. The dangers that were attendant upon it, if the prey was hunted too closely, also met the need for manliness and heroism that other field sports could not.

The vogue for blood sports may or may not have anticipated the bloodlust that was only satiated in 1914. What is interesting is that many British soldiers initially saw war in sporting terms. Take, for example, Richard Meinertzhagen. As Elspeth Huxley wrote of him, the tally of slaughtered animals presented in his journals in such astonishing abundance is nauseating. "He had only to see an animal, provided he was reasonably sure it was a male, only to shoot it".

Meinertzhagen was the first to admit that he had been possessed of an "unashamed bloodlust" while serving in Africa. But, he added, it had kept him alive later in life: "After all, the hunting of men—war, is but a form of hunting wild animals and on many occasions during the First World War I thanked my God that I had learned several tricks of my trade when hunting wild and dangerous game".[27]

One of the first British experts of this trade was Hesketh Pritchard: "The smallest of big game animals do not present a smaller mask as the German face so sniping becomes the highest of all forms of rifle shooting".[28] The best weapon in the trenches was accurate to a range of 600 yards. Men worked in pairs. An observer using a 20× telescope worked out the ranges. The ammunition was hand-picked, with each bullet carefully prepared. Only one shot was possible at a time. On a good day snipers could fill a large bag. One man killed six Germans and wounded ten in a week. One First World War diary entry reads:

> December 9, 1915. Hazy. Cool. One leaning against tree. Tué. One 50 yards right. Fell across log. Shot 3 successive helpers. . . . December 16, 1916. Clear. Fire. Good hunting. 16 good shots. 7 known hits and feel sure of 4 more.

The British congratulated themselves on being amateur marksmen rather than professional sportsmen. The Germans did not, training specialists to do the job for them. They continued nevertheless to observe some of the amateur spirit for which their enemies were famous. One British officer was shot by a German marksman waving a signboard that read "87 not out".[29]

Desmond Young, who served at Cambrai at the same time as Ernst Jünger, took the latter's account of the battle as evidence of "how the German soldier has always taken war with a seriousness with which only sport is treated by the British".[30] In our postmodern age, of course, in which the citizen is no longer called up, sport has become even more of a sublimation of war. Today many sports writers might concur with Umberto Eco's belief that pent-up aggression is best expressed through sport rather than on the battlefield.

> I must say that I am not against the passion for soccer. On the contrary, I approve of it and consider it providential. Those crowds of fans, cut down by heart attacks in the grandstands, those referees who pay for a Sunday of fame by personal exposure to grievous bodily harm, those excursionists who climb, bloodstained from the buses, wounded by shattered glass from windows smashed by stones, those celebrating young men who speed drunkenly through the streets in the evening, their banners poking from the overloaded Fiat Cinquecento, until their crash into a juggernaut truck, those athletes physically ruined by piercing sexual abstinences, those families financially destroyed after succumbing to inane saltpeters, those enthusiasts whose cannon crackers explode and blind them. They fill my heart with joy. I am in favour of soccer passion as I am in favour of drag racing, of competition between motorcycles on the edge of a cliff, and wild parachute jumping, mystical mountain climbing, crossing oceans in rubber dinghies, Russian roulette and the use of narcotics. Races improve the race, and all of these games lead fortunately to the death of the best, allowing mankind to continue its existence serenely with normal protagonists of average achievement. In a certain sense I could agree with the Futurists that war is the only hygiene of the world except for one little correction. It would be if only volunteers were allowed to wage it. But unfortunately, war also involves the reluctant, and therefore, it is morally inferior to spectator sports.[31]

Moosbrugger, Serial Murder and the Enemy Within

If mankind could dream collectively, it would dream of Moosbrugger.
—Robert Musil, *The Man Without Qualities* (1942)

Perhaps the most famous serial murderer in twentieth-century literature is the carpenter Moosbrugger, who appears as one of the central characters of Robert Musil's novel *The Man Without Qualities*. A big man with enormous strength, Moosbrugger is also a psychopath, a mentally subnormal killer who murders a prostitute in a particularly horrifying manner. In the longest chapter of his introduction Musil traces in some detail the man's early life, that of an apparently decent, good-natured citizen.

The most striking feature of Moosbrugger as a man is the discrepancy between his quiet, modest appearance and the nature of his crime. It is his previously unblemished record that lies at the heart of the enigma that the carpenter poses: How responsible is he for his actions? A society that is none too healthy itself is embarrassed by the question.

A central theme in Musil's book is its hero's fascination for sex killers as a group. Are they quite as unusual as society would like to think? What astonishes Ulrich most is how alike he and Moosbrugger are, at least in his own eyes. Moosbrugger, Ulrich concludes, is the embodiment of the repressed urge common to all, the incarnation of everybody's fantasy about committing murder. Repression would appear to be the key:

> Well then, let those who believe themselves justified in doing so deal with him in their own way. Let them try him and condemn him and so re-establish the balance of their morality. . . .
>
> The split in him [Ulrich] was different. It lay precisely in the fact that he represented nothing and so could not help seeing that what the murderer's image faced him with something no stranger, or any less familiar, than any other image in the world and every one of them was just like his old image of himself.[32]

Ulrich's ruminations are prompted by his own distaste for a prostitute who accosts him in the street. After the incident he begins to understand how Moosbrugger's rage could have been triggered by a single incident, by a simple importuning in the street, just as Europe itself went to war in a sudden frenzy in the summer of 1914.

Is Moosbrugger sane? Is he a man whose madness frees him from moral responsibility, or is he in fact responsible for his actions? A similar question was asked about Europe after the First World War: Was the war so rationally planned that there had to be reason behind it despite its apparent insanity, or had the insanity been there all the time? Was the solid citizen before he became a murderer, the man who avoids prostitutes (and is egged on to commit his crime), really murderous? Had he succeeded for years in hiding his true character? Did the structure of early-twentieth-century Europe with its class divisions and social conflicts merely hide an innate pathological condition?

Such questions were posed in a particularly telling way not in Vienna but in Berlin. According to the Russian writer Ilya Ehrenburg, "hardly a month passed" in Weimar Germany "without some terrible murder becoming known".[33] Real Moosbruggers proliferated in the 1920s at an alarming rate.

Indeed, Weimar Germany was distinguished by a striking number of sexually motivated killings, particularly gruesome examples of what the Germans at the time euphemistically called *Lustmord*. The most famous were carried out by four serial murderers whose crimes were among the nastiest of the century. The extent to which they penetrated contemporary consciousness can be seen in the paintings and drawings of George Grosz and Otto Dix, both of whom painted the cities in which they lived as abattoirs, brothels or free-range lunatic asylums. Their pictures are populated by terrifyingly disfigured veterans, rampaging idiots, drug addicts, uniformed thugs and, apparently untroubled by the chaos raging outside, hard-faced industrialists and petty clerks. Grosz and Dix were only the most famous painters who found a compelling theme in the murders of the time. Rudolf Schlichter and Karl Hubbuch also painted pictures of rapes, slayings and murders that provide a fascinating testimony to the way artists gravitated to murder as a theme.

"O country of opposites and extremes", declares the narrator of Yvan Goll's *Sodom Berlin* as he reflects on Germany's place in history, a country that had produced the poet Friedrich Hölderlin and the psychopath Fritz Haarmann, one the model of self-sacrifice, the other the sacrificer of other people. Both were linked by blood: Hölderlin who opened his veins, and Haarmann who drank the blood of the young boys he killed. Berlin was the city were the two pathologies converged.[34]

Such correspondences came to the mind of a number of other writers of the time. In the early 1930s Thomas Mann's son found himself sitting across from Hitler at the Carlton tea rooms in Munich. He suddenly remembered whom he resembled:

> It was that sex murderer in Hanover, whose case had made such huge headlines. ... His name was Haarmann ... the likeness between him and Hitler was striking. The sightless eyes, the moustache, the brutal and nervous mouth, even the unspeakable vulgarity of the fleshy nose; it was indeed, precisely the same physiognomy.[35]

Berlin was not the only city that witnessed an outbreak of serial murders of the 1920s. A contemporary of Mann's suggested that Hanover, the scene of the grisly murders of Fritz Haarmann, should erect a monument to him. For had he not illustrated the enigma of the entire German nation? Was he not a 'lightning flash' that revealed the state-sanctioned serial killings that were soon to come?

What gave these gruesome murders such resonance in the popular mind was the extent to which the criminal dimension of life had been politicised at the end of the previous century. Criminals, wrote one mid-nineteenth-century writer were a race apart—"another people ... with its own habits, instincts and morals". Such celebrated phrenologists as Cesare Lombroso contended that many of the characteristics of the savage could be found in the criminal psychology and that "criminal anthropology" permitted the identification of this kind of criminal through such features as their "low cranial capacity ... prognathism ... anomalies of the ear ... and relative insensitivity to pain".[36]

Once criminality was identified in a person or an entire ethnic group it had to be purged if society were not to be poisoned or polluted. Crime, for the first time, came to be seen as a unique social problem that could only be eradicated by political means. Criminal anthropologists even went as far to identify criminals as a distinct race. They were prompted to do so by the discovery of Africa, which led to the rediscovery of themselves. As Claude Lévi-Strauss once wrote, the anthropologist is always in danger of becoming the object of his own observation. In the case of the Europeans, they saw in African 'savages' their own degenerate citizens—men who had relapsed into an earlier state of indigence. Criminal societies, wrote Lambroso, were distinguished like African tribes by

> the improvised rules of criminal gangs, the entirely personal influence of the chiefs; the custom of tattooing; the not uncommon cruelty of their games; the excessive use of gestures; the onomatopoeic language with the personification of the inanimate thing; and a special literature recording heroic times when crimes were celebrated and thought tended to cloak itself in rhythmic form.[37]

In addition, criminals were recognised by their long jaws, flattened noses and scanty beards and other peculiarities that supposedly denoted a reversion to savagery. Such thinking gave rise to the most bizarre theories. During the First World War one French anthropologist claimed that the entire German nation could be distinguished by its anatomical features. The Germans, wrote Edgar Berillon in 1915, were prone to excessive defecation and body odour, which gave them away whenever they engaged in spying, especially when masquerading as citizens of Alsace.[38]

Perhaps it was not entirely coincidental that Weimar Germany should have been the first mass society to produce serial killers in large numbers, men like Wilhelm Grossmann or the equally infamous Karl Denke. Grossmann was tried for the murder and cannibalism of fourteen women. Denke, "the mass murderer of Münsterberg", carried out thirteen murders over a period of twenty years until he was jailed on suspicion of murder. He committed suicide before he could be tried.

These murders were considered to be symptomatic of an intense social psychosis. Many newspapers covering the trials were more concerned with the threat of 'criminal contagion' than trying to understand the personal circumstances that had led to the murderers' actions. After the trial of one of the killers, Theodor Lessing claimed that many Germans were convinced that they had become a psychotic race, poisoned by a hideous epidemic that had previously been unknown. Lessing himself tried hard to rise above the trial, to challenge the theory that the killings were the result of a social malaise rather than the pathology of a single murderer. But he too entered into the discourse of contagion when he suggested that the only way the community could come to terms with the situation was to turn the physical violence that had been directed at the victims against the murderer himself, by allowing the mothers of the murdered youths to break through the bars and despatch him themselves as an unorthodox form of catharsis.[39]

Weimar Germany apparently had an urgent need to designate its murderers as psychopathological cases, a break with the norm, to call men monstrous rather than ill and so obscure the source of their pathology—society itself. The murders of Fritz Haarmann were considered doubly grave because he was a homosexual and his victims were homeless young men. Homosexuals of course were among the first people to be sent to the concentration camps in Hitler's Germany. Their crime was not only to be sexual outsiders but also 'corrupters' of youth. Once they were classified as criminals their fate was sealed.

In a long speech in November 1937 Himmler explained what should be done with them. In the old days, he reminded his SS audience, they had been drowned in swamps, with no feeling of hate or revenge on the part of the executioner. The punishment was 'natural'. The victims sank of their own weight into the swamp. No human hand held them down. So, wrote George L. Mosse, the outsider was simply "snuffed out", and if that actual mode of execution in the early 1940s could no longer be reproduced, during the Holocaust at least the language could be recycled. The Jews too were snuffed out or extinguished, their memory eradicated as though they had never existed. They too were to drown "without human assistance", to be asphyxiated in the gas chambers of Auschwitz.[40]

Was it also coincidental that the serial killers even anticipated the industrial nature of the holocaust? In the flat of Karl Denke the police found barrels of smoked human flesh, crates of human bones and jars of human lard. Denke had even set up a modest business in cured meat. Brecht believed that he had the measure of the age when he described the crimes as "the processing of victims", the recycling of meat, using the most modern industrial methods. Denke, he added,

> killed people in order to use their corpses. He cured the meat and made soup from the fat, buttons from the bones and purses from the skins. He placed his business on a scientific footing and was extremely surprised when, after his apprehension, he was sentenced to be executed.
>
> I contend that the people of Germany, those who condemn Denke, fail to recognise the qualities of true German genius the fellow displayed . . . namely, method, conscientiousness, cold-bloodedness and the ability to place one's every act on a firm, philosophical foundation . . . they should have made him a PhD.[41]

As a Marxist, of course, Brecht saw Denke's murders as an illustration, if a perverse one, of the capitalist mode of production. If we read his work as an anticipation of what was to come, however, we may treat it a little more seriously. Haarmann too had "recycled" his corpses, cleaned his victims' clothes and sold them for cash, and even boiled down and potted their flesh for sale. Only by pure chance was he apprehended: when the mother of one of his victims recognised the jacket his landlady's son was wearing as the one she had bought for her own son.

As I suggested in the first chapter of this book, ideas are "in the air". Private and public actions are not easily distinguished. Patterns of behaviour, even pathological ones, reflect the consciousness of the time. One way of coping with fear is to escape into another fear that offers more security. Fear was one of the defining themes of the modern age. Before the First World War people feared the possibility of revolution or social conflict. After the war they feared the state's "finding them out" and sending them once again to the front. European society also produced its own unique fears—fear of the enemy within. It was a fear that could take many forms—fear of the heretic, the fifth columnist, the traitor or the outsider or simply the Jew.

What distinguished the modern age was that it transformed an occasional danger that was more or less threatening into a permanent nightmare all the more terrifying because enemies could not always be identified—the fellow traveller, or the assimilated Jew, or the carpenter turned murderer, a serial killer—an enemy of society, a Moosbrugger rather than a Raskolnikov.

The German people were in that sense prepared for the horrors to come long before Hitler made a public appearance. It is that anticipation that historians continue to find so fascinating about the rise of national socialism. Indeed, one of Hitler's most chilling remarks was in a speech he made in the late 1930s in which he pointed out, with disarming frankness, the extraordinary circumstances in which, out of so many millions, the German people had discovered him, and how he, in turn, had discovered them. Was this not another example of the discovery finding the discoverer?

Child Abuse in Fin-de-Siècle Vienna and the Totalitarian Mentality

At the next corner . . . I saw a little girl run into the street in front of a van. Her mother stood petrified on the other side of the street until the girl ran up to her unscathed. Then she grabbed her by the arm and gave her a spanking. The child howled with pain, her eyes were slits, her mouth a perfect square. It was only too obvious. Fear or no fear, mother was taking her revenge. And if motherhood is the pride of humanity, what must the rest of us be like?
—M. Ageyev, *Novel with Cocaine* (1919)

Child abuse is a relatively recent social phenomenon, at least in polite society. Long before it was suspected to exist, of course, the same societies had done little to prevent physical cruelty to children, to prohibit their being sent down mines or forced into factories to work. Indeed, in the 1840s Schopenhauer found cruelty to children so widespread that he was moved to ask whether "the admitted necessity for a so anxiously guarded European balance of power" did not already contain a confession that "man is a beast of prey which will pounce upon a weaker neighbour as soon as he notices his existence".[42]

'Child abuse', however, as we understand the term today, was not discussed publicly until 1962 with the publication of an article entitled 'The Battered Child Syndrome', which appeared in the *Journal of the American Medical Association*. Since then hardly a year has passed when it has not been aired in court cases, newspaper articles and television documentaries. It has become part of our contemporary consciousness.

In Vienna at the turn of the century this was certainly not the case. That is why the reporting of a series of court cases about child battering and murder proved so sensational. Four of them form the case studies of an excellent book on the century's-end Viennese mind, *Postcards from the End of the World* by Larry Wolff. For the social critic Karl Kraus, the cases were merely another indication that Europe was heading for perdition. Where Vienna led, the world would follow; Vienna, he said, had become "an experimental laboratory for the end of the world".[43]

The second of Wolff's studies involves two parents, Juliane and Josef Hummel, who came to court accused of murdering their five-year-old daughter Anna. The body, which had been examined six months before, was described for the public in excruciating detail at the trial—a tear on the left ear, another laceration cutting through the upper jaw, the front teeth missing, a collarbone and a seventh rib broken. The third, fourth and fifth fingers of both hands were deformed, and there were countless abrasions on the forehead, cheeks, chin, nose, arms and thighs. At her death the emaciated body of the young girl weighed only twenty pounds. In reporting the Hummel case, one newspaper accused the parents of being "dedicated to the destruction of the five-year-old girl", an accusation that troubled a society that never before had come to terms with the extent of child abuse in its midst.

What were the facts of the case? Josef Hummel was a day labourer who worked in a laundry; Juliane his wife did the washing and ironing. Anna, their first child, had been born out of wedlock and sent off for care. Only after Josef and Juliane married and had a second child was Anna returned to her parents. They were reported to the authorities for excessively punishing their daughter when she was only four, a year before she died. Thereafter Juliane told a friend that they had beaten the child in such a way as to avoid visible bruising.

The public response showed how unaware it was of the conditions of the slums that produced child abuse—overcrowding and malnutrition as well as the fact that doctors were too expensive to call in case of serious illness. The only middle-class witness called by the prosecution, a doctor who testified to the condition of the corpse, would never have come across the child while she was alive. One witness testified that she had reported the child's condition to the police four times but they had never bothered to check the story. Only her death had brought them out.

The jury was told about the child's fate in harrowing detail: how she had often been tied to a tree and beaten, how her mother had poured hot water over her hands or in winter forced her to stand in cold water barefoot. The parents insisted that the abuse was no more than discipline. Their defence was that the death of their child was an accident, not murder. The prosecution attributed the excessive punishment to evidence of murderous intent. The jury unanimously agreed. The couple were condemned to death.[44]

The Hummels came from the underclass in Vienna, a class that the bourgeoisie rarely encountered or even read about in their papers. It was a class, however, that Hitler knew well. In *Mein Kampf* he wrote, rather movingly, not about child abuse so much as the suffering of children amidst the social misery of Viennese poverty:

> Imagine, for instance, the following scene:
> In a basement apartment consisting of two stuffy rooms dwells a worker's family of seven. Among the five children there is a boy of, let us assume, three years. This is the age in which the first impressions are made on the consciousness of the child. Talented persons retain traces of memory from this period down to advanced old age. . . . At the age of six the pitiable little boy suspects the existence of things which can inspire even an adult with nothing but horror.

The conditions in which the children of the urban proletariat lived and were brought up may have been their redeeming quality—or more likely an extension of his own experience as an unloved son of a petty bourgeois family denied love by his father and subjected to excessive discipline whenever his drunken father deemed that he had misbehaved.[45]

Hitler himself was not born into the Viennese underclass. But he drifted into it by chance; he came to know it well. The experience seems to have been a traumatic one. He was an outcast, a tramp, an alienated individual who formed no friendships with others. As a man he was possessed of a dream, "the need of the outsider to be let in".[46]

Another Bohemian who wrote at length about the phenomenon of child abuse, this time psychological rather than physical, was Franz Kafka, who experienced a particularly unhappy childhood. In one of his most famous letters, a manuscript consisting of forty-five typewritten pages written in November 1919, he set out in detail the reasons for the troubled relationship between him and his father. He wrote of a "sense of nothingness that often dominates me", which he traced to his father's influence. He vividly recalled one occasion when his father picked him up and left him outside on the balcony to stop him crying: "Even years afterwards I suffered from the tormenting fancy that the huge man, my father, the *ultimate authority,* would come almost for *no reason at all* ... to carry me out onto the balcony".[47]

He then went on to detail his father's obsession with his own authority; he was a man who could maintain his own self-esteem only by putting others down:

> You were capable, for instance, of running down the Czechs, and then the Germans and then the Jews and what is more, not only selectively, but in every respect and finally there was no one left but yourself. For me you took on the enigmatic quality that all tyrants have whose rights are based on their person and not on their ideas.

In a later passage Kafka added:

> Hence the world was for me divided in three parts: one in which I, the slave, lived under laws that had been invented only for me and which I could, I did not know why, never completely comply with: and a second world which was infinitely remote from mine, in which you lived, concerned with government, with the issuing of orders and with annoyance about their not being obeyed. ... I was continually in disgrace; either I obeyed your orders and that was a disgrace for they applied after all only to me, or I was defiant, and that too was a disgrace, for how could I presume to defy you, or I could not obey because for instance I had not your strength, your appetite or your skill, in spite of which you expected it of me as a matter of course: this was, of course, the greatest disgrace of all.[48]

In these circumstances it is not surprising that Kafka concluded, "I had lost my self-confidence where you were concerned and in its place had acquired a boundless sense of guilt".

As Elias Canetti adds, of all writers in the twentieth century Kafka is the most representative because he was preoccupied with the century's main theme—power and one of its central motifs: the humiliation of the man who victimises himself.[49] In *The Trial* Joseph K. is told that the court requires nothing from him. It will receive him when it wishes and dismiss him when he goes. K. protests against his treatment and tries many different ways of influencing the progress of his case, but he never tries simply walking away. And when at the end a group of what appear to be third-rate actors haul him off for execution, he takes care to steer them away from a policeman who might have intervened to save him.

In one of Kafka's most powerful short stories, 'In the Penal Colony', the image of the condemned man and his chains is epitomised in one sentence: "In any case the condemned man looked so like a submissive dog that one might have thought he could be left to run free on the surrounding hills and would only need to be whistled for when the execution was due to begin".[50]

Perhaps it was a uniquely Jewish experience, or rather one felt most intensely by Jews, at the turn of the century. The most famous Jewish victim of the time, Alfred Dreyfus, had also, like Joseph K., been summoned unexpectedly to a meeting at 9:00 A.M., arrested for a crime of which he was innocent, and stripped of his insignia until his tattered uniform looked like the rags of the Wandering Jew. He was mocked by journalists for his Jewish physiognomy, and he was kept in chains on Devil's Island—a form of physical torture. The importance of Dreyfus's fate in Kafka's imagination can be inferred from his story 'In the Penal Colony', in which the torture machine is located on a French-speaking island in the Tropics, the machine that inscribes on the prisoner's back the crime of which he is accused, the crime of existence, of posing as a man that he is not—the Jew as a Frenchman.

What we find in these two instances of childhood, that of the abuse of the underprivileged child and that of the humiliation of privileged children in middle-class households, is something that echoes the totalitarian mentality that found its political expression in the middle years of the twentieth century.

In the case of the bourgeois family we can also see some of the features of a totalitarian state—the presumption of guilt (rather than innocence); the arbitrary power of the state, or of the father; the humiliation of the citizen, or the of child, to the point of even encouraging self-victimisation. And in Kafka's letter we find something else—the idea that freedom is merely a stay of execution. In *The Trial* the painter Tironelli reminds Joseph K. that even if he is acquitted and allowed to walk out of the court a free man he is only "ostensibly free, or more exactly, provisionally free. For the judges of the lowest grade haven't the power to grant a final acquittal; that power is reserved for the highest court of all, which is quite inaccessible to you, to me and to all of us. What the prospects are up there we do not know and, I may say, do not want to".

In other words, guilt had become existential. No crime needed to be identified since it was a crime to be alive. It was a feeling that many children were encouraged to experience for themselves, constantly reminded, as they were, that they were always in the wrong. If guilt was boundless, if nothing a child ever did seemed to please its parents (whom the child rarely saw anyway), and if in addition the child had no way of finding out why he had been punished, how could he develop any confidence in himself as an authentic person with a separate identity of his own?

We may take as evidence of the first the extent to which social misfits were defined as children. One writer talked of applying "the often repeated comparison of savages to children in their moral and intellectual condition".[51] For Jeremy Bentham criminals were "flawed children, persons of unsound mind", from which it did not take much of an intellectual leap to conclude that children were really criminals.[52] Edith Balfour, on visiting

Ireland, concluded that the Irish were still children listening to old fairy tales: "They are like children who are afraid to walk alone, who play with fire, who are helpless; like children who will not grow up". The childhood status of the Irish mind in English thinking suggested the only remedy, that applied to unruly children.[53]

Even the need to control the masses, one of the persistent themes of the age, was often justified in terms of childhood. In *The Crowd* Gustave Le Bon, while acknowledging that some crowds could act morally, insisted that they tended in the main to display childlike features: "impulsiveness, irritability at reasoning, absence of judgement . . . exaggeration of sentiments". In an analysis twenty-five years later, Freud congratulated Le Bon for pointing out the similarity between the crowd and children, for pointing out that "in groups the most contradictory ideas can exist side by side and tolerate each other without any conflict arising from the logical contradiction between them". In his eyes this was typical of "the unconscious mental life" of a child.[54]

In similar vein H. G. Wells imagined the masses as a "vacillating crowd of children", not adults or equal men. Like children they tended to be victims like Mr. Kipps: "I see through the darkness the soul of my Kippses as they are . . . little ill-nourished ailing ignorant children . . . children who feel pain, who are naughty and muddled and suffer and do not understand the reason why".[55]

What is especially interesting is that in war soldiers were frequently seen as children too. Siegfried Sassoon described how his own life was changed by the expression of total trust and self-surrender visible in the faces of his men, looking up at him as they squatted cross-legged while he inspected their feet after a long route march.[56] As so often in his response to the war he deceived himself, for he would have known at first hand that soldiers were not treated like favoured sons. They were shouted at on parade and in the field, constantly humiliated and reduced to a condition where they were amenable to almost any command. Off the drill square their unimportance as individuals was a constant theme. To ram the point home, they ate out of enamel bowls without knives or forks, and then only after being forced to engage in a free-for-all in a stampede to the cookhouse.[57]

As with children, it was also considered best to keep them busy. They were constantly engaged in endless patrols and reconnaissance missions to keep them "up to the mark". Even in the more enlightened 1940s they were occupied most of the time. In Italy in 1944 British forward companies would send out one fighting patrol of about fifteen men every night, and soldiers could expect to take part in such ventures every nine or ten days.[58]

By the time the Cold War set in, an entire society found itself being treated like children. One of the most famous child psychiatrists of the century was Melanie Klein. If Freud discovered the repressed child in the adult,

Klein discovered the infant, or what was already repressed in the child. Inner states of consciousness, she maintained, were more important than outer ones. The relationships we form are always structured by internal, unconscious fantasies and desires that mediate our experience of the external world.

For Klein the centre of the infant's experience was the death drive, an anxiety generated by the threat that governs an infant's development. In 1946 she wrote that the "anxiety that arises from the operation of the death instinct within the child is felt as a fear of annihilation (death) and takes the form of fear of persecution". She went on to argue that we are all born with death in our hearts, that destructiveness and aggression are simply part of the human condition. The anxiety that the threat of annihilation produces often leads to defensive strategies or strategies of survival in which our destructive feelings are projected onto the external world, which thus becomes the source of persecution. Childhood helps the child come to terms with these feelings. Bonding with parents leads to a wider bonding with society. The potential for destructiveness that lies within every individual can be contained by social relationships.

The problem in the Kleinian universe is that the external environment is not always supportive enough to allow a progression from the paranoid schizoid to depressive reconciliation. There is a danger of disintegration, "of the return to primordial childhood". Our persecutory fantasies may have internal origins, but if they are confirmed by the brutality of the outside world they will be even more powerful. The upshot will invariably be the disintegration of the personality. A man will revert to childhood, or remain a child, his development half aborted.[59]

Klein's ideas today are widely challenged within the profession. I cite them because they were formulated in the late 1940s: in the age of nuclear deterrence, the ultimate totalitarian experience. They may, as Stephen Frosh has noted, seem bizarre and unbelievable, but they do possess the ability to convey an experience of the modern world that was in itself bizarre and unbelievable, a world that included such stark, unqualified images of destruction as Auschwitz and Hiroshima.[60]

With regard to the Final Solution, Bruno Bettelheim (a child psychologist himself), who had experienced life in the concentration camps of Dachau and Buchenwald, described the purpose behind the creation of an extreme situation. The arrests, torture and confinement were a deliberate attempt to "make the prisoners like children", to accelerate the transformation of adults into adolescents.[61] After Germany's defeat the philosopher Karl Jaspers warned the Allies that in the course of twelve years of national socialism the German people had been reduced to the status of children whose judgement was unformed. As a people, they could no longer be trusted with their own future.[62]

The dilemma did not end with Hitler's defeat. It was carried over into the postwar world. The division of Germany in 1945 was meant to be temporary. Its permanence helped to underline the impermanence of the peace. In the Cold War that followed, the horror of childhood reasserted itself in the popular imagination. All the terms that Melanie Klein identified in childhood—'a balance of terror', 'anxiety', 'the need for social containment', above all 'self-discipline'—were terms that were frequently used in the discourse of nuclear deterrence.

What conclusions can we reach on the basis of the preceding discussion? Perhaps we can see the illiberal conscience as a manifestation of an existential need: to declare 'open season' on certain nations or races; to punish the criminal element in society by methods similar to, but far different in scope from those of the serial murderers themselves in 1920s Germany; to articulate a totalitarian mentality that sought to treat citizens as errant children rather than responsible adults. In the case of hunting, the analogy between the mass slaughter of animals and the even greater slaughter of people at the front a few years later was noted even at the time. Blood sports did indeed appear to writers like Nietzsche to be a sublimation for the real thing: war.

Child abuse also revealed that all known forms of civil society are plagued by endogenous sources of incivility, especially in the home. We have become inured to what our own generation calls 'family violence'. The fact that liberal societies do not go to war as often as others and rarely against each other should not disguise the fact that domestic incivility seems to be a chronic feature of civil societies, one of their normal conditions, and therefore a chronic obstacle to their complete 'civilisation'.[63]

Serial murder—or more precisely the response to the phenomenon in Germany—reflected two dimensions of the same phenomenon. Social crime was seen as a virus poisoning the body politic. It was a virus that had to be isolated quickly, especially in the eyes of those writers who regarded politics in pathological terms. Ideas and images were thought to spread through the masses by means of contagion, an automatic process that produced a state of transitory madness in the multitudes of Europe's overcrowded cities, one that made them peculiarly susceptible to the ideologies of extremist political movements, which in turn tried to unmask the enemy within.

I have cited Kafka as one of a select number of writers who anticipated many of these trends. But it is important to recognise that he lived and wrote from "an inner plight", a constant tension that fed his imaginative universe. In a diary entry in early February 1922 he wrote: "Looked at with a primitive eye the real, incontestable truth, a truth marred by no external circumstances (martyrdom, sacrifice of oneself for the sake of another) is only physical pain".[64] In a letter to Max Brod in the same year, 1922, he wrote: "I have been dashing about or sitting as petrified as a desperate animal in his burrow. Enemies everywhere".[65]

Kafka, however, had no interest in political causes. He did not see politics as a source of relief, as a strategy for avoiding internal anxiety. He chose to confront his demons on his own. They continued to haunt him until the end of his life precisely because they could not be identified or explained. The sense of guilt that tortured him to the end remained unspecified in his writings. He considered it a natural condition of being.

Many others, however, were encouraged to confront the violence of modern life by externalising their anxieties. Many were receptive to external explanations of their plight. Many others sought and found simplistic explanations for their alienation that often provoked them to think in terms of violent solutions in political life.

The Identity Crisis and European Nationalism

We have, whether we like it or not, to realise our 'personage', our vocation, our vital programme, our 'entelechy'—there is no lack of names for the terrible reality which is our authentic 'I'.
—José Ortega y Gasset, *The Dehumanisation of Art and Other Writings on Art and Culture* (1956)

If the modern age was deeply interested in the unconscious, it had to be. What we are discussing is a feature of modernity, the internalisation of experience. In the course of the nineteenth century consciousness changed in a way that distinguished the classical from the modern mind. It became ego related. The modern identity was marked by what the philosopher Charles Taylor has called 'the inner horizon' of man. It was characterised by a set of inner drives and goals, or destinies and aspirations. Identity became highly reflective as subjective experience became the cornerstone of reality. The emphasis on subjective experience as the arbiter of reality meant not only that identity became more strongly individuated but also that the narrative form most expressive of the modern sense of self was the confession, the diary or the autobiography.

Late-nineteenth-century authors spent a great deal of time trying to understand themselves in the hope of imposing some order on the chaos of their subjective growth. As a theme, that is what is most telling in such seminal works as Nietzsche's *Genealogy of Morals* and Dostoyevsky's novels, in particular *The Possessed*. Kierkegaard's probing, in turn, both foreshadowed and influenced Freud's theories of the subconscious.

One interesting aspect of the Hummel trial, however, is the fact that Freud, who was at that time engaged in writing his book *The Interpretation of Dreams*, ignored the case completely, as he did the three other cases of child abuse that Wolff discussed in *Postcards from the End of the World*. The omission is striking, for he was quite prepared to propose the contrary idea—that children wish the death of their parents. He also anticipated the response of his readers, the denial that they had ever had such a thought themselves. "We must distinguish", he pleaded, "between what the cultural standards of filial piety demand of this relationship and what everyday observation shows it, in fact, to be. More than one occasion for hostility lies concealed in the relations between parents and children".[66]

The Interpretation of Dreams was not received favourably at the time. Only 350 or so copies were sold in the first six years of publication. But the book soon became one of the key texts in the establishment of psychology and psychoanalysis as reputable scientific professions. Its publication marked the transition from the energy of the nineteenth century to the painful introspection of the twentieth. Until then the interest in dreams was determined by the insight they were supposed to provide into the future. With Freud dreams became important no longer in terms of prediction but in the analysis of the dreamer's character. They were no longer of interest for what they said about the future but for what they revealed about the past. They were seen to be crucial in confronting the difficulty of reconciling past certainties with the desperate uncertainty of modern life.

In retrospect the historical importance of his work on dreams was profound. It was a commentary on the crisis of identity that played perhaps the decisive role in moulding the illiberal search for national authenticity.

It is in the nature of modernity, of course, to provoke crises of identity. That is what modern is about it; that is what constitutes its inventiveness. Without such crises there would be no self-questioning and therefore no change. But this is also what produces the terror of modernity. Rapid social transformation leaves few areas of certainty or arenas in which individuals can control their own destiny. One response in the 1920s was fascism, a regressive desire to return to a pristine, purified state that never existed. Fascism also offered a chance to deny the contradictions of modern life, a chance to forge a conflict-free society, one absorbed in a fantasy of completeness and social unity.[67]

What fascism demanded was a complete or authentic human being. The quest for 'being' reached its apotheosis in the philosophy of national socialism. It was given credence, if not respectability, by the language of the hour, the language of collective consciousness that was to be found in the works of philosophers as distinguished as Husserl and Heidegger.

Being and Time (1927) was Heidegger's first and most significant systematic work. It is his philosophical programme aimed at a return to the "single question of the essence of Being". Why, he asked, "are there entities of being at all, and not nothing"? "Is being a mere word in its meaning, or does that which is named 'being' conceal the spiritual fate of the West?" If his aim was to answer these central questions, he believed that the unique circumstances of the 1930s offered the best time to venture in search of the answers.

What Heidegger found in national socialism was a convincing language of political discourse. Individuals, he said, had 'fates', communities had 'destinies'. And the individual's true identity is derived from membership in a community. In national socialism he found an authentic German move- ment, one that promised to allow the German people to be themselves, to appreciate their own "inner truth and greatness".

In this respect, he told his students in 1934, Hitler was an existential fig- ure. He *was* Germany. As Jonathan Stern adds, Heidegger introduced the concept of personal authenticity into the public sphere and proclaimed it as the chief value and sanction of politics. That is what he meant when he added that membership in the Nazi movement was a question of "wanting ourselves", a question of fulfilling the destiny of an entire people.[68]

For Heidegger destiny had to be grasped. It involved a decisive break with the past, or a moment of transcendence. Whereas man experiences a series of empty 'nows', an authentic existence would elevate the people above this state by offering them a vision or a moment of discovery. War was one way in which a people could grasp its destiny and thus recognise itself for the first time.

This language was in wide circulation at the time. It was part of the po- litical vernacular of conservative political movements and writers like Jünger and Spengler. In the words of Pierre Bourdieu, both men used a par- ticular language in pursuit of "an unfocused objectification of a collective mood". Jünger's preferred words included 'intuitive insight', 'the percep- tion of essence' or 'personal experience' that enabled the hero on a battle- field to grasp his identity and thus be himself. The key words in his work are 'Gestalt', 'Typus', 'Total', and 'Totalität', all of them the language of the political discourse of struggle. Even Karl Jaspers talked of the nation 'obey- ing' its destiny and submitting itself to history's 'commands'. History, he in- sisted, demands that we act as 'warriors' with the "strength to make deci- sions under the most extreme conditions". Authenticity requires that we realise our identity by taking risks, that we see ourselves as men of action.[69]

The phenomenologists' search for the authentic being of man was the ex- pression of a particular historical consciousness. The quest for authenticity, or for the essence of man, was dictated by a much larger crisis of identity. We need look no further for its origins than the teeming slums of Vienna, the city that produced the great hunter the Archduke Franz Ferdinand, the serial killer Moosbrugger, the first publicly recorded instances of child abuse, and above all, the two defining representatives of the debate over identity: Hitler and Freud.

In Hitler's case the quest for authenticity was profound. His account of his discovery of the Jews was dramatically introduced by a single sentence in *Mein Kampf.* "Then I came to Vienna". In Vienna he found that 10 per-cent of the citizens were Jews, many of them highly recognisable in the distinctive kaftans of those who had recently migrated from Russia and Eastern Europe. "Once as I was strolling through the inner city", he recalled, "I suddenly encountered an apparition in a black kaftan and black hair locks. Is this a Jew, was my first thought".

Many of the Jews who flooded into Vienna at the end of the nineteenth century were relegated to its underclass. Others, freed from rural poverty, tried to assimilate themselves into bourgeois culture. One Jewish sociologist of the early twentieth century, Arthur Ruppin, contended that "large towns are one of the great factors of assimilation—veritable hotbeds of the process". Ruppin himself feared that intermarriage would eventually erase the Jewish identity, that as a people, the Jews might disappear altogether.[70] He did not foresee that their disappearance might be occasioned by a quite different turn of events.

For the most part assimilation did not take place. Jews largely associated with one another. The writer Stefan Zweig noted that nine-tenths of his friends were Jewish. Freud's son Martin recalled how most of his father's patients and business colleagues were mostly Jewish as well. With them, he shared "the clear consciousness of an inner identity".[71] It was not one that he chose but one that was forced upon him. Martin recalled in particular the atmosphere of the University of Vienna at the turn of the century when German nationalist students would break into the lecture halls shouting *"Juden hinaus!"* and keep it up until the Jewish students gathered up their books and filed out in despondency.[72]

Of his own year of service in the army Medical Corps in 1882 Arthur Schnitzler recalled: "Among the army medical students, as in almost every unit of those serving for one year only, and where not?—there was ... a clear-cut division between gentiles and Jews, or, since the national factor was being stressed more and more, between the Aryan and Semitic elements".[73] Freud himself tried hard for many years to escape his Jewish identity, or at least to make light of it. He was a firm believer in cultural assimilation. He did not, he tells us, find his Jewishness irresistible until 1895, when it gave him a sense of belonging "as well as the clear consciousness of an inner identity", or what he called in the language of psychology the "familiarity of the same psychological structure".

Freud too had been scarred by childhood. Growing up in the 1860s in the world of the Leopoldstadt, he had experienced poverty, cultural deprivation and racial humiliation at first hand. As he wrote in his *Autobiographical Study:* "I found that I was expected to feel myself inferior and an alien because I was a Jew. I refused absolutely to do the first of these things. I had never been able to see why I should feel ashamed of my descent or, as people were beginning to say, of my race".[74] He added that he had parted

with his Jewishness without much regret even at the cost of the nonaccep-
tance by his own community, "for it seemed to me that in spite of this exclusion an active fellow worker could not fail to find some nook or cranny
in the framework of humanity".

Unfortunately, after the victory of the anti-Semitic Christian Socialist
Party in 1895, he discovered that assimilation was not going to happen, or
not soon, as he had hoped. Cruelly disappointed by politics, he assigned
himself the intellectual task of "neutralising politics by reducing it to its
psychological category". By the end of the nineteenth century he knew that
the assimilation he craved was likely to elude him completely. By the late
1920s he recognised that the Jews were in danger of being dispossessed of
their humanity as well. In 1926 he told a friend, "My language is German,
my culture, my attainments are German. I considered myself German intellectually".[75] But at the same time he recognised that he would never be accepted as a German by his confrères.

Peter Gay concludes that it was only in 1926 that Freud chose to call
himself a Jew rather than a German. But the change of heart surely dates
back much earlier to the 1890s. Carl Schorske's masterly analysis of the
progression of his thought traces the genesis of his theory of repression as
manifested in particular in the *Interpretation of Dreams* as going hand-in-
hand with his own intellectual withdrawal from Viennese life. The book itself bears a Latin epigraph from Virgil's *Aeneid:* "If I cannot bend the Gods
above I shall stir up hell". The epigraph had previously been chosen by the
social democratic writer Ferdinand Lassalle for his 1859 pamphlet 'The
Italian War and the Task of Prussia'. We know that Freud read Lassalle. As
Schorske puts it, "Lassalle . . . threatened 'those above' with the latent
forces of national revolution. . . . Freud transferred the hint of subversion
through the return of the repressed from the realm of politics to that of the
psyche".[76]

In his theory of repression, Freud put forward the idea of the uninte-
grated self, the person who has no identity except as a mishmash of
thoughts and feelings that flow from the past into the future or prevent us
from having a future at all. The concept of identity was an abstract, even a
metaphysical one for which, according to Sartre, the Jews showed a particular talent as a consequence, not a cause, of their exclusion from the traditions of the culture in which they lived on such tenuous terms. There was,
in that sense, something specifically Jewish about the response to nationalism. The Jews were not creative writers until the twentieth century. They
spent centuries commentating on the great texts—on the Hebrew Bible and
the scholarly reflections of the great rabbis. Freud and Kafka should be
seen, perhaps, as the last commentators of this Jewish tradition.

Seen in this light, *The Interpretation of Dreams* was a commentary, a
very Jewish creative act. Freud, of course, was heir to the methodology and

epistemology of the great commentaries on revealed scripture, the 'unending analyses' that formed the Jewish contribution to biblical exegesis. The technique of teasing meaning out of the text, of liberating language to make it transparent to the light, has its antecedents in scriptural exegesis. For Freud the text was not the Bible but man himself. To find the meaning of man and to make him transparent, to expose the clothes in which he hides under the labels of race, nation or tribe, to deconstruct the text of history, were all part of Freud's great project of deconstructing man.[77]

In Jean-François Lyotard's critique of Heidegger, he cites by name the other Jewish thinkers of the century who took part in that endeavour, who were also among the most prominent thinkers who challenged the idea of an authentic person, or a fully integrated human being: "Benjamin, Adorno, Arendt, Celan—the great non-German Germans, these non-Jewish Jews who not only questioned but betrayed tradition, mimesis, the immanence of unveiling in its roots; whom emigration, dispersion and the impossibility of *integration* make despair of any return . . . expelled, doomed to exodus".[78]

Hitler's insistence that an authentic personality could be forged and a New Order constructed was occasioned by his experience of Vienna as a young adult. In an essay written after the *Anschluss* (1938) Thomas Mann went so far as to suggest that the event itself was prompted by Hitler's particular loathing for Freud and those Jewish writers who had raised disturbing questions about the supposed authenticity of any nation-state: "I quietly suspect that the frenzy which drove him into . . . [Vienna] was aimed at the old analyst who lived there, his true and most personal enemy, the philosophical man Freud who had revealed the nature of neurosis and administered sobriety and sobering knowledge even about 'genius'".[79]

The upshot of all this was that after the war the Germans pursued a quite different tack, that of making themselves good Europeans. "Whoever wishes to be a German", declared the German nationalist politician Franz-Joseph Strauss in the 1950s, "must ensure that he becomes a European while there is still time".[80]

Conclusion

What can we conclude from this discussion? Psychology is vitally important in any analysis of the illiberal conscience. As Peter Gay insists, the subjective dimension can never be far from the mind of the historian. There is some repression in all social relations, some projection in all political activity, some sublimation in all aesthetic enterprises. The springs of action that are invisible are often more consequential than those that parade their power. In ways that historians have not yet fully grasped, all history must, in some measure, be psychohistory.[81]

In this chapter I have perhaps raised more questions than answers, and some of these I hope will be taken up in further research by writers more qualified than I. Part of what I have tried to do is to pursue some of the questions raised some time ago by Susan Sontag when she looked at the cultural construction of health and sickness.[82] What did the *perceived* new phenomena of serial murder, child abuse and blood sports on an unprecedented scale tell the Europeans about their own collective unconscious? What did they reveal about the sociopathology of modern Europe? And did that pathology predispose the Europeans to take seriously the illiberal critique of modernity? Did it ensure that illiberal ideas would strike a popular chord even when they were articulated by intellectuals?

Chapter Seven

War, the Liberal Conscience and the Postmodern Era

The Horsemen of the Apocalypse rode on. They had only held manoeuvres for the Judgement Day. The supreme crisis was not yet.
—Heinrich Mann, *The Man of Straw* (1918)

[Every] nation begins to show its age . . . even if it possessed a thousand Napoleons it would refuse nonetheless to compromise its repose or that of other nations. With failing reflexes whom would it terrorise and how?
—E. M. Cioran, *The Temptation to Exist* (1954)

Two books appeared in 1934 that are of importance in this study. I have discussed the first, Leonard Woolf's *Quack, Quack*, an archetypal, intellectually weak but passionately argued critique of the illiberal imagination. The second is J. B. Priestley's *English Journey,* a book of a very different mettle, a quiet, reflective commentary on liberal England dozing away as the world began the long countdown to war.

Priestley was as dismissive of continental thinking as Leonard Woolf was. "The typical English mind", he wrote, "mistrusts clear cut formulas, a logical pattern, severely rational boundaries and likes to move delicately in a slight haze".[1] There was no haze about Priestley's journey through England the year before which he undertook an attempt to study the impact of the Depression on English life. His book offers us a journey through his native land, a journey that helped to define an entire era. From the drowsy, rural idyll of the Cotswolds to the dark satanic landscapes of the north, he journeyed through a country that only six years later would once again find itself at war.

In the wartime years his voice became that of the nation—the influence of his broadcasts was only exceeded by those of Churchill himself. As a broadcaster he became the articulator of the agreed public meaning of the war. As a writer he brought its emotional consequences within the scope of the collective imagination. His speeches, wrote A.J.P. Taylor, were more representative in their cheerful understatements, but more representative also in their assumption that a people's war would necessarily be followed by a people's peace.[2]

In the pages of *English Journey* Priestley recorded his encountering at first hand the traditional England of the history books, the England of Churchill's heroic purpose, the imperial power guided by a sense of its own destiny. He also told of encountering a second England distinguished by the mean streets, industrial grime and industrial squalor of the north—the England of socialism and class conflict.

To his surprise, however, he had encountered a third England, that of the future, a modern twentieth-century nation, shapeless and unplanned. It was peopled by a new generation without a Churchillian consciousness of a mission or a class consciousness of the Marxist kind. What they represented was a technocratic, less political, more materialistic England that had little time for historical struggles.

It was that England, wrote John Plumb, that found after the war that Churchill's "pasteboard pageantry" indicated very little. Churchill's oratory may have served him particularly well in his dialogue with the nation in 1940. By the time he served his second time as prime minister, however, he was already irrelevant as a political figure. His rhetoric, in Plumb's words, while still grandiloquent, "dictated neither action nor belief."[3] To cite the main themes of this study, it neither appealed to England's conscience nor rang true in its consciousness.

Priestley himself was never much in sympathy with the heroic view of English history. He confessed that he had become, or perhaps always had been, a 'Little Englander'. It was a term of abuse, but he would have been delighted to accept it as a description of himself. "That *little* sounds the right note of affection".

He was adamant in his insistence that he had always disliked the 'Big Englanders', the "red faced, staring, loud voiced fellows, [who wanted] to go and boss everybody about all over the world". The latter, of course, were men Priestley despised all his life—the imperial braggarts, the 'Empire' men, the believers in 'the white man's burden', in the right to rule others in the name of those 'higher' values that a Greater Britain was presumed to represent.

But the Big Englanders also included men of Leonard Woolf's stamp, liberal internationalists and Fabian socialists, and braggarts like Wells, the custodians of the liberal conscience. Most of them saw the world as an immense tabula rasa that could be shaped according to the ideas of the liberal canon.

The Empire men, of course, lost their voice long before the empire collapsed. The liberal internationalists, by contrast, were confirmed in their first principles by Britain's victory in the Second World War. They remained assertive until the end of the Cold War, even if the United States, not Britain, was loudest in its affirmation of the liberal creed.

Long before the end of the Cold War, however, the West had begun to develop that 'postmodern' mentality that Priestley had discovered in the 1930s without, of course, fully appreciating its significance even at the time of his death in 1974. We can trace that sensibility back much earlier than the 1930s. We can find it in the book I quoted at the very beginning of this study—Chesterton's *Napoleon of Notting Hill*.

It is a book that posits three quintessential postmodern themes. The first is that the English people had lost faith in revolution. All revolutions are doctrinal. You cannot upset all existing things, customs and compromises unless you believe in something outside them. The problem was that the English has lost all belief: "All theoretical changes have ended in blood and ennui. If we change we must change slowly and safely as the animals do. . . . Nature's revolutions are the only successful ones. There has been no conservative reaction in favour of tails".

Chesterton also anticipated another change in the liberal consciousness. The coercive force maintained to govern others had grown smaller and had almost vanished. The military had been reduced to a minimum and would, he predicted, vanish altogether. One day the English people would lose interest in heroic themes. One day they would no longer be prepared to fight their way into history, or fight their way out.

Even the liberal historical consciousness was no longer what it had been in the past. The Englishman had come to believe in "the vague and somewhat depressed reliance upon things happening as they always have happened . . . a mood [that] had become an assumed condition. There was really no reason for any man doing anything but the thing he had done before".[4]

Chesterton, in short, caught a glimpse of a future world. These were all, of course, liberal objectives—the hope that war would be eliminated from political discourse, that nations would no longer go to war to realise their historical destiny, that evolution rather than revolution would become the principal medium of change. Our success in achieving these objectives, however, has been paid for in a higher currency than most liberals expected: the undermining of our own ground of action.

In the present chapter I shall look at three dimensions of this change in the liberal consciousness that both Chesterton and Priestley anticipated:

1. Even among the radical left the West lost faith in revolutionary action, as the events of 1968 showed all too clearly. The revolutionaries on the Left

Bank were playacting. They were no longer moved by real revolutionary impulses.

Our postmodern age seems to have no time for the revolutionary tradition of 1789. There is no longer a role for the heroic in its thinking. Our terms of engagement with history are far more modest. History is no longer seen as Hegel's 'bloody dialectic' of war and revolution.

2. In addition the liberal world has repudiated the authority of the great metahistorical texts that once dominated the Western imagination. We know that we have reached the end of an era and have embarked upon a new one, but we have no idea what the present era signifies. History has become simply too unpredictable to be shaped by any narrative. Or perhaps our range of vision is simply too narrow and confined to allow us to grasp its essential rhythm.

3. Finally, our citizens are no longer willing to be conscripted to fight in defence of their own first principles. Writing in 1977 Michael Howard posed what he called 'the liberal dilemma': could a peaceful and prosperous community of liberal democracies preserve its interests and extend its influence in pursuit of its highest ideals if it abjured the use of armed force? At the end of the century that question is beginning to be answered in a way that many find disturbing.

Even during the Cold War, the United States found in Vietnam that it could no longer send a conscript army into the field with the same confidence that it had in the past. Rather forlornly one writer at the time entitled the chapter of a book 'The Revolt Against Obligation'.

The Postrevolutionary Age

"I see that you are very sceptical about the struggle of the young against the old", I said. Kafka smiled.

"My scepticism does not alter the fact that the struggle is usually only shadow boxing".

"What do you mean shadow boxing?"

"Age is the future of youth, which sooner or later it must reach. So why struggle? To become old sooner? For a quicker departure?"

—Gustav Janouch (ed.), *Conversations with Kafka*

In his novel *Doctor Faustus* Thomas Mann records a conversation between his hero, the composer Adrian Leverkuhn, and a circle of friends studying theology at Halle. The idea of youth, Leverkuhn is told by one of his companions, is a prescriptive right of the German people. German deeds have the spirit of youth and immaturity. Not for nothing were the Germans the people of the Reformation, rather than the Renaissance. The latter was the product of a mature society; the former, the product of a young society. Perhaps, speculates Leverkuhn, it was only the fact that the nation was united late in its history and developed a national consciousness later than most other European states that deluded it into the notion of its uncommon youthfulness.

It was probably something else, replies Leverkuhn's friend:

> "Youth in the ultimate sense has nothing to do with political history, nothing to do with history at all. . . . To be young means to be original, to have remained nearer to the sources of life; it means to be able to stand up and shake off the fetters of an *outlived* civilisation, to die—through dying to allow others to be reborn. . . . To plunge into the elemental."
>
> "Is that so in Germany?" asked Adrian.
>
> "Rebirth was once called *renascimento* and went on in Italy. And 'back to nature', that was first prescribed in France."
>
> "The first was a cultural renewal", answered Deutschlin. "The second a sentimental pastoral play."
>
> "Out of the pastoral play", persisted Adrian, "came the French Revolution." [5]

The German people were undoubtedly restless for much of their history. History, observed Spengler, had used them "sparingly". Unfortunately, they were not to spare themselves in the course of the twentieth century. Nearly 15 million forfeited their lives, sacrificed needlessly by men like those in Leverkuhn's circle who talked into the night about Germany's elemental power, will to life and youthful energy. What impressed visitors most about the Third Reich was its youthfulness. In 1936 the English diplomat Sir Robert Vansittart returned from Berlin convinced that the German people were "the most formidable proposition that has ever been formulated". [6]

In the end, of course, the Third Reich was overwhelmed by two even younger nations, the United States and the Soviet Union, the two superpowers waiting in the wings. Both had entered history within a few months of each other in 1917, when Lenin took Russia out of the war and Woodrow Wilson took the United States into it.

It was not their youth that counted for most in the end, however, but their material wealth. Nazi Germany was quite literally overwhelmed by American industrial production and Soviet manpower (those hundreds of extra divisions that the Wehrmacht stumbled upon in the first months of Operation Barbarossa).

After the *Götterdämmerung* of the Third Reich the Germans engaged in a very different project: transforming their country into the most formidable economy in Europe. At the same time the liberal spirit triumphed in the country that had done so much to challenge it.

By then most Europeans had mined their revolutionary potential. They had exhausted their intellectual annuities; they were no longer able to live off them. The Third World had become the real home of revolution and produced all the revolutionary icons from Che Guevara to Mao, whose 'Little Red Book' sold by the thousands in West Berlin and the Boulevard St. Michel.

Not everyone believed in the verities of liberal capitalism, of course. Germany, bemoaned its young radicals in the 1960s, had become an *'Ersatzvaterland'*, a society in which the maximisation of wealth seemed to be the only purpose of government. When the young rebelled in 1968 one of their leaders claimed that it was the only way to survive the fear of "dying of boredom".[7]

It was symbolically fitting nevertheless that the last revolutionary gasp should have fizzled out so pathetically in 1968 not in Bonn or Berlin but in Paris, where the revolutionary tradition was first conceived. It was no less important that the revolt achieved almost nothing of lasting importance—with one exception. It confirmed the authority of a new generation of French writers who have captured the high ground of postmodernity as Hegel, Schopenhauer and Nietzsche had seized the high ground of the modern era. Lyotard, Derrida, Foucault, Lacan, Bourdieu, Baudrillard—this litany of names dominates the debate as the German phenomenologists Heidegger and Husserl once dominated the philosophical discourse in the first half of the twentieth century. The great difference is that the French school has become the great exponent of inaction, of deconstructionism.

Perhaps the main reason the 1968 revolt failed was provided by a distinguished psychoanalyst at the time who accused the revolutionary students in Paris of "functioning as a regressive group".[8] They were regressing because they were looking back. They were demonstrating something very strange in the young: a nostalgia for the past rather than an expectation of the future.

They demonstrated something else too, something that was also unusual in the young. As Umberto Eco wrote at the time, they did not want to destroy the past. They wanted to revisit it, this time "with irony". Irony and revolution, of course, do not go together; one is a negation of the other.[9]

The student revolt would probably have vindicated Walter Benjamin in his opinion that history in the West had become a reflection of two social activities: war and festival. If the modern age expressed itself most forcefully through war, the postmodern has turned its back on war and embraced the festival instead. As Octavio Paz recognised, the Paris revolt had begun as a mutiny and turned into a festival instead—"a festival of youth".[10]

Sartre, who was one of the great champions of the revolt from the beginning, compared it to the Paris insurrection of 1944, which represented, in his mind, the archetype of the *'fête'*, a spontaneous fusion of individual freedom into an assertion of the collective will.[11] His enthusiastic call to the students to "wreck the system" no matter to what end, to live purely for the present not the future, transformed him into a postmodern thinker even though the students rejected his philosophy in favour of the surrealism of André Breton. '*Les évènements*', the events, as they were called at the time, turned into a festival or, in the parlance of the time, 'a happening'—one in which nothing, of course, actually happened.

The students chose an unlikely hero in Breton. In the first manifesto of surrealism, which he had published in 1924, he had established the right to become the leader of a movement that had its origins in the third year of the Great War—in Zurich in 1916, the city where Joyce was engaged in writing *Ulysses,* and Lenin, his study *Imperialism: The Highest Stage of Capitalism.* From Breton's point of view, more significant still, it was the city in which a young Romanian who called himself Tristan Tzara invented Dadaism, from which surrealism emerged.

The extremism of the various artistic movements that grew up during and in the wake of the First World War was the product of being young in a world in which the values of the older generation had apparently produced only ruin. But the revolt of youth failed. So many young men perished in the war that the old men quite literally took over. Surrealism, for all its power to shock, proved to have no revolutionary stamina. Benjamin, fa- mously, was able to find the revolt in surrealism—but not the revolution. Victor Serge dismissed Breton and his friends as 'café activists'; Antonin Ar- taud more critically as 'toilet paper' revolutionaries.[12]

Sartre could never reconcile himself to surrealism and its offspring. He berated Breton for his optimism. Camus, another critic, more compellingly saw what was so hollow at the heart of his philosophy. Breton, he wrote, "wanted, at the same time, revolution and love, which are incompatible".[13] But then Breton always was more of a poet than he was a Marxist, which is why Sartre so despised him. The one good poet who emerged from the sur- realist movement, Paul Eluard, certainly had an instinct for stringing to- gether evocative lines about love. The editor of the *Pléiade* edition of his works describes his poems as like "the wings of a butterfly dazzling with dawn"—but like a butterfly too, they have a very brief life in the mind after one has read them.

In the end the revolt of 1968 represented a revolution of free love, a ring- ing affirmation of the brotherhood of man, though one entirely different in spirit from that to be found in the Declaration of the Rights of Man. It was different again, of course, from the asceticism of Saint-Just, who had dealt with the men of love, Danton and Desmoulins, by despatching them to their death.

The 1968 revolt was not really a political revolt at all. Any shock value it possessed lay in the rhetoric of its leaders, not their actions. It was in political terms nihilistic, for it was incompatible with the central theme of modernity: transcendence. Transcendence assumed that history was a single linear trajectory, that it illustrated a single theme and that it involved a single protagonist. As a Marxist, Sartre, for example, knew that the theme of history was class struggle and that its most important protagonist was not the bourgeoisie but the proletariat—the only class that wanted its own abolition, and that in achieving it, it would make history for the first (and last) time.

The young in the late 1960s shared few of these concerns, even though they tried to make common cause with the workers, with indifferent success. Most could not see beyond their youth—a short-term perspective that anchored them firmly in the present, not the future. As Saint-Just had insisted, to be truly revolutionary a people had "to drop its anchor in the future".[14] In the same spirit Sartre declared in his autobiography that he felt himself "anchored in the future", as a true revolutionary should. Youth ironically was condemned to treat the present as its bedrock. It could not even be the protagonist of history. Unfortunately, the young cannot 'become' anything else. They can only 'be' what they are, for the young grow old—or, perhaps, grow up.

Sartre's fate serves as a useful illustration of the fate of the radical intellectuals who had once embraced illiberal ideas. "Why are you so afraid of looking foolish?" Sartre had once asked Raymond Aron. Aron's fear of making a fool of himself left Sartre and his colleagues the philosophical arbiters of the Left Bank and the spiritual fathers of some of the century's most monstrous regimes, including that of the Khmer Rouge in Cambodia.

By 1968 it was Sartre himself who looked foolish, not only to his detractors on the right but, more significantly, to the young. Sartre failed to spot that the Zeitgeist had changed or moved on and that it had abandoned the intellectual elite it had succoured for so long.

East of the Iron Curtain, of course, intellectual life was more serious. In the figure of writers like Kundera exiled in Paris, or playwrights like Havel, or novelists like Konrád, the intellectuals of Eastern Europe played a critical and honourable role in the movements that brought down the communist regimes in 1989, the same year (appropriately enough) as the bicentennial of the French Revolution. But then the people too were not the same. They were not playacting. Their revolt was genuine, not surreal. Those who took to the streets of Leipzig, Prague and East Berlin were true revolutionaries.

What distinguished them most from the ersatz rebels of Paris was their wish to escape from the tyranny of nineteenth-century ideas and tasks. Where they differed most from the radicals of '68 was their impatience for the twentieth century to begin.

The Posthistorical Agenda

An American major refuses to sleep in the same compartment as a negro who is also wearing an American uniform. The German guard, a Swabian, is ordered to find a bunk somewhere else for the black victor. The guard nods, implying, "OK, you don't need to put it into words"; then, he is hunting through the corridors, not without a gloating grin which he does not conceal from us. Still, it is not directed against the negro himself—just against the way things are: the real problem, re-education. (World History has not yet reached its end).
—**Max Frisch, Sketchbook, 1946–1949**

In retrospect it would seem that the surrealists did anticipate the postmodern age in one respect, in asserting the alleged meaninglessness of history. Raymond Queneau with Breton was one of the main voices of the movement. Although considered a surrealist he began as a Hegelian. Hegel indeed is the presiding philosopher of Queneau's most important book, *The Sunday of Life* (1951). In the course of the work its principal character, Valentin Brû, on a tour of Germany, visits the battlefield of Jena, where Napoleon had prevailed. Later he visits Goethe's birthplace. Both were men of the hour, two of Carlyle's heroes. The title of Queneau's book is an epigraph from Hegel, who in meditating on the world of Dutch painting had spoken of "the Sunday of life which levels everything and rejects everything bad". The problem of the postmodern age, however, is that history is becoming increasingly difficult to decipher: "Local people, having no new stories to tell except to the extent they were participating in History, now only really came to confide to him the more and more petty details of a life pulverised by newspaper headlines".[15]

The novel is about many things, but one is the battle of Jena (1806). It is even mentioned on the first page as Private Brû's virtually sole thought: "Private Brû . . . in general thought of nothing, but when he did had a preference for the battle of Jena", at which Napoleon had defeated the Prussians and gone on to enter Berlin. In 1940 Hitler, in turn, defeated France and spent half a day visiting Paris.

Napoleon's defeat of Prussia is a mirror image of the defeat to be suffered by France a century later. The Prussians, of course, got their revenge. So did the French in 1944. Jena is a metaphor not for victory but for the momentary defeat "of everything bad" that human life in its timeless succession of Sundays outlasts. "The days which pass which turn into the time that passes, are neither lovely nor hideous, but always the same". So much, in the end, for Hegel's glorification of history.

Eight years later Queneau published another novel, *Zazie in the Metro* (1959). It is his most famous work. It describes a group of tourists scouring

Paris to see the 'sights', on a grand tour through the museum of history. Zazie is not among these foolish tourists, gaping at a past that is already beyond their comprehension. She does not 'take in' the gothic cathedrals or Napoleon's tomb but frequents the present, the Metro.[16] For her the highlight of the trip is a meeting with her Uncle Gabriel, who is to be found in a gay bar, the ultimate point of rendezvous, perhaps, of the postmodern era, with his tutu, lipstick and meticulously manicured nails, dancing the part of the 'Dying Swan'.[17]

The conclusion had been reached much earlier by a far more systematic thinker, the Romanian philosopher E. M. Cioran. Cioran was much too cynical to fight for any cause. Although he had dabbled with fascism when young he had perceived that it offered little prospect of transcending any condition. As a philosophy student he had shocked his tutor by wanting to write a thesis on the futility of history that he had intended to call 'A General Theory of Tears'.

Cioran's themes were also Nietzsche's. And like Nietzsche he had a profound distrust of the way in which nations tended to appropriate history in order to speak in its name. France, England, Germany, now Russia and the United States, each had an age of expansion and madness. Each had taken to the field to vindicate their respective beliefs. This was the fate, Cioran added, of most *young* nations, who tended to see matters from the viewpoint of action. "Sacrificing comfort to adventure, happiness to efficiency, they do not admit the legitimacy of contradictory ideas, the coexistence of antinomic positions".[18]

In that respect, Cioran believed that the superpowers were as much a danger to themselves as they were to each other. In Soviet Russia he saw the real heir of the French Revolution, a power that wished to impose its ideas on a world that was not especially happy to accept them. Indeed, its proselytising mission was even greater than that of revolutionary France.[19]

The Russians, he added, were so haunted by themselves that they posed themselves as a unique historical problem. They had already "introduced the Absolute into politics" long before Lenin set out for the Finland station: that was the Russian people's challenge to the world. They felt what they thought. Their truths were stimulants to action. They were not troubled by self-doubt. They had not subjected their obsessions to rigorous self-questioning.[20] As for the United States, it was a society that had not yet mastered itself. It offered its citizens only "the sterility of uninterrupted good fortune". "In order to cease being a superficial master, she requires an ordeal of major scope".[21]

Was that not the threat, however, of nuclear war? "Having lived outside hell, she was prepared to descend into it". Writing in 1949, Cioran had little hope that the twentieth century would be survived or a nuclear war averted. His only advice to mankind was that it "should prepare for bad times".[22]

What is most remarkable today, looking back on his writing in the 1950s, is Cioran's foresight in anticipating the coming of the postmodern era. He was one of the first writers to recognise that the Europeans had abandoned the call of history. If they were interested in a better future they were so "only on condition it came from somewhere else, on condition that they need not bother to conceive it themselves". They had once been prepared to die for the absurdity of glory. Now they were willing to abandon themselves to the "frenzy of small claims". They were tempted by happiness, not ambition. Even France, the home of the revolutionary age, had become an 'old' society whose historical reflexes had begun to fail it.

For Cioran, France in the 1960s was a society that was postmodern to the core. It had once been a country which, far from husbanding its resources, had been prepared to squander them in a cause. Now it had surrendered everything to the wish to live well. In the process it had become "a sum of individuals, a society rather than a historic will". It had left the stage to pursue a more provincial destiny.[23]

Writing thirty years later, another Parisian exile, Milan Kundera, arrived at a similar conclusion. In his first post–Cold War novel, *Immortality* (1991), he describes the lives of two of his female protagonists. Bettina von Arnim stands in the Paris Metro with a collection box, begging. What impels her to help others is not a passion for good deeds but a longing to enter into direct, personal contact with God, whom she believes to be incarnate in history. Kundera contrasts her with Laura, another kindhearted lady who sits on the boards of charitable organisations. She is not in the habit of giving money to beggars. She passes them by though they are only a few feet away. She suffers from "the defect of spiritual farsightedness". Africans a thousand miles away are nearer in her imagination than the beggars she passes every day in the streets.

> What to Bettina was an intervention in history, was to Laura merely a charitable deed. But this was not Laura's fault. World history, with its revolutions, Utopias, hopes and despair had vanished from Europe, leaving only nostalgia behind. That is why the French have made charitable actions international. They were not led (like the Americans for example) by Christian love for one's neighbours, but by a longing for lost history, a longing to call it back and to be present in it, if only in the form of a red collection box for blacks.[24]

By the end of the Cold War, indeed some time earlier, the West had begun to undergo a change of consciousness. In its response to the civil war in Bosnia we caught a glimpse of a world that had begun to suspect that the ground of its own history had changed for good.

What do I mean by the ground of history? With the arrival of modernity history replaced nature as the principal explanation of reality. Modernity sought the ground of history not in nature but in man. But having mastered nature, having subdued it to his own will, he was dismayed to discover that he had nowhere to stand, that he had no firm ground beneath him. He was compelled accordingly to ask what the ground of history was.

The Cold War, in this respect, can be seen as a disagreement about the nature of history. Marxism grounded history on the class struggle, which it predicted would end in the victory of the proletariat, just as Nazism had tried to ground history on the struggle between the races. Liberalism, in turn, grounded history on the idea of progress, on the basis of the claim that economic prosperity was the best 'ground' of freedom.

With the end of the Cold War we no longer have the confidence to ground history in a specific process. The posthistorical condition is one in which the ground of history has largely shifted under our feet. The liberal world has begun to suspect that history no longer has a goal or purpose that can be anticipated in advance of the future. History is no longer determined by a generic individual—the proletariat, for example, or the bourgeoisie, or for that matter the West, all of whom were once encouraged to see themselves as the meaning of history and who, as a result, believed that they were able to determine what history would become. "Our time", writes a contemporary French philosopher, "is no longer the time of history and therefore history itself appears to have become part of history. . . . History is suspended without movement and we can appreciate only with uncertainty or with anxiety what will happen if it moves forward again".[25]

The key words here are 'movement' and 'anxiety'. Is history going forwards or backwards? As an anonymous Pentagon official put it in 1990, "history is happening in a way it is not supposed to".[26] The destruction of Bosnia revealed that it has become unpredictable, even dangerous. It defies analysis. We no longer know where it is heading, or what lies ahead.

The liberal powers were paralysed in their response to the destruction of Bosnia (and will be paralysed again when the next crisis comes) because of a second feature of the posthistorical world that also denies them any ground of action. They no longer believe that they live in *the* moment of history. Our time is no longer able to feel and represent itself as the time in which history is made. We tend to see it only as a period in which history will make of us whatever it will. We can no longer explain why we are *here*—in the present. We no longer understand our presence in history as a way station to a future that we can anticipate, even if we may not live to see it.

We live instead with the disconcerting truth that although we now know that everything is historically determined, we do not know how determination works. We cannot unlock the key of history or even decode its message. Its meaning seems forever out of reach.

I think Jean-Luc Nancy sums up the point succinctly when he writes, "One could say that everything is historical but also that nothing is 'historic'".[27] What does 'historic' mean? It means significant or memorable.

We can no longer consciously initiate events that will be remembered because of their significance for a future generation. We can no longer make the present significant for ourselves because we can no longer determine what the future will find of note or not. We have to live with the prospect that we may be forgotten.

In short, the liberal world has lost faith or interest in history itself. In an agnostic age the 'will to power' has been devalued by the suspicion that there is nothing to will for. If there is no single truth behind history, then the 'will to truth' seems even more questionable. As Cioran recognised, if the Western powers are still interested in a better future they are so only on condition that it comes from somewhere else, on condition that they need not bother to conceive it themselves.

A Postmilitary Society

At a conference in November 1972 on the work of Hannah Arendt, Mary McCarthy, one of Arendt's closest friends, questioned her about the sharp distinction she insisted on drawing between the political and the social worlds. It was particularly noticeable in her book *On Revolution,* in which she had sought to demonstrate that the failure of the French and Russian Revolutions, compared with the American, was to be explained by the fact that both had been far more concerned to redress social and material suffering than to promote the political liberty of the citizen. McCarthy responded:

> It seems to me that if you once have a constitution and you have had the foundation and you have a framework of laws, the scene is set for political action. And the only thing that is left for a political man to do is what the Greeks did: make war. . . . If all questions of economics, human welfare . . . anything that touches the social sphere are to be excluded from the political scene, then . . . I am left with war".[28]

Arendt acknowledged that in some respects McCarthy was right. The Greeks has busied themselves with more than just waging war. Their philosophy and literature were incomparable. But, for good or ill, war was the most profound phenomenon to have shaped the Greek consciousness, just as it was the most profound experience of the modern world.

At the centre of Arendt's political philosophy is the idea that true freedom can be attained only through political action—which must necessarily include war. Her criticism of American liberal thinking in the 1960s was that it had become profoundly preoccupied with socioeconomic programmes and activities. She particularly deplored the growth of the positive liberal bias in social science, which had obscured the role that conflict still played in political life. What she was criticising, unconsciously to be sure, was the passing of the modern age.

Liberal societies had spent most of the twentieth century engaging illiberal regimes in battle. Those conflicts were fought—on both sides—by citizen armies. The conscription of the citizen made possible the "requisitioning of an entire people", in the words of Carnot, the French minister of war in the early years of the Revolution. By the mid–twentieth century the process had reached the stage where military historians had begun to write no longer about armies in battle but about entire societies at war. In the course of the twentieth century, however, it became increasingly difficult for modern societies, liberal and illiberal alike, to motivate their citizens to fight. The industrial world had recourse to a series of strategies.

1. In the case of the illiberal world, and especially Nazi Germany it was to *demodernise* warfare, to transform it into what it had been in the past—an absolute, existential struggle. In order to continue fighting for the last three years of the war with Russia even the German army had to depart from its blitzkrieg strategy, with its emphasis on heavy armour and the rapid, relentless thrust. It chose to change the terms of engagement completely.

After 1943 the German army reverted to the infantry tactics of the Great War, digging in, fighting for every square foot of ground, refusing to admit defeat. In its tactics it showed the same grim determination that had been displayed by the soldiers on the Hindenburg Line (1917), perhaps even more. Frequently they fought in conditions of physical exhaustion much grimmer than those its forebears had sustained in the last phase of the First World War. Unlike the German army at the end of the Great War, the *Ostheer* did not collapse.

On the eastern front war became a condition of life, a Darwinian struggle that offered only one choice, that of killing or being killed. This in turn made the rank and file highly susceptible to ideological indoctrination. As the military historian Omer Bartov has noted, the Germans had to substitute "a ruthless, fantastic, amoral view of war for material strength and rational planning". There was an anarchic element in this celebration of death and the return to savagery among the frontline troops, one that combined a growing contempt for traditional values with "a powerful rage to annihilate both one's enemies and oneself".[29]

Bartov quotes at length from the diaries and journals of contemporary German soldiers. "Orders are not given any more", wrote one young man; "leadership has reverted to its original form". It was, he claimed, "a battle for survival", in which everything was allowed that might prevent the extinction of the individual soldier, and by extension that of his comrades, his unit, his country and his race.

It became, indeed, much more than that. In the attempt to overcome the material demodernisation of the front as well as the hopelessness of their situation, battle became a condition to be glorified as the real, supreme essence of being.

It was, of course, the last time Germany was able to put such an army into the field. The demodernisation of warfare resulted in the destruction of the German state and its partition between the superpowers. Hitler's purge of the officer class after the July 1944 plot also destroyed, more effectively than the Allies would have done, the warrior caste that had been such a distinguishing feature of Prussian 'militarism'.

2. By the time of the Second World War, it was becoming clear that citizens in the democratic West were also becoming increasingly disinclined to fight with the enthusiasm, or the mass resignation, that their predecessors had shown on the western front.

Conscripted troops in the democracies had already begun to show a disinclination to fight on terms the generals would have liked. A British commander in the Middle East complained that the British army had lost its 'fighting spirit'. The generals insisted, in response, on cripplingly conservative margins of strength before they would attack. Even then, they complained about the 'unwillingness' of their men to fight with the same tenacity of purpose they had shown twenty years earlier when they had commanded them on the western front.

Two of these commanders, Archibald Wavell and Harold Alexander, were themselves products of the First World War experience that proved so traumatic, particularly for the British, because during it they had fielded for the first and last time in their history a continental army that had successfully engaged the main body of enemy troops. Wavell confessed that he was not really "interested in war"; Alexander hated it, according to his contemporaries.[30]

The U.S. army was somewhat different. Some of its generals, such as Mark Clark in Italy, did not think that a victory in battle was worth much unless it had been purchased at a high price in terms of casualties. Fifteen years later its resolve began to falter. In Vietnam, the last war in which a democracy fielded a conscript army, its strategy was not to demodernise it but to make it postmodern.

In its style, wrote Paul Fussell, the Vietnam War can be seen not as a modern war at all, but as the world's first postmodern conflict. By postmodern he means a war that went beyond the modern into something more sceptical, even nihilistic, which destroyed the last vestiges of patriotism on which modern warfare had been grounded. One characteristic of the postmodern agenda in the arts is a self-consciousness bordering on a contempt for the medium or genre in which the artist is working. Lionel Trilling once spoke of the 'modern' movement in culture as the "legitimation of the subversive". Today that phenomenon is deeply entrenched. Historians, for example, claim that their work is no truer than fiction; novelists refuse to draw a distinction between high and low culture.

In Indochina the United States tried to sanitise the conflict by disguising its true nature. Terms such as 'protective reaction' allowed soldiers to differentiate their actions from the routine killing of the enemy. 'Free fire zones' were intended to provide a 'killing ground' in which everything that moved could be shot. Even within American ranks the deception was maintained. Soldiers were not killed, but 'attrited'. The accidental death of South Vietnamese, on whose behalf the United States was ostensibly fighting, was dismissed as 'collateral damage'. Even in the description of war psychosis the medical authorities did what they could to disguise cases of illness by recourse to euphemism. 'Post-traumatic stress disorder' was the favoured term to describe the panic attacks, the nightmares and dry dysphoria that takes the joy out of life and makes it difficult to associate with other people. The term of course was never meant to include a collective disorder, but it was used by the military nonetheless.[31]

Once a nation de-heroises war it subverts it as a moral exercise. The result is likely to be a profound disenchantment among the soldiers who are called upon to fight the war, especially when they are conscripts, not volunteers. Disenchantment was to prove particularly devastating in Vietnam. 700,000 veterans suffered from trauma, from symptoms of delayed stress, on returning to the United States. Of the married veterans 38 percent were divorced within six months of their return. By the early 1980s there were 40,000 registered heroin addicts among the veterans in New York City alone. In retrospect, what was particularly striking about the war in Vietnam was the collapse of morale off the field, rather than on it.

3. The third response to war has been to privatise it—to contract out to the private sector, or to allow the private sector to contract in. In some countries soldiers are ex–national servicemen under short-term contract. In others national service in peacetime has been abandoned altogether. Private companies now regularly bid for contracts that include everything from the servicing of ships to the maintenance of tanks.

In the 1870s Nietzsche warned of the consequences of the decline of the ethical effects of political obligation when he counselled his readers against the privatisation of life: "Henceforth the individual will see only the side of it [the state] that promises to be useful or threatens to be harmful to him. . . . Distrust of all government . . . will impel men to quite a novel resolve: the resolve to do away with the concept of the state, to the abolition of the distinction between private and public". Private companies, he predicted, would step-by-step absorb the business of the state. The great professions would become trades. The sense of 'vocation' would be rendered anachronistic or would be seen as a throwback to an earlier era. Even the most resistant reminder of what was formally the work of government (for example, its responsibility for protecting the private person from the private person) would, in the long run, be taken care of by private contractors.[32]

The 'civilian powers' or trading states the democracies have become will doubtless live up to their own first principles. They will probably prefer to contract out to industry rather than maintain large forces, or to hire others to do the fighting for them, as the German and Japanese taxpayers paid the United States to defend their interests in the Gulf War. Even the United States is not averse to buying off its opponents, paying one Somali warlord $30 million during the brief return of its troops to Somalia in February 1995, as a bribe to discourage him from firing on American troops.

Does the civilianisation of the liberal world matter? Does it matter if liberal societies redefine freedom in negative terms, not as the power to remake the world on its terms but as the right to be left alone, the right to suffer from its own mistakes, not from the malice of others?

It may matter a great deal if history returns when least expected. The problem with history is that it can flare up at any moment. The West may soon discover that it does not live only in one time zone—its own, the postmodern era; it also lives in several overlapping ones as well, simply by living in the imagination of a labour-surplus world. If capital will not go to the societies that have an excess of labour, labour will visit societies that are capital intensive. History is fast becoming an interaction between two historical time zones, rather than a dialectic within one.

In the future the West would do well to read not Clausewitz but Machiavelli. Machiavelli was always mindful of the fact of a serious decline of parental, religious and civic authority in fifteenth-century Italy. With it went a lack of good military organisation. To meet the challenge he advocated schooling the citizens in civic discipline by establishing citizen armies. It was the only sure way to arrest the process of internal disintegration.

Machiavelli also tells us about the fate of a postmodern society in a modern world. He considered the city-states of late-fifteenth-century Italy to have forfeited their own independence because their citizens had been too proud to fight themselves, because they preferred hiring mercenaries, Swiss or Italian *condottieri*, to fight for them, paying them off at the end of each year. Like other medieval city-states Machiavelli's own, Florence, had suffered from increasing prosperity and the refusal of the wealthy to bear arms. The result had been a general reliance on mercenaries who did not hesitate to blackmail or betray the state that had hired them, if profits were involved. Some even seized power themselves.

The *condottieri* of course were in the business of fighting. They were not a warrior class; they were businessmen who made a point of not killing each other. Machiavelli recounts one battle in which no one was killed. He describes another that lasted four hours in the course of which one soldier accidentally lost his life when he fell off his horse and was trampled to death by his own cavalry.

Given such behaviour, the Florentine commissioner of war proposed that the mercenary commanders should be given viva voce examinations to ascertain whether in fact they knew anything about war. His suggestion did not meet with favour, in part because if they had been found wanting there was no one else to take their place.[33]

What happened in the end to fifteenth-century Italy Machiavelli tells us in his book *The Art of War*. Something that had not been suspected happened in 1494 when the big powers, France and Spain, arrived in the peninsula. It was from their incursion that historians date the decline of the city-states and the disappearance of Italy as a major actor in European politics for the next three hundred years. It is also the year, incidentally, from which the historian Arnold Toynbee dated the beginning of 'modern' war.

Conclusion: Liberalism and the Tragic Spirit

Liberalism had never accepted the Leninist premise that this was an age of wars and revolution. Where the communists saw class war, civil war, pictures of catastrophe, we only saw temporary aberrations. Capitalist democracies could never be at home with a catastrophe outlook. . . . Worshippers of progress, its dependants, we are unwilling to reckon villainy and misanthropy, we reject the horrible—the same as saying we are anti-philosophical.
—Saul Bellow, *The Dean's December* (1982)

As early as the 1960s the Marxist critic Henri Lefebvre noted that after every period of dogmatism comes a moment of irony. Dogmatism conjures up its own opposite and triggers off its own opponent. At the time he was writing, he added, one of the casualties of the ironic spirit of the times was the intellectual community itself. Once they were no longer "functionaries of the Absolute" they no longer had a function. They ceased to be the pedagogues of society, relaying the lessons of history through books or the press. They no longer created effective images that could answer ideological needs. They had been shut off in intellectual ghettos.[34]

Not only had the antipositivist revolt failed, positivism too yielded place to cynicism or irony. The chief casualty was Marxism, with its claims that socialism was 'scientific' and therefore universally true. But the liberal conscience did not escape unscathed. It was undermined even as the illiberal critique crumbled. At the end of the twentieth century the liberal world urgently needs to rethink some of its own first principles if it is to meet the challenge of the future.

We seem to have undergone a change of consciousness that may be as significant as that of 1910 chronicled by Virginia Woolf. The result is a marked lack of commitment by the West to exporting its own message. Its terms of engagement with history have changed significantly. What distinguishes it at the end of the century is its historic reticence, the modesty of its aims.

In our postmodern age we are no longer divided on the great questions that once distinguished the political debate: socialism, liberalism, capitalism and individualism. The talk now is of 'inventing', 'representing', 'construing' and 'deconstructing'. Our political philosophy can, at best, define questions. It cannot provide answers. Intellectuals (when they dare proclaim themselves such) are no longer willing to put forward general conclusions or general truths. In this sense we are living not in a potential world but in an existing one that has lost much of its potential.

All this is demoralising for those who still have ideas of what history should be about, or how societies should behave. The pursuit of private satisfaction cannot be reconciled with the pursuit of meaning on which real happiness (as Mill insisted) depends. Market demands have left values unprotected; inadequate spiritual outlooks have left them unanchored except in the bogus spirituality of the New Age movement.

The problem of course is that belief is a value, not an interest, or it is talked of as such. And as Locke pointed out, no one can be forced to believe or not believe. Similarly no one can be forced to find history meaningful. Perhaps history never really deserts those it has chosen for great tasks. It is the community that rejects its responsibilities. Everything depends on the strength of its inner life, the strength of its convictions. Collective action stems from the dictates of an inner voice. In the West that voice is getting weaker by the year.

The reader will by now have gathered that I am not an unqualified admirer of every writer who claimed to speak on liberalism's behalf. At the end of the twentieth century no one can afford to be. The dialectic between the illiberal and liberal imaginations came near to embroiling us all in a catastrophic encounter. Many liberal intellectuals, like their illiberal counterparts, were wont to act, in Marx's words, as "paid wage labourers" who were forced to sell their labour to political movements in order to make a difference, to escape the threat of intellectual redundancy. As the twentieth century draws to a close it is perhaps time that we adopt a tragic vision of international relations. What is tragedy if not the irony that the attempt to create order often results in greater disorder still; that the attempt to make the world safe for democracy often ignores the fact that democracy is often unsafe for the world; that the belief in human rights often ignores human needs and ultimately, of course, that an attempt to postulate abstract variables such as sovereign right ignores those more abrasive realities with which the liberal world was brought into contact in the course of the twentieth century?

If we have overlooked the tragic this is because liberalism has discouraged us from thinking in tragic terms. As William Kaufmann admitted in his book *Life at Its Limits* (1973) philosophy is a branch of literature in which suffering and extreme situations have traditionally been ignored. The social sciences have compounded the problem by engaging in an untragic discourse about politics.

Social science, unlike philosophy, is largely an Anglo-American invention. If the United States has been the home of social science it has also been the home of refugees from Europe, fleeing from the Old World. In George Steiner's apt phrase, the new immigrants were determined to opt out of history altogether, "to abdicate from the historicity of injustice, of suffering, of material and psychological deprivation".[35] American history, wrote Henry Adams, was replete with *contingent* disaster, a fault that could be amended if only social circumstances could be changed.[36]

The great tragedians, by contrast, were suspicious of any theoretical impulse with a passion to transform enigmas into problems with solutions. They were even more opposed to the wish to dissolve mystery altogether so that one could impose one's own voice on history. For the most part liberal writers ignored this message; their illiberal counterparts did not.

Hegel, for example, was one of the first writers to assert that the true political life, or the dialectic of history, was innately tragic. At the centre of the great Greek tragedies we find not the tragic hero but the tragic collision—a conflict not between good and evil but between two one-sided positions, each of which embodies some good. In Greek tragedy the character that participates is often not at issue. The positions of the characters usually are.

Indeed, in the great tragedies of the past, is not our admiration affected by the view that there is not some good in the positions of both protagonists? There may well be one of those occasions in which right struggles against right, or if you like, wrong against wrong. Here is no simple case of sharp black-and-white distinctions but of those diverse shades of grey that make up the colour of history.

Often what makes a conflict 'tragic' lies in the fact that both sides may be honest in their own way. Is it not their inability to escape from the implications of their actions that is most moving? In a sense the ultimate verdict and punishment of the hero or heroine is an anticlimax. It is the struggle itself rather than its outcome that engages our sympathies most.

In many of the Greek plays we find this position: right clashing against right. Euripides' favourite method was to take a one-sided point of view, a noble half-truth, and exhibit its nobility, and then to exhibit the disaster to which it leads its blind adherents because, in the end, it is only part of the truth. William Arrowsmith speaks of a "head-on collision" between those who, for all their piety, represent the full-blown tyranny of conforming tradition and the arrogant representative of the ruthlessly antitraditional mind.

The poetic power of another of Euripides' plays, the *Bacchae*, adds Kaufmann, also constitutes a powerful warning against being blind to the sweeping power of irrational experience. The tragedy revolves, nevertheless, not around the single tragic hero but around a conflict between two one-sided views, the belief in absolute irrationality and the belief in the absolutely rational.

Sophocles' *Antigone* in particular is about the clash of two rights. It was for that reason Hegel's favourite play. If Creon were only a tyrant he would not be worthy of Antigone's challenge. If Antigone's cause were worthless, he would not be a tragic figure. What the dual tragedy holds out is the promise of an eventual reconciliation or resolution. It is only after their death that the conflict between private and public morality, the familial and the civic, the dead and the living, can be enacted on a richer level of consciousness from that which arose from the cause of the conflict between them. It is only in the future, in other words, that both sides to the conflict may feel a contradiction in their own arguments for the first time.

Such thinking, of course, hardly commended itself to a liberal world that during the Cold War years was encouraged to believe in right versus wrong. Yet the most influential liberal philosopher of all recognised early on in the conflict that the future might be more complex. Isaiah Berlin was among the first to acknowledge that one day the Western world might encounter ideas equally sacred that nonetheless were in conflict with its own. One day, he predicted, the liberal world might have to abandon one of its most compelling assumptions: that somewhere in the past or future, in this world or the next, in the speculations of metaphysics or the philosophy of social science, there was to be found a final answer to the question of how man should live.

Berlin issued a challenge to his liberal contemporaries to recognise that we live the life that is good for us and accept the value of it for that and no other reason. We must accept that others have the right to live the lives that they want to. For most of the century, this was unacceptable. Nevertheless Berlin was brave enough to assert that these might be the only terms on which liberalism might survive.[37]

In the 1950s Albert Camus also contended that the tragic, as opposed to the melodramatic, was that the forces confronting each other are, in their own light, equally legitimate and equally justified. The perfect tragic formula would be "all can be justified, no one is just".[38] That is why the chorus in classical tragedy generally advises prudence. It knows that up to a certain limit everyone is right and that the person who oversteps this limit is heading for catastrophe if he persists in his desire to assert a right he thinks that he alone possesses. The constant theme of classical tragedy is that limits must not be transgressed.

Tragedy poses a particular challenge, of course, to a creed as interventionist as liberal internationalism. As Aristotle reminds us, tragedy works on the spectator. It is we—the spectators—who find life tragic. This is not necessarily true for those involved in the events we see on our television screens at night who may see their condition as part of the natural order, or accept it as the price to be paid for salvation in this world, or the next.

The irony, of course, is that tragedy is performed with utter disregard for the audience. What transpires on stage admits of no intervention. How can we warn Oedipus or advise Antigone? It is in their nature to act as they do. The effect, writes Gadamer, is the other way, tragedy effects *us*.[39] It is *we* who are overcome by misery and terror. It is we who often do not want what we see on the stage to be true. What overwhelms us most is that there is little we can do about it.

An understanding of the tragic would be the most mature way of taking liberalism into the twenty-first century. It would not be, contrary to what many may think, an anticommunitarian creed. As Jean-François Lyotard wrote, "The community of the world is not a place of safety. It is a place of tragedy".[40] One of the conditions of the tragic enumerated by Aristotle is precisely its domestic condition. Relationships are ultimately tragic because they occur in the family. It is in the family that incest, patricide and matricide, the great themes of Greek tragedy, occur. Tragedy, in fact, is not really possible outside the family framework. It is an essential part of family life. Recognising that the tragic is a part of international life might offer an affirmation rather than a denial of liberalism's international creed.[41]

Ultimately a tragic vision is consistent with the liberal idea, for what did the Greeks tell us but that life is about assuming responsibility for our misfortunes and learning to overcome them rather than finding solace in a political programme offering us a spurious form of redemption, or promising us that we can transcend our tragic condition—at a price? However appalling our circumstances, or however violent the world we live in, we can still insist on the right to make choices for ourselves and live with the consequences. It was on this ground, after all, that the liberal world engaged its enemies and, in the end, prevailed.

Notes

Preface

1. Cited in Jon Glover and Jon Silkin, *The Penguin Book of the First World War* (London: Viking, 1989), pp. 349–354.

2. Wyndham Lewis, *The Art of Being Ruled* (Santa Rosa, Calif.: Black Sparrow Press, 1989), p. 139.

3. Ibid., p. 328.

4. Cited in Germaine Brée, *Camus and Sartre: crisis and commitment* (London: Calder and Boyars, 1974), pp. 185–186.

5. Ibid., p. 195 n. 24.

6. Ibid.

7. Lewis, *Art of Being Ruled*, p. 221.

8. George Lichtheim, *Marxism in Modern France* (New York: Columbia University Press, 1966), p. 194.

9. Joachim Fest, *Frankfurter Allgeimene Zeitung*, 30 December 1989. Reprinted in *German Comments* (19 June 1990), pp. 88–93.

10. Ralf Dahrendorf, *Society and Democracy in Germany* (New York: Doubleday, 1969), p. 192.

11. Cited in Brée, *Camus and Sartre*, p. 238.

12. Cited in Brée, *Camus and Sartre*, p. 254.

13. Something of this dilemma comes out in a poem by Osbert Sitwell called 'The Next War'. It was written twenty years before the outbreak of the Second World War. "Rushing eagerly into the street / The kindly old gentleman cried to the young / Will you sacrifice through your lethargy / What your fathers died to gain? / The world must be made safe for the young / And the children went." Osbert Sitwell, *Left Hand, Right Hand* (London: Penguin, 1984), p. 291.

14. Michael Howard, *War and the Liberal Conscience* (New York: Rutgers University Press, 1978).

15. D. H. Lawrence, *Kangaroo* (London: Heinemann, 1950), p. 249.

16. Carlton Hayes, *A Generation of Materialism* (New York: Harper and Brothers, 1941). Cited in Daniel Gasman, *The Scientific Origins of National Socialism: social Darwinism in Ernst Haeckel and the German Monist League* (London: Macdonald, 1971), p. 122.

17. Cited in Malcolm Bradbury, *Dangerous Pilgrimages: trans-Atlantic mythologies and the novel* (London: Secker & Warburg, 1995), p. 341.

18. Fritz Stern, *The Failure of Illiberalism: essays on the political culture of modern Germany* (Chicago: University of Chicago Press, 1971).

19. Friedrich Nietzsche, *Daybreak: thoughts on the prejudices of morality*, transl. R. J. Hollingdale (Cambridge: Cambridge University Press, 1992), No. 299, p. 304.

20. Georg Lukács, *Essays on Thomas Mann* (Atlantic Highlands, N.J.: Humanities Press, 1979), p. 89.

21. Cited in Claudio Magris, *Danube: a sentimental journey from the source to the Black Sea* (London: Harvill Collins, 1990), p. 188.

22. Peter Gay, *The Bourgeois Experience: from Victoria to Freud*, vol. 3, *The Cultivation of Hatred* (New York: Norton, 1993).

23. See Philip Gold, 'Does complex technological information alienate us from our humanity? Lessons from the study of despair', in Philip Windsor, ed., *The End of the Century: the future in the past* (Tokyo: Kadansha, 1995), pp. 117–157.

Chapter One

1. W. D. Rubinstein, *Capitalism, Culture, and Decline in Britain* (London: Routledge, 1993), p. 2.

2. Cited in Felix Markham, *Napoleon and the Awakening of Europe* (London: English University Press, 1965), p. 175. For Scott, see John Buchan, *Sir Walter Scott* (London: Casell, 1933), p. 312. One of Napoleon's generals, Gaspard Gourgand, the First Ordnance Officer in the 1812 campaign in Russia, did not think it laudatory enough. He took such offence that he threatened to challenge the author to a duel. Scott rose to the occasion: "It is clear to me that what is least forgiven in a man of any mark . . . is want of that article blackguardedly called pluck. And the fine qualities of genius cannot make amends for it. We are told the genius of poets especially is irreconcilable with that species of grenadier accomplishment. If so 'quel chien de génie'." He selected Will Clerk as his second and saw that Napoleon's own pistols, which he possessed, were in order. But the challenge never arrived.

3. Cited in Walter Houghton, *The Victorian Frame of Mind, 1830–1870* (New Haven: Yale University Press, 1975), p. 309. The former warden of All Souls College, Oxford, liked to recount the following story. "As a boy a Fellow of All Souls the Hon. Edmund Bertie . . . saw Napoleon when the *Bellerophon* moored in Torbay on its way to St. Helena. He was very willing as an old man to recall the scene . . . a scene now familiar to many through Orchardson's picture: the solitary figure on the deck plunged in thought, in recollection it may be of his past triumphs or anticipation of his years of exile. When Bertie was an old man junior Fellows of All Souls . . . would egg him on . . . to give his recollection of the scene, well knowing what it was they were going to get from him. 'Tell us, can you sum up the impression the Emperor made upon you?' The answer never varied. 'You could tell at once that he was *not* a university man'." (John Sparrow, 'Reflections on memory', *The Listener*, 12 April 1979, p. 513.)

4. G. K. Chesterton, *The Secret of Father Brown* (London: Penguin, 1974), p. 172.

5. G. K. Chesterton, *The Napoleon of Notting Hill* (London: Penguin, 1982), p. 8.

6. See Arthur Danto, 'Some remarks on the *Genealogy of Morals*', in Robert Solomon and Kathleen Higgins, eds., *Reading Nietzsche* (Oxford: Oxford University Press, 1988), pp. 13–14. Leonard Woolf's attitude towards Nietzsche was nevertheless typical of the time. H. L. Stewart, in *Nietzsche and the Ideas of Modern Germany* (London, 1915), found in the philosopher one of the causes of the German

state of mind, which he held responsible for the Great War. F.J.C. Hearnshaw, in *Germany: the aggressor throughout the ages* (New York, 1941), referred to "the poisonous fallacies of maniacs such as Nietzsche" (p. 235). Robin D. Butler, in *The Roots of National Socialism* (London: Faber & Faber, 1941), found "nothing less than the Nietzschean transvaluation of values: the education of Germans in Germanity, the nihilistic revolution which would not stop at smashing countries but would wreck the very heart of man utterly, destroying the civilisation of the West" (p. 295). Crane Brinton, although much fairer than the others, ended his book *Nietzsche* (Cambridge, Mass.: Harvard University Press, 1941) with the observation: "Nietzsche like the Nazi leaders was never really housebroken" (see the chapter 'Nietzsche and the Nazis', pp. 200–231). For all citations above, see Eric Voeglin, 'Nietzsche, the crisis, and the war', *Journal of Politics* 6 (1944), pp. 177–212.

7. Patrick Bridgewater, 'English writers and Nietzsche', in Malcolm Pasley, ed., *Nietzsche: imagery and thought* (London: Methuen, 1978), p. 222.

8. Lewis, *The Art of Being Ruled* (Santa Rosa, Calif.: Black Sparrow Press, 1989), p. 174.

9. Mulk Raj Anand, *Conversations in Bloomsbury* (Oxford: Oxford University Press, 1991), pp. 106–107.

10. Ibid., p. 109.

11. Leonard Woolf, *An Autobiography,* vol. 2, *1911–1969* (Oxford: Oxford University Press, 1980), p. 12.

12. Duncan Wilson, *Leonard Woolf: a political biography* (London: Hogarth Press, 1978), p. 21, citing Woolf's *Autobiography.*

13. H. D. Lewis, ed., *G. E. Moore: essays in retrospect* (London: George Allen, 1968), p. 40. The twentieth century, of course, brought the realisation that language that misleads its readers can be dangerous for both parties. In *The Idea of the Holy* (1917), Rudolph Otto illustrated the danger of metaphysical terms entering common currency and being devalued as a result. He listed the criteria of what he called the "irrational" in German philosophy: the contingent in contrast to the necessary; power and the will in contrast to reason and knowledge; impulse and instinct in contrast to insight and reflection; mystical depths and the stirrings of the soul; intuition and prophesy. (Rudolph Otto, *The Idea of the Holy*, transl. James Harvey [London: Oxford University Press, 1923], p. 58.)

14. Cited in Peter Wilson, 'Leonard Woolf and international government', in David Long and Peter Wilson, eds., *Thinkers of the Twenty-Year Crisis: interwar liberalism reassessed* (Oxford: Clarendon Press, 1995), p. 146.

15. Leonard Woolf, *Quack, Quack* (London: Hogarth Press, 1935), p. 60.

16. Ibid., p. 193. Woolf performs a typical trick here (intentionally or not?), namely, guilt by association, in mentioning Spengler in the same breath as the Nazis. It should be noted of course that Spengler was a critic of national socialism. In *The Reconstruction of the German Reich* he condemned German race theories as more dangerous than anything else. "Members of one's own race are more dangerous than strangers". And of Hitler, he wrote that Germany needed a "hero, not a heroic tenor". (See H. Stuart Hughes, *Oswald Spengler* [New York: Charles Scribner, 1952], pp. 124–127.) As for Nietzsche's nationalism, that too has been much misinterpreted. He called nationalism "a forcibly imposed state of siege" that required force and falsehood to maintain "a front of respectability". Once men recog-

nised the fact that they would work for a united Europe, they would not be afraid to proclaim themselves "good Europeans". (From *Human, All Too Human,* transl. R. J. Hollingdale [Cambridge: Cambridge University Press, 1986], No. 467.) In a 1931 edition of *Thus Spake Zarathustra* the German-born Jew Oscar Levy wrote: "In England for a long time they discredited Nietzsche by giving out not only that he lost his reason after publishing his books but that he lost it even when writing the most important of them". Levy called Nietzsche the only "innocent German" in contrast to the prophets of "the German state church". "A disciple of Nietzsche belongs to no country and has no right to defend one country, least of all that in which he was born." (From *Thus Spake Zarathustra,* 6th edition [London: Unwin, 1931].) Suspect because of his origins, Levy was expelled from Britain in 1921 and allowed to return only some years later. In a true Nietzschean spirit of revenge he published a journal, *The Good European.*

17. Woolf, *Quack, Quack,* p. 160.

18. Ibid., p. 140.

19. Ibid., p. 145. Whatever their problems with Spengler's main theme and his methodology, contemporary writers were much influenced by the poetic power of his work. Northrop Frye described *The Decline of the West* as "German romanticism at its corniest", full of Halloween imagery about "the dark goings on of nature and history". Still, he confessed that as a young man he had slept with it under his pillow. The Dutch historian Johan Huizinga found Spengler quite "absurd", yet he acknowledged himself at times quite "bewitched" by him: "He compels us to forget that we know better". (From William Dray, *Perspectives on History* [London: Routledge and Kegan Paul, 1980], p. 100.) For Hitler as a "medicine man", see Norbert Elias, *The Germans* (Cambridge: Polity Press, 1996): "Hitler was in essence an innovative political medicine man ... and since the Nazi regime represented a particularly malignant form of social mythology and magical manipulation of society, it throws into fuller relief the stage of development reached in our time regarding the capacity of people to handle their own social affairs and to solve their own special problems" (p. 389).

20. George Santayana, *Egoism in German Philosophy* (London: Dent and Sons, 1916), p. x. For a critical account of Santayana's misreading of German philosophy, written by an American during the Second World War, see the essay by Edward Schaub in Paul Schilpp, ed., *The Philosophy of George Santayana* (Evanston, Ill.: Northwestern University Press, 1940).

21. J. S. Mill, 'Comparison of the tendencies of French and English intellect', *Monthly Repository* (New Set 7, 1833), p. 802.

22. Cited in Houghton, *Victorian Frame of Mind,* p. 116.

23. Ibid.

24. Friedrich Nietzsche, *The Twilight of the Idols* (London: Penguin, 1990), p. 103.

25. Cited in Daniel R. Ahern, *Nietzsche as Cultural Physician* (University Park: Pennsylvania State University Press, 1995), p. 103.

26. See P. K. Kavanagh, ed., *The Essential Chesterton* (Oxford: Oxford University Press, 1987), pp. 94–99.

27. Friedrich Nietzsche, *Beyond Good and Evil* (New York: Vintage, 1984), No. 228.

28. Cited in Ahern, *Nietzsche as Cultural Physician,* p. 69.

29. Nietzsche, *Twilight of the Idols*, No. 112, 'Maxims and Arrows'.

30. Friedrich Nietzsche, *Ecce Homo* (London: Penguin, 1992), p. 119.

31. Nietzsche, *Beyond Good and Evil*, p. 189.

32. Eldon Eisenach, *The Two Worlds of Liberalism: religion and politics in Hegel, Locke, and Mill* (Chicago: Chicago University Press, 1981), p. 216.

33. Friedrich Nietzsche, *On the Genealogy of Morality*, ed. Keith Ansell-Pearson, transl. Carol Diethe (Cambridge: Cambridge University Press, 1994), p. 119. The British were very empirical even when speculating on the grandest themes. Thus Arnold Toynbee's monumental ten-volume *Study of Civilisation*, which took thirty years to complete, differed radically from Spengler's *Decline of the West*. One of his American critics in the *Herald Tribune* (28 October 1934) pronounced: "There is a radical difference in spirit and method between Spengler and Toynbee: Spengler is a prophet; Toynbee an enquirer. In his boldest attempts the British scholar remains an empiricist, a Baconian".

34. Friedrich Nietzsche, *Notebooks* (1880). Cited in Stanley Roseman, *The Mask of Enlightenment: Nietzsche's Zarathustra* (Cambridge: Cambridge University Press, 1995), p. 5.

35. Erich Heller, *The Importance of Nietzsche: ten essays* (Chicago: Chicago University Press, 1988), p. 157. Karl Popper made a similar observation in his autobiography when he attributed the death of logical positivism to the decline of interest by its practitioners in great problems. It had perished because of its obsession with the meaning of words and semantic puzzles. It had died because of its "scholasticism". (Popper, *Unending Quest: an intellectual autobiography* [London: Routledge, 1993], p. 90.)

36. Michael Hamburger, *A Proliferation of Prophets: essays on German writers from Nietzsche to Brecht* (Manchester: Carcanet Press, 1983), p. 10.

37. Milan Kundera, *Testaments Betrayed: an essay in nine parts* (London: Faber & Faber, 1995), pp. 224–226. A much more convincing portrayal of a totalitarian state is Rex Warner's *Aerodrome* (London: Harvill Collins, 1996; originally published in 1941). Its hero, the narrator Ray, unlike Winston Smith, is a three-dimensional figure who can veer between the totalitarian and the liberal vision. The village, disorderly, dirty and apparently irredeemable, contrasts markedly with the aerodrome on its outskirts, which is clean, ordered and in many ways inviting. But as Roy discovers, the attempt to order life can only end in disaster, as it does in the novel. Life in the end is 'forgiving' of human frailty. Order is not.

38. Cited in E. E. Sleinis, *Nietzsche's Revaluation of Values: a study in strategies* (Urbana: University of Illinois Press, 1994), p. 55. Theodore Zeldin puts the point very well: "Artists were not armies, their purpose was not to give security or defend prejudice; on the contrary, they were guerilla fighters, impossible to restrain, always on the move; and they showed how to acquire the strength to live with insecurity, to derive joy from its challenge". (Zeldin, *Happiness* [London: Harvill Collins, 1988], p. 268.)

39. See Russell Kirk, ed., *The Portable Conservative Reader* (London: Penguin 1982), p. 470.

40. Michael Oakeshott, 'The fortunes of scepticism', *Times Literary Supplement*, 15 March 1996, pp. 14–15.

41. Henry Statten, *Nietzsche's Voice* (Ithaca: Cornell University Press, 1990), pp. 78–79.

42. L. T. Hobhouse, *The Metaphysical Theory of the State: a criticism* (London: Routledge, 1993), p. 6.

43. André Malraux, *Anti-memoirs* (New York: Holt, Rinehart and Winston, 1968), p. 417.

44. Arthur Koestler, *The Trail of the Dinosaur* (New York: Vintage, 1994), pp. 134–135.

45. Cited in Daniel Boorstin, *The Creators: a history of the imagination* (New York: Vintage, 1992), p. 715.

46. Cited in Adam Piette, *Imagination at War: British fiction and poetry, 1939–1945* (London: PaperMac, 1995), pp. 179–180.

47. Leonard Woolf, *The Journey Not the Arrival Matters: an autobiography of the years 1939–1969* (London: Hogarth Press, 1969), p. 178.

48. Cited in Felipe Fernandez-Armesto, *Millennium: a history of the last thousand years* (London: Bantam Press, 1995), p. 469.

49. H. G. Wells, *Selected Short Stories* (London: Penguin, 1958), p. 686. I am reminded of Mountbatten's use of the same language in an entry he made in his diary on taking the Japanese surrender in Singapore in 1945: "I have never seen six more villainous, depraved or brutal faces in my life. I shudder to think what it would have been like in their power. When they got off their chairs and shambled out they looked like a bunch of gorillas with great baggy breaches and knuckles almost trailing on the ground". (Cited in Philip Ziegler, *Mountbatten* [London: Fontana, 1985], pp. 303–304.)

50. Cited in Peter Gay, *The Bourgeois Experience: from Victoria to Freud,* vol. 3, *The Cultivation of Hatred* (New York: Norton, 1993), p. 267.

51. Vincent Cheng, *Joyce, Race, and Empire* (Cambridge: Cambridge University Press, 1995), p. 32.

52. Ibid.

53. Arthur Conan Doyle, *The Lost World* (Oxford: Oxford University Press, 1995 [1912]), p. 26.

54. Houghton, *Victorian Frame of Mind,* p. 197.

55. Ibid., pp. 204–205, n. 34.

56. George Bernard Shaw, *The Simpleton of the Unexpected Isles,* in *Plays Extravagant* (London: Penguin 1991). In the preface Shaw wrote, "Is Everyman the creator of social values or a parasite? . . . the moral of the dramatic fable *The Simpleton* is clear enough . . . it is time for us to reconsider our Visions of Judgement and see whether we cannot change them from old stories in which we no longer believe . . . to serious and responsible public tribunals" (pp. 127–129).

57. Cited in Eric Bentley, *The Cult of the Superman* (London: Robert Hale, 1947), p. 166.

58. James Drennan, *Oswald Mosley and British Fascism* (London, 1934), p. 291.

59. See Jorge Luis Borges, *Other Inquisitions: essays, 1937–1952* (Austin: University of Texas Press, 1973).

60. Norman Mackenzie and Jean Mackenzie, *The Life of H. G. Wells: time traveller* (London: Hogarth Press, 1987), pp. 162–165.

61. Ibid.

62. Ibid.

63. Clive Bell, *Civilisation* (London: Chatto and Windus, 1928), p. 33.

64. John Hersey, *The Call: an American missionary in China* (London: Weidenfeld and Nicholson, 1985), p. 47.

65. G. L. Mosse, *Nationalism and Sexuality: respectability and abnormal sexuality in modern Europe* (New York: Howard Fertig, 1985), p. 116.

66. John Carey, *The Intellectuals and the Masses: pride and prejudice among the literary intelligentsia, 1880–1939* (London: Faber & Faber, 1992), pp. 162–165.

67. Mackenzie and Mackenzie, *Life of H. G. Wells,* p. 445.

68. In a very different work Eric Havelock describes the liberal temper: the preference for negotiation instead of war, for affection in place of competition, for complex political societies in which some adjustments between the powers of the strong and the needs of the many can be worked out. In the Greek writers of the fifth and fourth centuries B.C. he claims to find "a consistency of temper" in their approach to politics and life. (Havelock, *The Liberal Temper in Greek Politics* [London: Jonathan Cape, 1957], p. 32.)

69. What is consciousness and its relationship with conscience? Freud connects the words *'Gewissen'* and *'Wissen'*. "For what is conscience? On the evidence of language it is related to that of which one is most certainly conscious". In some languages the words are not distinguished. See Paul Ricoeur, *Freud and Philosophy: an essay in interpretation* (New Haven: Yale University Press, 1970), p. 204 n. 46.

70. J.G.A. Pocock, *Politics, Language and Time: essays on political thought and history* (New York: Atheneum, 1972), pp. 15ff.

71. Virginia Woolf, 'Mr. Bennett and Mr. Brown', in *Collected Essays,* vol. 1 (London: Hogarth Press, 1966), pp. 320–321. Woolf is the great novelist not of the master consciousness (like Proust and Joyce) but of streams of consciousness. Each of her novels is a new experiment with the self.

72. Cited in Thomas Harrison, *1910: the emancipation of dissonance* (Berkeley: University of California Press, 1996), p. 145.

73. Henri Lefebvre, *The Production of Space* (Oxford: Blackwell, 1993), p. 302.

74. Robert Musil, *The Man Without Qualities* (London: Picador, 1979), p. xv (see introduction by Eithne Wilkins and Ernst Kaiser). See also Jacques Darras: "The real artistic movement of the period—modernism—had nothing to do with the First World War and indeed predated its outbreak by several years. Already Picasso and Braque were experimenting with Cubism, while Matisse and Kandinsky were freeing colour from line. Stravinsky followed the lead of Debussy, adding savage rhythmic vitality to subtle orchestral texture, while the Dadaists in Zurich were taking poetry in directions unimaginable to the nineteenth century formalists against whom they were rebelling. Thus to the French the War, when it came in 1914, was in aesthetic terms at least an almost supernumerary event breaking out anachronistically after the real upheaval had taken place". (Darras, *Beyond the Tunnel of History* [London: Macmillan, 1990], p. 65.)

75. Cited in Harrison, *1910: emancipation of dissonance,* p. 67.

76. Cited in Lefebvre, *Production of Space,* p. 304. Illiberal societies, of course, such as the Soviet Union, never reconciled themselves to the new thinking. The Soviet state found it necessary to deny all scientific thinking after Darwin. After Hugo de Vries introduced chance into biology, contrary to the rules of Darwinian determinism, the Soviets, in Camus's classic phrase, entrusted the geneticist Lysenko with

"the task of disciplining the chromosomes"—with disastrous results for agriculture in the 1950s. (Camus, *The Rebel* [London: Penguin, 1991], p. 188.)

77. Miroslav Holub, *The Dimension of the Present Moment and Other Essays* (London: Faber & Faber, 1990), p. 132.

78. Musil, *Man Without Qualities*, p. 172.

79. Gerald Kennedy, *Imagining Paris: exile, writing, and American identity* (New Haven: Yale University Press, 1993), p. 202.

80. Donald Mitchell, *The Language of Modern Music* (London: Faber & Faber, 1976), pp. 74–76. Schoenberg was a nationalist in his early years. He called the New Music "a battle cry" and hoped that it would allow Germany to dominate music for another century (p. 27).

81. George Steiner, *No Passion Spent: essays, 1978–1996* (London: Faber & Faber, 1996), p. 249.

82. Hamburger, *Proliferation of Prophets*, p. 22.

83. Steven Ascheim, *The Nietzsche Legacy in Germany: 1890–1990* (Berkeley: University of California Press, 1992), p. 259.

84. Friedrich Nietzsche, *Human, All Too Human*, transl. R. J. Hollingdale (Cambridge: Cambridge University Press, 1986), p. xv.

85. Franz Kafka, *Stories, 1902–1924* (London: Futura, 1988), pp. 251–252.

86. Cited in Lewis, *Art of Being Ruled*, p. 57.

87. Maurice Merleau-Ponty, *The Phenomenology of Perception* (London: Routledge and Kegan Paul, 1962). See the preface, pp. viii, xxi. Richard Hughes, in an additional chapter to his uncompleted trilogy *The Human Predicament*, puts into the mind of one of his characters the following thoughts: "Perhaps it is the same with all Hitler's innermost thoughts: they are always whatever that man imagines his hearers are thinking themselves, so that hearing the Führer confide in you comes to no more than seeing yourself distorted in Hitler's unflattering mirror. . . . That makes the whole nature of Hitler's 'greatness' merely a pre-natural empathy, turning him into a caricature of yourself whoever you are—and even, however many you are: an incarnate caricature of the whole German nation". (Hughes, *The Wooden Shepherdess* [London: Harvill Collins, 1995], p. 434.)

88. Elias Canetti, *The Tongue Set Free* (London: Andre Deutsch, 1979), p. 25.

89. Milan Kundera, *The Art of the Novel* (London: Faber & Faber, 1987), p. 116. For sheer interest I must add an episode recounted by W. H. Auden while living in the United States. In an entry in his *Tabletalk* dated 11 December 1946 we find the following: "I had occasion once to visit the Pentagon and really that's straight out of Kafka. When I was just going through a gate to get out, a guard stopped me and said, 'Hey, where do you think you're going?' I answered, 'I want to get out'. And then, he said, 'You're out already'." (*The Tabletalk of W. H. Auden* [London: Faber & Faber, 1989], p. 11.)

90. August Strindberg, *Son of a Servant*.

91. Musil, *Man Without Qualities*, p. 17. José Ortega y Gasset said much the same of Spengler's great work, *The Decline of the West*. He condemned the simple mindlessness of those who thought Spengler had invented the idea of decline. "Before his book appeared everyone was talking of this matter, and it is well known the success of his book was due to the fact that the suspicion about relativism was already existing in people's minds in ways and for reasons of the most heterogeneous

kinds". (Ortega y Gasset, *The Revolt of the Masses* [Notre Dame, Ind.: University of Notre Dame Press, 1985], transl. Anthony Kerrigan, p. 9.)

92. Gustav Janouch, ed., *Conversations with Kafka* (London: Quartet, 1985), p. 143.

93. See Francis Haskell, *History and Its Images in Art: an interpretation of the past* (New Haven: Yale University Press, 1993), p. 494.

94. Cited in Stephen Kern, *The Culture of Time and Space* (New York: Oxford University Press 1994), p. 288.

95. Johan Huizinga, *Dutch Civilisation and the Seventeenth Century* (London: Collins, 1968), p. 107.

96. Lawrence Langer, 'Kafka as Holocaust prophet: a dissenting view', in *Admitting the Holocaust: collected essays* (Oxford: Oxford University Press, 1995), 109–124.

Chapter Two

1. John Maynard Keynes, *Essays in Biography* (New York: Norton, 1951), pp. 72–77.

2. Robert C. Tucker, *Stalin in Power: the revolution from above, 1918–1941* (New York: Norton, 1991), p. 93.

3. Theodore Zeldin, *An Intimate History of Humanity* (London: Sinclair Stevenson, 1994), p. 141.

4. John Keegan, *A History of Warfare* (London: Hutchinson, 1993), pp. xlii–xliii.

5. Leo Tolstoy, *War and Peace* (New York: Oxford University Press, 1983), p. 654. Hugh Walpole, who was present on the eastern front during the First World War, was one of the few Western intellectuals to find the Cossacks redeeming. "Wonderful sight", he wrote to his mother, "Cossacks swimming with their horses in the lake. Hundreds of horses, hundreds of the finest men in the world flashing naked in the sun—such colour and peace and happiness, the Cossacks playing with one another like babies". (Cited in Peter Vansittart, *Voices from the Great War* [London: Jonathan Cape, 1981], p. 76.)

6. Henri Barbusse, *Under Fire*, cited in Jon Silkin and Jon Glover, *Anthology of the First World War* (London: Viking, 1989), pp. 189–205.

7. Colin Wilson, *The Outsider* (London: Picador, 1978), p. 214.

8. Isaac Babel, *Diary 1920*, ed. Carol Avins (New Haven: Yale University Press, 1995), pp. 68–77.

9. Isaac Babel, *Collected Stories* (London: Penguin, 1994), p. 356.

10. Ibid., p. 347.

11. Norman Mackenzie and Jean Mackenzie, *The Life of H. G. Wells: time traveller* (London: Hogarth Press, 1987), p. 325.

12. John Reed, *The War in Eastern Europe* (New York: Charles Scribner, 1916), pp. 123–124.

13. Babel, *Collected Stories*, p. 263.

14. Ibid.

15. Neal Ascherson, *Black Sea* (London: Jonathan Cape, 1995), pp. 100–102.

16. Ibid., p. 362.

17. See Harry B. Henderson, '*The Red Badge of Courage:* The search for histori-cal identity', in Donald Pizler, ed., Stephen Crane, *The Red Badge of Courage* (New York: Norton, 1994), p. 238.

18. Ibid.

19. Vital Shentalinsky, *The KGB's Literary Archive* (London: Harvill Collins, 1995). For Munblit's comments, see Cynthia Ozick, 'Isaac Babel and the identity crisis', in *Portrait of the Artist as a Bad Character* (London: Pimlico, 1996), p. 227.

20. Thomas Mann, *Doctor Faustus* (London: Everyman, 1992), p. 397.

21. Friedrich Nietzsche, *A Nietzsche Reader*, transl. R. J. Hollingdale (London: Penguin, 1977), p. 65. In a letter to Mann's son, Gottfried Benn justified his deci-sion to join the Nazi movement, arguing that he was inspired by a longing for ag-gression, for a liberation from the intellect. That is why he had "placed [himself] at the disposal of those to whom Europe . . . denies recognition". Gustav Sack's motto was "I'd rather be a brute than spiritualised". Benn's Dr. Ronne yearns for the hap-piness of regression and commits murder to attain it. (Walter Sokel, *The Writer in Extremis: expressionism in twentieth-century German literature* [Stanford Univer-sity Press, 1959], p. 96.) See also S. D. Stirk, ed., *The Prussian Spirit: a survey of German literature and politics, 1914–1940* (London: Faber & Faber, 1942).

22. Mann, *Doctor Faustus,* p. 436.

23. See Gordon A. Craig, 'The Mann nobody knew,' *New York Review of Books,* 29 February 1996, p. 36.

24. Siegfried Sassoon, *Memoirs of an Infantry Officer* [the second volume of the trilogy] (London: Faber & Faber, 1930), p. 130.

25. Ibid.

26. Dagmar Banouw, *Weimar Intellectuals and the Threat of Modernity* (Bloom-ington: Indiana University Press, 1988), p. 30.

27. Friedrich Nietzsche, *On the Genealogy of Morality*, ed. Keith Ansell-Pearson, transl. Carol Diethe (Cambridge: Cambridge University Press, 1994), p. 184.

28. Cited in Saul Bellow, *It All Adds Up: from a dim past to an uncertain future* (London: Penguin, 1990), p. 90.

29. Milan Kundera, *Testaments Betrayed: an essay in nine parts* (London: Faber & Faber, 1995), p. 165.

30. H. G. Wells, *The War of the Worlds* (1898). Wells's novel is an apt descrip-tion of a continent that was hell-bent on war. One of the most powerful battleships of the day was HMS *Polyphemus*. It appears in the book under the transparent alias HMS *Thunderchild*. The *Polyphemus* is also the only weapon capable of resisting the onslaught of the Martians, hurling itself furiously against the wading war ma-chines crossing the Thames estuary before finally being despatched by a heat ray. See Jan Morris, *Fisher's Face* (London: Penguin, 1996), p. 79.

31. Hans-Georg Gadamer, 'Literature and philosophy in dialogue', in *Essays on German Literary Theory* (Albany: State University of New York Press, 1994), p. 90.

32. Curzio Malaparte, *Kaputt* (London: Picador, 1982), p. 21.

33. Cited in Ian Adams, *Political Ideology Today* (Manchester: Manchester Uni-versity Press, 1993), p. 231.

34. Karl Polanyi, *The Great Transformation: the political and economic origins of our time* (London: Beacon Press, 1994), p. 29.

35. Ibid., p. 53.

36. John Steinbeck, *A Russian Journal* (London: Minerva, 1994), pp. 120–121. German cities of course were devastated too at the end of the war. The Swiss playwright Max Frisch saw the extent of the destruction when he visited Frankfurt the same year. "At the railroad station. Refugees lying on all the steps. . . . Their life is unreal, a waiting without expectation, and they no longer cling to it, rather life clings to them, ghostlike. . . . It breathes on the sleeping children as they lie in the rubble, their heads between bony arms, curled up like embryos in the womb, as if longing to return there". (Max Frisch, *Sketchbook, 1946–1949* [New York: Harvest, 1983], p. 22.)

37. Jeremy Reed, *Madness: the price of poetry* (London: Peter Owen, 1989), p. 142.

38. Ibid., p. 140.

39. George Steiner, *Language and Silence: essays, 1958–1966* (London: Faber & Faber, 1985), p. 139.

40. Primo Levi, *The Drowned and the Saved* (London: Michael Joseph, 1988), p. 18.

41. Cited in Carolyn Forche, *Against Forgetting: the twentieth century and the poetry of witness* (New York: Norton, 1993), p. 88.

Chapter Three

1. Paul Ricoeur, *Time and Narrative,* vol. 2 (Chicago: Chicago University Press, 1985), p. 709.

2. Albert Camus, *Lyrical and Critical Essays,* ed. Philip Thody (New York: Vintage, 1968), p. 282.

3. Ricoeur, *Time and Narrative,* p. 710.

4. Clive Gamble, *Time Walks: the prehistory of global colonisation* (London: Penguin, 1995), p. 17.

5. François Guizot, *The History of Civilisation in Europe* (London: Penguin, 1997), p. 44, p. 249 n. 9.

6. Cited in Peter Osborne, 'Small scale victories, large scale defeats', in Andrew Benjamin and Peter Osborne, eds., *Walter Benjamin's Philosophy: destruction and experience* (London: Routledge, 1994), p. 86.

7. Ibid.

8. Ibid.

9. Ibid.

10. Cited in Robert Calasso, *The Ruin of Karsch* (Manchester: Carcanet, 1994), p. 51.

11. G.W.F. Hegel, *The Philosophy of Right,* transl. T. M. Knox (Oxford: Oxford University Press, 1979). Such thinking persisted well into the 1950s. The French philosopher Maurice Merleau-Ponty, for example, saw history as a process of natural selection. "History has meaning only in that there is a logic of human co-existence that . . . as if by natural selection, finally eliminates those that act as a diversion in relation to the permanent needs of humanity". (Cited in Raymond Aron, *History, Truth, and Liberty: selected writings of Raymond Aron,* ed. Francizek Draus [Chicago: University of Chicago Press, 1985], p. 49.)

12. G.W.F. Hegel, *The Philosophy of History,* transl. J. Sibree (New York: Wiley, 1944), p. 350.

13. Cited in John F. Laffey, *Civilisation and Its Discontented* (Cheektowaga, N.Y.: Black Rose Books, 1993), pp. 33–34.

14. See the introduction by Jonathan Spence to André Malraux, *The Temptation of the West* (Chicago: University of Chicago Press, 1992), pp. vii–xi.

15. Jacques Nanterre, *Here and Now* (Paris: Pleon, 1970), p. 107.

16. Shlomo Avineri, ed., *Marx on Colonialism and Modernisation* (New York: 1969), p. 132. Many of these concepts persisted right up to the late 1960s—and were not the prerogative of Marxist scholars. See Lloyd I. Rudolph and Susanne Hoeber Rudolph, *The Modernity of Tradition* (Chicago: University of Chicago Press, 1967), pp. 17ff. Marxists always hated small people asserting their right to a voice in the making of the twentieth century. Engels proclaimed that the south Slavs were "nothing more than the national refuse of a thousand years of mentally confused development". His conclusion was that a "war of annihilation and ruthless terrorising" might be necessary against such "an unhistoric people". Rosa Luxemburg, writing of the First World War, complained that the "would-be nations" were asserting their false claim to statehood. They were "rotted corpses" rising from centuries-old graves. She complained that "unhistoric peoples" were getting in the way of change. (See Mark Almond, *Europe's Backyard War: the war in the Balkans* [London: Mandarin, 1994], p. 71.)

17. Zsigmond Moricz, *Be Faithful unto Death*, transl. Stephen Vizinczey (Prague: Central European University Press, 1995), p. 177.

18. Avineri, *Marx on Colonialism*, p. 229.

19. D. Ross Gandy, *Marx and History: from primitive society to the communist future* (Austin: University of Texas Press, 1979), p. 20.

20. Avineri, *Marx on Colonialism*, p. 230.

21. See Elie Kedourie, *Hegel and Marx: introductory lectures* (Oxford: Blackwell, 1995), pp. 134–135.

22. Steven Smith, *Hegel's Critique of Liberalism: rights in context* (Chicago: University of Chicago Press, 1989), pp. 159–160.

23. Adolf Hitler, *Mein Kampf* (London: Pimlico, 1992), p. 61.

24. Jay W. Baird, *To Die for Germany: heroes in the Nazi pantheon* (Bloomington: Indiana University Press, 1990), p. 183.

25. Ibid., pp. 240–242.

26. Ibid.

27. Cited in Joachim Fest, *The Face of the Third Reich* (London: Pelican, 1972), p. 9.

28. Alexis de Tocqueville, *Democracy in America*, vol. 1, ed. Francis Bowen (Cambridge: Sever and Francis, 1864), p. 435. See also William D. Richardson, 'Racial equality in America', in Ken Masugi, ed., *Interpreting Tocqueville's Democracy in America* (Savage, Md.: Rowman & Littlefield, 1991), p. 456.

29. Clyde Milner, ed., *The Oxford History of the American West* (Oxford: Oxford University Press, 1994), p. 813. "It may be regarded as axiomatic", wrote the historian Milo M. Quaine in 1916, "that when a superior and an inferior race come into contact a struggle for domination will ensue ... [yet] no government ever entertained more enlightened and benevolent intentions towards a weaker people than did that of the United States towards the Indians". Quaine made his proud boast only three years after the U.S. government at last agreed to release an entire people,

the Chirichau Apaches from their twenty-seven-year confinement in prisoner-of-war camps. (Mark Apley, 'Tales of the dispossessed', *Times Literary Supplement*, 16 February 1996, p. 6.)

30. Michael Hereth, *Alexis de Tocqueville: threats to freedom in democracy* (Durham, N.C.: Duke University Press, 1986), p. 149.

31. The wars were not wars so much as skirmishes or mêlées. In the Red River War (1874–1875) the army lists fourteen pitched battles; however, it was not battle but attrition that wore the Indians down. They were expensive operations. It cost the government, according to its own estimates, $1 million to kill each Indian and $2 million to keep a regiment fed, clothed and maintained on the plains for a year. (Ralph Andrist, *The Long Death: the last days of the Plains Indians* [New York: Collier, 1993], p. 295.) In the end modernity displaced the Indians. Their buffalo hunts came to an end when cattlemen began fencing off the high plains with barbed wire. As Andrist writes, it is not completely coincidental that the Sioux who fell at Wounded Knee—the last engagement with the American army—died at the close of the same year in which the superintendent of the census announced that the frontier—until then the dominant theme of American life—had ceased to exist. "The Indian of the Old West was a creature of the other side of the frontier, the dwindling side, and when it finally pinched out there was no place left for him. He became in truth the vanishing American" (p. 354). See also Robert Wiebe, *The Opening of American Society: from the adoption of the constitution to the eve of disunion* (New York: Vintage, 1985); Stephen Ambrose, *Crazy Horse and Custer: the parallel lives of two American warriors* (New York: Doubleday, 1975), pp. 322–323.

32. Cited in Milner, *Oxford History of the American West*, p. 176.

33. Cited in Carey McWilliams, *Brothers Under the Skin* (Boston: Little, Brown, 1964), pp. 68–69.

34. René Dubos, *So Human an Animal* (New York: Charles Scribner, 1968), p. 138.

35. Octavio Paz, *On Poets and Others* (London: Paladin, 1992), p. 11.

36. Joseph Manzo, 'Native American, European American: some shared attitudes to life in the prairies', *American Studies* 23:2 (Fall 1982), p. 46.

37. Julie Roy Jeffrey, *Frontier Women: the trans-Mississippi West, 1840–1880* (New York: Vintage, 1979), p. 52.

38. Cited in Robert F. Berkhofer Jr., *The White Man's Indian: images of the American Indian from Columbus to the present* (New York: Vintage, 1979), p. 89.

39. George Fredrickson, *The Black Image* (New York: Praeger 1985), p. 305.

40. Jonathan Raban, *Hunting Mr. Heartbreak* (London: Harvill Collins, 1990), pp. 18–19.

41. George Steiner, *In Bluebeard's Castle: some notes towards the redefinition of culture* (New Haven: Yale University Press, 1971), p. 140.

42. Cited in Kathryn Tidrick, *Empire and the English Character* (London: J. B. Tauris, 1990), p. 85.

43. Hannah Arendt, *The Origins of Totalitarianism* (London: George Allen and Unwin, 1967), p. 197. Arendt adds, quoting from C. W. de Kiewiet's *History of South Africa* and Leonard Barnes's *Caliban in Africa*, "Here they were cured of the illusion that the historical process is necessarily 'progressive', for if it was the course of older colonisation to trek to something, 'the Dutchman trekked away from everything'; and if 'economic history once taught that man had developed by grad-

ual steps from a life of hunting to pastoral pursuits and finally to a settled and agricultural life', the story of the Boers clearly demonstrated that one could also . . . [revert back] 'to becom[ing] a herdsman and a hunter'" (pp. 206–207).

44. See Carl G. Jung, *Memories, Dreams, Reflections,* ed. Aniela Jaffe (New York: Vintage, 1989), pp. 238–247.

45. Ibid.

46. Paul Fussell, *The Great War and Modern Memory* (Oxford: Oxford University Press, 1975), pp. 112–113.

47. D. H. Lawrence, *Studies in Classic American Literature* (London: Penguin, 1977), p 56.

48. Ibid.

49. Elazar Barkan, *The Retreat of Scientific Racism: changing concepts of race in Britain and the United States between the two world wars* (Cambridge: Cambridge University Press, 1992), pp. 82–84. Such views were widely held. Take the German philosopher Carl Gustav Carus, who later influenced Jung. He thought the relation of the passage of the sun to any given area influenced the character of those living there. According to Carus (who was one of the first formulators of the idea of the unconscious) the new inhabitants of a geographical area acquired the characteristics of its previously unrelated inhabitants. (See Andrew Samuels, *The Political Psyche* [London: Routledge, 1993], p. 315.)

50. Erich Heller, *The Disinherited Mind: essays in modern German literature and thought* (Cambridge: Bowes and Bowes, 1952), p. 83.

51. Gaston Blanchard, *The Poetics of Space* (Boston: Beacon Press, 1994), p. 191.

52. Michael Weston, *Kierkegaard and Modern Continental Philosophy* (London: Routledge, 1994), p. 28.

53. Patrick Gardner, *Kierkegaard* (Oxford: Oxford University Press, 1988), p. 86.

54. Cited in David Chandler, *The Campaigns of Napoleon* (London: Weidenfeld and Nicholson, 1965), p. xi.

55. Cited in André Maurois, *A History of France* (London: Methuen 1964), p. 348.

56. Peter Fenves, *'Chatter': language and history in Kierkegaard* (Stanford: Stanford University Press: 1993), pp. 31–35.

57. Cited in Paul Britten Austin, *1812: the Great Retreat* (London: Greenhill Books, 1996), p. 425.

58. John Erickson and David Dilks, *Barbarossa: the Axis and the Allies* (Edinburgh: Edinburgh University Press: 1994), pp. 254–274.

59. Cited in David Jablonsky, *Churchill and Hitler: essays on the political-military direction of total war* (London: Frank Cass, 1994), p. 186.

60. Justin Kaplan, *Lincoln Steffens: a biography* (London: Jonathan Cape, 1975), p. 249.

61. Ibid., p. 329.

62. Robert B. Pippin, *Modernism as a Philosophical Problem: on the dissatisfactions of European high culture* (Oxford: Basil Blackwell, 1991), p. 43.

63. Cited in Sjepan Mestrovic, *A Coming Fin de Siècle: an application of Durkheim's sociology to modernity and post-modernity* (London: Routledge, 1991), p. 61.

64. Ibid., p. 71.

65. Albert Camus, *Between Hell and Reason: essays from the Resistance newspaper 'Combat', 1944–1947*, ed. Alexandre de Gramont (Hanover, N.H.: Wesleyan University Press, 1991), pp. 32–35.

Chapter Four

1. Octavio Paz, *Convergences: essays on art and literature* (London: Bloomsbury, 1990), p. 157.

2. J. H. Plumb, 'Churchill as historian', in A.J.P. Taylor, ed., *Churchill: four faces and the man* (London: Allen Lane, 1969), p. 121.

3. Paz, *Convergences*, p. 157.

4. See E. M. Cioran, *Tears and Saints* (Chicago: University of Chicago Press, 1995), pp. xvii–xxv. Such thinking still persists. In a 1995 publication by the Clubul Acoladelor, a political association, the reader is told that the association is dedicated to the following: collective destiny; the war against economic and technological totalitarianism; the study of traditional Indo-European and Greco-Latin culture; a geopolitical teleology; the defence against liberal utilitarianism; cultural ecology; anti-Americanism and anti-Marxism; ethnic existentialism and personal destiny; sociobiological imagination; and the pursuit of a heroic historical vision. (*Refuzul Americanizarii*, April 1995, ISBN 973-95612-6-8.)

5. Cioran, *Tears and Saints*, p. xix.

6. Cited in Noel Mostert, *Frontiers: the epic of South Africa's creation and the tragedy of the Xhosa people* (London: Pimlico, 1993), p. 480.

7. Cited in G. Totemeyer, 'Political groupings in Namibia: their role and changes', *International Affairs Bulletin* 2:1 (1978).

8. Cited in David Chandler, *The Campaigns of Napoleon* (London: Weidenfeld and Nicholson, 1965), p. 736.

9. Cited in Peter Vansittart, *Voices from the Great War* (London: Jonathan Cape, 1981), p. 55.

10. Michael Howard, 'War and the nation state', *Daedalus* 108 (Fall 1979), p. 102.

11. See the excellent discussion of nationalism (or absence of it in Napoleonic Europe) in Charles Esdaile, *The Wars of Napoleon* (London: Longman, 1995), pp. 261–264.

12. Yael Tamir, *Liberal Nationalism* (Princeton: Princeton University Press, 1993), p. 5.

13. Hans Sluga, *Heidegger's Crisis: philosophy and policy in Nazi Germany* (Cambridge, Mass.: Harvard University Press, 1993), p. 32.

14. Hans Kohn, 'Arndt and the character of German nationalism', *American Historical Review* 54:4 (July 1949), p. 801.

15. Cited in Tzvetan Todorov, *On Human Diversity: nationalism, racism, and exoticism in French thought* (Cambridge, Mass.: Harvard University Press, 1993), p. 211.

16. Cited in Louis Dumont, *German Ideology: from France to Germany and back* (Chicago: University of Chicago Press, 1994), pp. 230–231.

17. Ibid.

18. Ernst Jünger, *The Adventurer's Heart* (Berlin, 1929), cited in Karl Löwith, *Martin Heidegger and European nihilism* (New York: Columbia University Press, 1965), p. 180.

19. Cited in S. D. Stirk, ed., *The Prussian Spirit: a survey of German literature and politics, 1914–1940* (London: Faber & Faber, 1942), p. 62. For Mann, see *Reflections of a Nonpolitical Man,* transl. Walter D. Morris (New York: F. Unger, 1982), p. 32.

20. Cited in Dumont, *German Ideology,* p. 65.

21. Nietzsche, *Ecce Homo* (London: Penguin, 1992), p. 91.

22. Friedrich Nietzsche, *Unfashionable Observations: The Utility and liability of history for life,* in *The Complete Works of Friedrich Nietzsche,* ed. Ernst Behler (Stanford: Stanford University Press, 1995), pp. 83–169. Anatole France, in a short essay entitled 'Wicker Woman', wrote that the result of defeat in war was often incalculable—even in liberal England. French scholarship was despised in English universities after France's defeat in 1871. The English refused to learn from the vanquished. They wouldn't even listen to a professor discussing the origins of Greek poetry unless he came from a nation that excelled at the casting of cannon. "Such are the results of military inferiority, slow moving and illogical, yet sure in their effects". Alas, it was only too true that "the fate of the Muses is settled by a sword thrust".

23. See my discussion of H. G. Wells in *War and the Twentieth Century: the impact of war on modern consciousness* (London: Brassey's, 1994), pp. 101–109.

24. Cited in Paul Leonard Rose, *Wagner: race and revolution* (London: Faber & Faber, 1992), p. 113.

25. Ibid., p. 182.

26. David Beetham, *Max Weber and the Theory of Modern Politics* (London: Polity Press, 1985), p. 143.

27. Stephen Turner, 'Weber, the Germans, and Anglo-Saxon conversation: liberalism as a technique and form of life', in Ronald Glassman, ed., *Max Weber's Political Sociology: a pessimistic vision of a rationalised world* (Westport, Conn.: Greenwood Press, 1984), p. 45.

28. Cited in Gunther Roth, 'Between cosmopolitanism and ethno-centrism: Max Weber in the Nineties', *Telos* 96 (Summer 1993), p. 160. Weber totally ignored the cultural vitality of the German Polish community at that time. See Lech Trzeciakowski, *The Kulturkampf in Prussian Poland* (New York: Columbia University Press, 1990).

29. Philippe Lacoue-Labarthe, *Heidegger, Art, and Politics* (Oxford: Basil Blackwell, 1990), p. 96.

30. Paz, *Convergences,* p. 117.

31. D. H. Lawrence, *Apocalypse* (London: Penguin, 1976), p. 32.

32. Wyndham Lewis, *The Art of Being Ruled* (Santa Rosa, Calif.: Black Sparrow Press, 1989), p. 281.

33. Nagai Takashi, *The Bells of Nagasaki* (Tokyo: Kodansha, 1984).

34. Frank Kermode, *The Sense of an Ending: studies in the theory of fiction* (Oxford: Oxford University Press 1968), p. 156.

35. Ibid.

36. Cited in Robert Thomas, *Serbia: still Europe's pariah?* (London: Institute for European Defence and Strategic Studies, 1996), p. 10.

37. John Lukacs, *The Last European War: September 1939–December 1941* (London: Routledge and Kegan Paul, 1976), p. 66.

38. Milan Kundera, *Testaments Betrayed: an essay in nine parts* (London: Faber & Faber, 1995), p. 192.

39. Cited in Neal Ascherson, *Black Sea* (London: Jonathan Cape, 1995), p. 160.

40. Zbigniew Brzezinski, *Power and Principle: the memoirs of the national security adviser, 1977–1990* (London: Weidenfeld and Nicholson, 1983), p. 541.

41. Czeslaw Milosz, *The Land of Ulro* (New York: Farrar, Straus and Giroux, 1984), pp. 270–272.

42. Jan Ciechanowski, *The Warsaw Rising of 1944* (Cambridge: Cambridge University Press, 1974), p. 256.

43. Czeslaw Milosz, *The Captive Mind* (London: Penguin, 1981), pp. 297–298.

44. Michael Howard, *War and the Liberal Conscience* (New York: Rutgers University Press, 1978), p. 10.

45. Michael Biddis, 'Nationalism and the moulding of modern Europe', *History* 79:257 (October 1994), p. 412.

46. John Gooch, *The Unification of Italy* (London: Methuen, 1986), p. 19.

47. Richard Bellamy, ed., *Pre-Prison Writings of Antonio Gramsci* (Cambridge: Cambridge University Press, 1994), pp. 244–245. See also Antonio Gramsci, *Selections from Cultural Writings*, ed. David Forgris (London: Lawrence and Wishart, 1985).

48. Carlo Levi, *Christ Stopped at Eboli* (New York: Noonday, 1989), p. 123. In the 1920s Norman Douglas wrote of the peasants of Calabria: "The adult Jesus . . . is practically unknown. He is too remote from themselves and the ordinary activities of their daily lives; he is not married like his mother, he has no trade like his father . . . moreover the maxims of the Sermon on the Mount are so repugnant to the south Italian as to be almost incomprehensible". *Old Calabria* (London: Picador, 1994), p. 274.

49. Cited in Adrian Lyttelton, *Italian Fascism: from Pareto to Gentile* (London: Jonathan Cape, 1973), pp. 225–227.

50. Curzio Malaparte, *The Skin* (London: Picador, 1988), p. 240.

51. Lyttelton, *Italian Fascism*, p. 24.

52. G. K. Chesterton, *Orthodoxy* (London: Hodder and Stoughton, 1996), p. 98.

53. Nietzsche, *Unfashionable Observations*, p. 93.

54. Nietzsche, *On the Genealogy of Morality*, ed. Keith Ansell-Pearson, transl. Carol Diethe (Cambridge: Cambridge University Press, 1994), p. 67.

55. Taylor, *Churchill: four faces and the man*, p. 51.

56. Sigmund Freud, 'On Transience', *Standard Edition of the Complete Psychological Works of Sigmund Freud*, ed. James Strachey (London: Hogarth Press, 1953–1974), vol. 15, pp. 305–307.

57. Harold James, *A German Identity, 1770–1790* (London: Weidenfeld and Nicholson, 1990), p. 215. Of course most nations thought in intellectual terms in the modern era. "In the world of action", wrote Ernest Barker on the eve of the Second World War, "apprehended ideas are alone elemental and the nation must be an idea as well as a fact before it can become a dynamic force". (Barker, *The Nation State and National Self-determination* [London: Fontana, 1969], p. 42.)

58. George Orwell, *Homage to Catalonia* (London: Secker & Warburg, 1938), p. 314.

59. George Orwell, *The Road to Wigan Pier* (London: Penguin, 1989). See the introduction by Richard Hoggart, pp. ix–x.

60. Ibid. For a similarly depressing picture of England by another writer on the left, see Cyril Connolly, *The Condemned Playground* (London: Routledge, 1929). In a diary entry dated July 1929 he wrote: "Landed at New Haven. Depressed at being back in England. . . . Everybody is so weak and knock-kneed, a race of little ferrets and blind worms. . . . Disgusted by the crowd at Brighton. So dull, so dead, so woe-begone . . . men all undersized and weedy" (p. 206). For Mass Observation, see Anthony Burgess, *Homage to QWERT YUIOP: selected journalism, 1978–1985* (London: Abacus, 1987), p. 120.

61. Cited in Paul Fussell, *Abroad: British literary travelling between the wars* (Oxford: Oxford University Press, 1987), p. 74.

62. Cited in Martin Green, *Children of the Sun: a narrative of decadence in England after 1918* (London: Constable, 1977), pp. 468–469.

63. Cited in Joseph Brodsky, *Less than One: selected essays* (London: Penguin, 1986), p. 310.

64. Cited in Mary Lago and P. N. Furbank, eds., *Selected Letters of E. M. Forster,* vol. 2 (London: Collins, 1985), p. 118.

65. E. M. Cioran, *The Temptation to Exist* (London: Quartet, 1984), p. 53.

Chapter Five

1. Oswald Spengler, *The Decline of the West* (Oxford: Oxford University Press, 1991), p. 81. Time was the key to Napoleon's career. Nietzsche once described him as a man who was more "unique and late born for his times than ever man had been before" (*On the Genealogy of Morality,* ed. Keith Ansell-Pearson, transl. Carol Diethe (Cambridge: Cambridge University Press, 1994), p. 36), a remark that captures the ambivalence of Napoleon as a timeless (unique) individual but also an anachronism by 1812—a man at odds with history.

2. William Hazlitt, *Selected Writings* (Oxford: Oxford University Press, 1991), p. 236.

3. Cited in Alan Schom, *One Hundred Days: Napoleon's road to Waterloo* (London: Penguin, 1994), p. 321.

4. Pieter Geyl, 'Latter day Napoleon worship', in Pieter Geyl, *Debates with Historians* (London: Fontana, 1970), p. 250.

5. E. B. Ashton and Theodor Adorno, *The Negative Dialectics* (London: Routledge and Kegan Paul, 1973).

6. Nigel Reeves, *Heinrich Heine: poetry and politics* (London: Libris, 1994), p. 88.

7. For a discussion of the role of the hero in the *Mahabharata*, see Ruth Cecily Katz, *Arjuna in the Mahabharata: where Krishna is, there is victory* (Columbia, South Carolina: University of South Carolina Press, 1989).

8. Wyndham Lewis, *The Art of Being Ruled* (Santa Rosa, Calif.: Black Sparrow Press, 1989), p. 287. Marx's great mistake, Sorel argued, was to have undervalued "the enormous power of mediocrity in history". The production of the hero and of the heroic was Sorel's constant preoccupation. See Herbert Read, ed., *Speculations: essays on humanism and the philosophy of art* (London: Routledge and Kegan Paul, 1924), pp. 249–260.

9. See Scott Burnham, *Beethoven Hero* (Princeton: Princeton University Press, 1995), pp. 5–9.

10. Cited in Frank Field, *British and French writers of the First World War* (Cambridge: Cambridge University Press, 1991), p. 181.

11. Thomas Carlyle, *Sartor Resartus* (London: Everyman, 1973), p. 135.

12. Thomas Carlyle, *On Heroes and Hero Worship* (London: Everyman, 1973), p. 467. In *Past and Present* his attitude was more ambiguous. He saw Napoleon's career as circular: "Your Napoleon is flung out, at last on St. Helena: the latter end of him sternly compensating the beginning". He compared him to the English buccaneer Howel Davies: "Howell Davies dyes the West Indian seas with blood; piles his decks with plunder; proves himself the expertest seaman; the daringest sea fighter; but he gains no lasting victory; lasting victory is not possessed for him". The fault of both men is that they did not have right on their side. "All fighting is the dusty conflict of strengths, each thinking itself the strongest or in other words, the justest of rights which do in the long run and forever will in this just Universe mean Rights" (pp. 164–166). This passage can be taken to mean that might equals right, but it can also be read differently, that only right is mighty in the long term.

13. Cited in Eric C. Hansen, *Disaffection and Decadence: a crisis in French intellectual thought, 1848–1898* (Washington, D.C.: University Press of America, 1982), p. 232.

14. George Steiner, *In Bluebeard's Castle: some notes towards the redefinition of culture* (New Haven: Yale University Press, 1971), p. 22.

15. Cited in Eric Bentley, *The Cult of the Superman* (London: Robert Hale, 1947), p. 23.

16. Walter Houghton, *The Victorian Frame of Mind, 1830–1870* (New Haven: Yale University Press, 1975), p. 330.

17. Hansen, *Disaffection and Decadence*, p. 24.

18. Cited in Henri Lefebvre, *Introduction to Modernity: twelve preludes, September 1959–May 1961*, transl. John Moore (London: Verso, 1995), p. 20.

19. Karl Marx and Friedrich Engels, *The German Ideology*, ed. C. J. Arthur (London: Wishart and Hart, 1996), p. 42.

20. See Jorge Luis Borges, 'The mirror of the enigmas', in *Other Inquisitions: essays, 1937–1952* (Austin: University of Texas Press, 1973), pp. 125–128.

21. Miroslav Holub, *The Dimension of the Present Moment and Other Essays* (London: Faber & Faber, 1990), pp. 56–58.

22. Claudio Magris, *Danube: a sentimental journey from the source to the Black Sea* (London: Collins Harvill, 1990), pp. 78–81.

23. Fyodor Dostoyevsky, *Crime and Punishment* (London: Penguin, 1951), p. 291.

24. Ibid., pp. 277–280.

25. Magris, *Danube*, p. 280.

26. See Philip Windsor, 'The clock, the context, and Clausewitz', *Millennium* 6:2 (1977), p. 192.

27. Cited in Bruce Detwiler, *Nietzsche and the Politics of Aristocratic Radicalism* (Chicago: University of Chicago Press, 1990), p. 2. "*Mein Kampf* . . . could hardly have been written without the aid of two of the great names of the colourful heritage of the West—Richard Wagner and Friedrich Nietzsche".

28. Nicholas Martin, 'Nietzsche under fire', *Times Literary Supplement*, 5 August 1994, p. 11. The two soldiers were very different from the young Edwin Muir, new from the world of the crofters, chancing in an Edinburgh bookstall on a worn-out copy of *Zarathustra* that was to transform his inner and outer life. (George Steiner, *On Difficulty and Other Essays* [Oxford: Oxford University Press, 1978], p. 203.)

29. Friedrich Nietzsche, *Beyond Good and Evil* (New York: Vintage, 1989), p. 199.

30. Friedrich Nietzsche, *Thus Spake Zarathustra* (London: Penguin, 1978), p. 49.

31. Friedrich Nietzsche, *The Twilight of the Idols* (London: Penguin, 1990), p. 104.

32. See Irving Zeitlin, *Nietzsche: a reexamination* (Cambridge: Polity Press, 1994), p. 143.

33. See Mark Warren, *Nietzsche and Political Thought* (Cambridge, Mass.: MIT Press, 1991), p. 67.

34. Nietzsche, *Twilight of the Idols*, p. 191.

35. See Stanley Rosen, *The Mask of Enlightenment: Nietzsche's Zarathustra* (Cambridge: Cambridge University Press, 1995), p. 108.

36. Cited in Alan White, *Within Nietzsche's Labyrinth* (London: Routledge and Kegan Paul, 1990), p. 35.

37. Nietzsche, *On the Genealogy of Morality*, I:16.

38. Tracy Strong, *Friedrich Nietzsche and the Politics of Transfiguration* (Berkeley: University of California Press, 1975), p. 199.

39. Friedrich Nietzsche, *The Will to Power*. See *The Complete Works of Friedrich Nietzsche*, transl. Oscar Levy, vol. 15 (London: Wren Press, 1910), p. 107.

40. Cited in Erich Heller, *The Importance of Nietzsche: ten essays* (Chicago: University of Chicago Press, 1988), p. 54.

41. Cited in Michael Hamburger, *A Proliferation of Prophets: essays on German writers from Nietzsche to Brecht* (Manchester: Carcanet Press, 1983), pp. 25–27.

42. Nietzsche, *Thus Spake Zarathustra*, p. 73.

43. Nietzsche, *Twilight of the Idols*, p. 76.

44. Corelli Barnett, *The Sword Bearers: studies in supreme command in the First World War* (London: Penguin, 1966), p. 274.

45. Ibid.

46. Azar Gat, *The Development of Military Thought in the Nineteenth Century* (Oxford: Clarendon Press, 1992), p. 166.

47. Joseph Chiari, *Twentieth-Century French Thought: from Bergson to Lévi-Strauss* (New York: Gordian, 1975), p. 36. For Bergson's political thought, see Ellen Kennedy, 'Bergson's philosophy and French political doctrines: Sorel, Maurras, Péguy, and de Gaulle', *Government and Opposition* 15:1 (Winter 1980).

48. Theodore Zeldin, *France, 1848–1945*, vol. 2, *Intellect, Taste, and Anxiety* (Oxford: Oxford University Press, 1977), p. 1143.

49. Ibid., pp. 13–14.

50. Cited in David L. Schalk, *Roger Martin du Gard: the novelist and history* (Ithaca: Cornell University Press, 1967), p. 156.

51. Cited in Mary Jean Green, *Fiction in the Historical Present: French writers and the thirties* (Hanover, N.H.: University Press of New England, 1986), p. 79.

52. Frank Field, *British and French Writers of the First World War: comparative studies in cultural history* (Cambridge: Cambridge University Press, 1991), p. 249.

53. Cited in Ray Monk, *The Duty of Genius* (London: Jonathan Cape, 1990), p. 137.

54. Ibid., p. 139.

55. Rush Rhees, ed., *Recollections of Wittgenstein* (Oxford: Oxford University Press, 1984), p. 197.

56. Ibid., p. 190.

57. Another artist wrote: "Whoever wants to possess his own life must not consider himself born and alive just because he was born". See Thomas Harrison, *1910: the emancipation of dissonance* (Berkeley: University of California Press, 1996), p. 76.

58. Ludwig Wittgenstein, *Tractatus Logico-Philosophicus* (London: Routledge, 1981), pp. 186–187.

59. Ibid.

60. Rhees, *Recollections,* p. 199.

61. Monk, *Duty of Genius,* p. 4.

62. Ludwig Wittgenstein, *Culture and Value* (Oxford: Basil Blackwell, 1980), p. 61.

63. Gottfried Benn, writing of the role of the intellectuals in 1947 at the outset of the Cold War, saw no ground for optimism. "The West is not being destroyed by the totalitarian systems ... nor by its material impoverishment, or its Gottwalds and Molotovs, but by the dog-like grovelling of its intellectuals before political concepts". (Cited in Hamburger, *Proliferation of Prophets,* p. 222.)

64. See Paul Ricoeur, *Political and Social Essays,* ed. D. Stewart (Athens: Ohio University Press, 1974), pp. 95–97.

65. Georges Bataille, *Literature and Evil* (London: Calder and Boyars, 1973), p. 88.

66. Judith Shklar, *Freedom and Independence: a study of the political ideas of Hegel's 'Phenomenology of Mind'* (Cambridge: Cambridge University Press, 1976), p. 176. See also Chris Arthur, 'Hegel and the French Revolution', *Radical Philosophy* 52 (Summer 1989), pp. 18–21, and Charles Taylor, *Hegel and Modern Society* (Cambridge: Cambridge University Press, 1992), p. 120.

67. Cited in Richard Sennett, *Authority* (London: Faber & Faber, 1993), p. 134.

68. Pierre Klossowski, *Sade My Neighbour* (London: Quartet, 1992), p. 49.

69. Ibid.

70. Michael Gillespie, *Nihilism Before Nietzsche* (Chicago: University of Chicago Press, 1996), p. 172.

71. Peter Berkowitz, *Nietzsche: the ethics of an immoralist* (Cambridge, Mass.: Harvard University Press, 1995), p. 265.

72. Cited in Thomas Keenan, 'Freedom: the law of another fable', in *Literature and the Ethical Question,* Yale French Studies No. 79 (New Haven: Yale University Press, 1991), p. 241.

73. Octavio Paz, *On Poets and Others* (London: Paladin, 1992), p. 47.

74. Cited in Mary Gluck, *Georg Lukács and His Generation, 1900–1918* (Cambridge, Mass.: Harvard University Press, 1985), p. 207.

75. Cited in Peter du Preez, *Genocide: the psychology of mass murder* (New York: Calder and Boyars, 1994), p. 103.

76. Jorge Luis Borges, 'Three versions of Judas', in *Labyrinths* (New York: New Directions, 1990), pp. 98–100.

77. See Jean Améry, *At the Mind's Limit* (Bloomington: Indiana University Press, 1980), pp. 25–26.

78. Jean Genet, *A Thief's Journal* (London: Penguin, 1982), p. 102.

79. Reinhold Niebuhr, *The Irony of American History* (London: Nisbet, 1952), p. 133.

80. Herbert Butterfield, *Christianity and History* (London: Bell, 1949), p. 88.

81. Ibid., p. 104.

82. Ali El-Kentz, ed., *Algeria: the challenge of modernity* (London: Cordesia Books, 1991), p. 8.

83. Felix Markham, *Napoleon and the Awakening of Europe* (London: English University Press, 1965), pp. 274–275.

84. See William Irvine, *The Universe of George Bernard Shaw* (New York: McGraw Hill, 1950), p. 179.

Chapter Six

1. Friedrich Nietzsche, *Human, All Too Human*, transl. R. J. Hollingdale (Cambridge: Cambridge University Press, 1986), p. 103.

2. Peter Gay, *The Enlightenment: an interpretation*, vol. 2, *The Science of Freedom* (New Haven: Yale University Press, 1969), pp. 1–12.

3. Cited in J. N. Enright, ed., *The Oxford Anthology of Death* (Oxford: Oxford University Press, 1983), pp. 233–234.

4. John Keane, *Reflections on Violence* (London: Verso, 1996), pp. 12–15.

5. Cited in Henri Lefebvre, *Introduction to Modernity: twelve preludes, September 1959–May 1961*, transl. John Moore (London: Verso, 1995), p. 1.

6. Cited in Roger Chartier, *Cultural History* (Cambridge: Polity Press, 1988), p. 92.

7. Norbert Elias, *The Civilising Process* (Oxford: Blackwell, 1994). See also the discussion of Elias's work by Keane, *Reflections on Violence*, pp. 24–31.

8. Cited in Paul Ricoeur, *Freud and Philosophy: an essay on interpretation* (New Haven: Yale University Press, 1970), pp. 304–305.

9. Ibid., p. 307.

10. Jacques Le Rider, *Modernity and Crises of Identity: culture and society in fin-de-siècle Vienna*, transl. Rosemary Morris (Cambridge: Polity, 1993), p. 39.

11. Peter Lowenberg, 'Germany: the home front: (1) The physical and psychological consequences of home front hardships', in Hugh Cecil and Peter Liddle, eds., *Facing Armageddon: the First World War experienced* (London: Leo Cooper, 1996), pp. 560–561.

12. Anne Frank, *The Diary of a Young Girl* (New York: Doubleday, 1967), cited in Thomas Mallon, *A Book of One's Own: people and their diaries* (London: Picador, 1984), p. 257.

13. Herbert Read, *The Innocent Eye* (1933), cited in Peter Abbs, *The Polemics of Imagination: selected essays on art, culture, and society* (London: Skoob, 1996), pp. 77–78.

14. Cited in Wolfgang Leppmann, *Rilke: a life* (Cambridge: Lutterworth, 1984), pp. 285–286.

15. Virginia Woolf, *Three Guineas* (London: Hogarth Press, 1938), p. 265 n. 3.

16. *The Sunday Times*, 11 November 1995.

17. Laurence James, *The Rise and Fall of the British Empire* (London: Little, Brown, 1994), p. 289.

18. Frank McLynn, *Hearts of Darkness: the European exploration of Africa* (London: Hutchinson, 1992), p. 110.

19. Ibid., p. 186.

20. *Pages from the Goncourt Journal*, ed. Robert Baldick (New York: Oxford University Press, 1988), p. 179.

21. McLynn, *Hearts of Darkness*, p. 353.

22. Ibid., p. 186.

23. Nietzsche, *Human, All Too Human*, No. 477, p. 176.

24. Cited in Brian Spittles, *Joseph Conrad: text and context* (London: Macmillan, 1992), p. 67.

25. Erich Fromm, *The Anatomy of Human Destructiveness* (London: Penguin, 1987), p. 185.

26. Stephen Marshall, *Norbert Elias: civilisation and the human self-image* (Oxford: Basil Blackwell, 1989), p. 3.

27. Richard Meinertzhagen, *Kenya Diary, 1902–1906* (London: Elan Books, 1984), p. 179.

28. Cited in Denis Winter, *Death's Men: soldiers of the Great War* (London: Penguin, 1979), p. 90.

29. Ibid., p. 91.

30. Desmond Young, *Rommel: the Desert Fox* (New York: Berkeley University Press, 1961), pp. 25–26.

31. Umberto Eco, *Travels in Hyperreality* (London: Picador, 1994), p. 168.

32. Robert Musil, *The Man Without Qualities* (London: Picador, 1979), p. 607.

33. Cited in Frank Whitboard, 'Killer as victim', *The Times Literary Supplement*, 30 October 1995, p. 9.

34. Anton Gill, *A Dance Between Flames: Berlin between the wars* (London: Abacus, 1995), p. 41.

35. Ibid., p. 196.

36. John F. Laffey, *Civilisation and Its Discontented* (Cheektowaga, N.Y.: Black Rose Books, 1993), p. 73.

37. Ibid.

38. Theodore Zeldin, *France, 1848–1945*, vol. 2, *Intellect, Taste, and Anxiety* (Oxford: Oxford University Press, 1977), p. 12.

39. Maria Tatar, *Lustmord: sexual murder in Weimar Germany* (Princeton: Princeton University Press, 1995), pp. 47–48.

40. George L. Mosse, *Nationalism and Sexuality: respectability and abnormal sexuality in modern Europe* (New York: Howard Fertig, 1985), p. 169.

41. Cited in Gill, *Dance Between Flames*, pp. 124–126.

42. Arthur Schopenhauer, *Essays and Aphorisms*, transl. R. J. Hollingdale (London: Penguin, 1988), pp. 138–139.

43. Larry Wolff, *Postcards from the End of the World: an investigation into the mind of fin-de-siècle Vienna* (London: Collins, 1989).

44. Ibid., p. 89.

45. Ibid., pp. 69–70.

46. Cited in Norman Manea, *On Clowns: the dictator and the artist* (London: Faber & Faber, 1992), p. 34.

47. Cited in Anthony Storr, *Churchill's Black Dog, Kafka's Mice, and Other Phenomena of the Human Mind* (New York: Grove Press, 1988), p. 63.

48. Ibid., p. 64.

49. Elias Canetti, *Kafka's Other Trial: the letters to Felice* (London: Calder and Boyars, 1974), p. 36.

50. Franz Kafka, *Wedding Preparations in the Country and Other Stories* (London: Penguin, 1978), p. 34.

51. Laffey, *Civilisation and Its Discontented*, p. 53.

52. Cited in Michael Ignatieff, *A Just Measure of Pain: the penitentiary in the industrial revolution* (London: Penguin, 1989), p. 66.

53. Vincent Cheng, *Joyce, Race, and Empire* (Cambridge: Cambridge University Press, 1995), p. 27.

54. Gustave Le Bon, *The Crowd* (New Brunswick, N.J.: Transaction Publishers, 1995).

55. John Carey, *The Intellectuals and the Masses: pride and prejudice among the literary intelligentsia, 1880–1939* (London: Faber & Faber, 1992), p. 144.

56. Cited in John Keegan, *The Face of Battle* (London: Penguin, 1976), p. 225. The intellectual capacity of many working-class soldiers was not very high. A pre-war study found that some of the soldiers of the British army had a mental age of ten to thirteen years. Troops going home on leave were marched to stations and put on the right trains because of the difficulties they experienced in doing this unaided. (Len Deighton, *Blood, Tears, and Folly: an objective look at World War II* [London: Jonathan Cape, 1993], p. 121.)

57. Winter, *Death's Men*, p. 41.

58. John Ellis, *The Sharp End of War: the fighting man in World War II* (London: Pimlico, 1993), p. 55.

59. Melanie Klein, 'Notes on some schizoid mechanisms', in Melanie Klein, *Envy and Gratitude and Other Works* (New York: Delta, 1975), p. 4.

60. Stephen Frosh, *Identity Crisis: modernity, psychoanalysis, and the self* (London: Macmillan, 1991), p. 52.

61. Bruno Bettelheim, *The Informed Heart: autonomy in a mass age* (London: Penguin, 1986), p. 181.

62. Cited in David Watson, *Hannah Arendt* (London: Fontana Press, 1992), pp. 60–61.

63. Keane, *Reflections on Violence*, p. 63.

64. Cited in Lawrence Langer, 'Kafka as Holocaust prophet: a dissenting view', in *Admitting the Holocaust: collected essays* (Oxford: Oxford University Press, 1995), p. 121.

65. Ibid.

66. Le Rider, *Modernity and Crises of Identity*, p. 241.

67. Frosh, *Identity Crisis*, p. 191.

68. Cited in Hugo Ott, 'A distant command: the political dimension of Heidegger's philosophy', *German Currents* 17 (January 1990), p. 87.

69. Pierre Bourdieu, *The Political Ontology of Martin Heidegger* (Cambridge: Polity Press, 1991), p. 24.

70. Cited in Marsha Rozenblit, *The Jews of Vienna, 1867–1914: assimilation and identity* (Albany: State University of New York Press, 1983), p. 4.

71. Ibid., p. 9.

72. Robert S. Wistrich, *The Jews of Vienna in the Age of Franz Joseph* (Oxford: Oxford University Press, 1990), p. 60.

73. Rozenblit, *The Jews of Vienna*, p. 9.

74. Cited in Wistrich, *The Jews of Vienna*, p. 539.

75. Cited in Peter Gay, *Freud, Jews, and other Germans: masters and victims in modernist culture* (Oxford: Oxford University Press, 1979), pp. 90–91.

76. See Le Rider, *Modernity and Crises of Identity*, pp. 12–13.

77. George Steiner, *No Passion Spent: essays, 1978–1996* (London: Faber & Faber, 1996), p. 23. See also Harold Bloom: "I do not think that the psyche is a text, but I find it illuminating to discuss texts as though they were psyches, and in doing so I consciously follow the Kabbalists". (Cited in Cynthia Ozick, 'Isaac Babel and the identity crisis', in *Portrait of the Artist as a Bad Character* [London: Pimlico, 1996], p. 137.)

78. Jean-François Lyotard, *Heidegger and the Jews,* transl. Andreas Michel and Mark S. Roberts (Minneapolis: University of Minnesota Press, 1990), p. xxiv.

79. Cited in Patrick Carnegy, *Faust as Musician: a study of Thomas Mann's novel 'Doctor Faustus'* (London: Chatto and Windus, 1973), p. 89.

80. Cited in William Pfaff, *Barbarian Sentiments: how the American Century ends* (New York: Will and Wang, 1989), p. 58.

81. Peter Gay, *Art and Act* (New York: Harper & Row, 1976).

82. Susan Sontag, *Illness as a Metaphor* (London: Penguin, 1979); *AIDS and Its Metaphors* (London: Penguin, 1990).

Chapter Seven

1. J. B. Priestley, *English Journey* (London: Mandarin, 1994).

2. A.J.P. Taylor, *English History, 1914–1945* (Oxford: Oxford University Press, 1965), p. 489.

3. J. H. Plumb, 'Churchill as historian', in A.J.P. Taylor, ed., *Churchill: four faces and the man* (London: Allen Lane, 1969), p. 121.

4. G. K. Chesterton, *The Napoleon of Notting Hill* (London: Penguin, 1982), pp. 14–15.

5. Thomas Mann, *Doctor Faustus* (London: Everyman, 1992), pp. 119–120.

6. Cited in G. T. Waddington, 'Hassgegner: German views of Britain in the late 1930s', *History* 81:261 (January 1996), p. 38.

7. The point was put elegantly by Wittgenstein: "Resting on your laurels is as dangerous as resting when you are walking in the snow. You doze off and die in your sleep". *Culture and Value* (Oxford: Basil Blackwell, 1980), p. 35e.

8. See Andrew Samuels, *The Political Psyche* (London: Routledge, 1993), p. 9.

9. Peter Abbs, *The Polemics of Imagination: selected essays on art, culture, and society* (London: Skoob, 1996), p. 17.

10. Octavio Paz, *On Poets and Others* (London: Paladin, 1992), p. 37.

11. Germaine Brée, *Camus and Sartre: crisis and commitment* (London: Calder and Boyars, 1974), p. 110.

12. See Roger Caldwell, 'The pope of surrealism', *Literary Review* (October 1995), pp. 45–46.

13. Ibid. The surrealists sought to push poetry to its utmost limits of possibility, to blur the distinction between art and life and thus explode the outer limits of human freedom. To quote Benjamin, they were the first to challenge "the liberal-moral-humanistic ideal of freedom" because they believed in absolute freedom—in unrestricted or "free love", unbounded by social conventions. The surrealists were interested in the *poetics,* not the politics of revolution. See Paul Auster, *The Red Notebook* (London: Faber & Faber, 1995), p. 60. Camus reminds us that the French revolution 170 years earlier had been very different. It did not see the birth of a new art, only the journalism of Desmoulins and the 'under-the-counter' works of Sade. The followers of Saint-Simon may have demanded "a socially useful art", but they did not get it. "The only poetry of the time was the guillotine". (Camus, *The Rebel* [London: Penguin, 1991], p. 219.)

14. Cited in Richard Sennett, *Authority* (London: Faber & Faber, 1993), p. 134.

15. Raymond Queneau, *The Sunday of Life,* transl. Barbara Wright (London: John Calder Publishing, 1976).

16. Raymond Queneau, *Zazie in the Metro,* transl. Barbara Wright (New York: Harper & Row, 1960).

17. Cf. Kierkegaard's celebrated comment: "What a great thing is a police station. The place where I have my rendez-vous with the state". *The Present Age,* transl. Alexander Dru (New York: Harper & Row, 1962), p. 35.

18. E. M. Cioran, *The Temptation to Exist* (London: Quartet, 1987), pp. 48–50. Cioran is not much known in the English-speaking world, but he was a major figure in France. Octavio Paz writes of him, "a spirit apparently at the margins of our age but one who has lived and thought in depth and, for that reason, quietly". (Paz, *On Poets and Others,* p. 45.)

19. E. M. Cioran, *Anathemas and Admirations* (London: Quartet, 1992), pp. 68–69.

20. Cioran, *Temptation to Exist,* p. 65.

21. Ibid., pp. 53–54.

22. Ibid.

23. Ibid., p. 50.

24. Milan Kundera, *Immortality* (London: Faber & Faber, 1991), pp. 184–185.

25. Jean-Luc Nancy, *The Birth to Presence* (Stanford: Stanford University Press, 1993), p. 144.

26. Cited in Edward Mortimer, *European Security After the Cold War,* Adelphi Paper 271 (London: International Institute for Strategic Studies, 1992), p. 1.

27. Nancy, *Birth to Presence,* p. 159.

28. Richard Bernstein, *Philosophical Profiles: essays in a pragmatic mode* (Cambridge: Polity Press, 1986), p. 250.

29. Omer Bartov, *Hitler's Army: soldiers, Nazis, and war in the Third Reich* (Oxford: Oxford University Press, 1991), pp. 13–28.

30. See A. D. Harvey, *Collision of Empires: Britain in three world wars, 1793–1945* (London: Phoenix, 1992), pp. 626–629.

31. Paul Fussell, *The Bloody Game* (New York: Scribner, 1991), p. 656.

32. Friedrich Nietzsche, *Human, All Too Human,* transl. R. J. Hollingdale (Cambridge: Cambridge University Press, 1986), p. 103.

33. See Felix Gilbert, 'Machiavelli: the renaissance of the art of war', in Edward Mead Earle, ed., *Makers of Modern Strategy: military thought from Machiavelli to Hitler* (Princeton: Princeton University Press, 1943), pp. 3–25; J. R. Hale, *War and Society in Renaissance Europe, 1450–1620* (London: Fontana, 1985), p. 71.

34. Henri Lefebvre, *Introduction to Modernity: twelve preludes, September 1959–May 1961,* transl. John Moore (London: Verso, 1995), p. 48.

35. George Steiner, *No Passion Spent: essays, 1978–1996* (London: Faber & Faber, 1996), p. 284. Few historians refer to the tragic in political life. One exception is Jacques Droz. In explaining why the English, unlike the French, managed to escape revolution in the nineteenth century, he writes that the ruling class was able to grasp "the tragic nature" of politics and thus was prepared to make compromises. Understanding the tragic is the element of a "true political culture", or we might add, a liberal one. (Droz, *Europe Between Revolutions, 1815–1848* [London: Fontana, 1967], p. 142.)

36. After visiting the United States Charles Dilke wrote that the chief task of its universities appeared to be to declare war on crime, sin and death. (Dilke, *Greater Britain: a record of travels in English-speaking countries* [Philadelphia: J. B. Lipincott, 1869], p. 172.)

37. Isaiah Berlin, *Against the Current: essays on the history of ideas* (Oxford: Oxford University Press, 1991), pp. 74–75.

38. Albert Camus, 'On the future of tragedy', in *Lyrical and Critical Essays,* ed. Philip Thody (New York: Vintage Press, 1990), p. 305.

39. Cited in Joel Weinsheimer, *Gadamer's Hermeneutics: a reading of 'Truth and Method'* (New Haven: Yale University Press, 1985), pp. 116–118.

40. Jean-François Lyotard, *Political Writings* (London: University College Press, 1993), p. 97.

41. See Philip Gold, 'Does complex technological information alienate us from our humanity?' in Philip Windsor, *The End of the Century: the future in the past* (Tokyo: Kadansha, 1995), p. 124.

Index